AF328061

STUDIES IN HIGHER EDUCATION

DISSERTATION SERIES

Edited by
PHILIP G. ALTBACH
Monan Professor of Higher Education
Lynch School of Education, Boston College

A ROUTLEDGEFALMER SERIES

Other Books in This Series:

Saving for College and the Tax Code
Andrew Roth

Resource Allocation in Private Research Universities
Daniel Rodas

I Prefer to Teach
An International Comparison of Faculty Preferences for Teaching
James J.F. Forest

Tenure on Trail
Case Studies of Change in Faculty Appointment Policies
William Mallon

From Here to University
Access, Mobility, & Resilience Among Latino Youth
Alexander Jun

Scholarship Unbound
Kerry Ann O'Meara

Technology Transfer Via University-Industry Relations
The Case of the Foreign High Technology Electronic Industry in Mexico's Silicon Valley
Maria Isabel Rivera Vargas

Black Student Politics: Higher Education and Apartheid From SASO to SANSCO, 1968–1990
Saleem Badat

State Governments and Research Universities
David Weerts

The Virtual Delivery and Virtual Organization of Postsecondary Education
Daniel M. Carchidi

Federalism and Länder Autonomy
The Higher Education Policy Network in the Federal Republic of Germany
Cesare Onestini

RESILIENT SPIRITS

Disadvantaged Students Making it at an Elite University

Latty Lee Goodwin

ROUTLEDGEFALMER
NEW YORK & LONDON

Published in 2002 by
RoutledgeFalmer
29 West 35th Street
New York, NY 10001

RoutledgeFalmer is an imprint of the Taylor & Francis Group.
Copyright © 2002 by Latty Lee Goodwin

All rights reserved. No part of this book may be reprinted or reproduced or utilized in any form or by any electronic, mechanical, or other means, now known or hereafter invented, including photocopying and recording, or in any information storage or retrieval system, without written permission from the publishers.

10 9 8 7 6 5 4 3 2 1

Library of Congress Cataloging-in-Publication Data

Goodwin, Latty Lee, 1950–
    Resilient spirits : disadvantaged students making it at an elite university / Latty Lee Goodwin.
        p. cm. — (Routledge/Falmer dissertations in higher education)
    Originally published as author's thesis.
    Includes bibliographical references.
ISBN 0-415-93384-6 (HB)
    1. University of the State of New York. Higher Education Opportunity Program. 2. Minorities—Education (Higher)—New York (State)—Case studies. 3. Immigrants—Education (Higher)—New York (State)—Case studies. 4. Academic achievement—New York (State)—Case studies. 5. College choice—New York (State)—Case studies. I. title: Disadvantaged students making it at an elite university. II. Title . III. studies in higher education, dissertation series.

LC3732.N5 G66 2002
378.1'9829—dc21
                                                                        2002020840

Printed on acid-free, 250 year-life paper
Manufactured in the United States of America

This book is dedicated to my husband, Dan, who has been
my rock, my anchor, and my light
through this project and our many years together,
and to my favorite daughter and son, Correy and Eric.

Contents

Acknowledgments

This research project is far more than just an academic exercise that culminates years of study. It has indeed been a substantial part of my life and of those who have surrounded me for these past years, and I hope that it will be a positive force for social justice. I am grateful for the blanket of understanding care and nurturing support from so many people that has wrapped around me in the many lonely hours of solitary work. For the times I could not be there for my family and friends, and yet they were there for me, I thank them all for understanding that this was just temporary. Special thanks to Lauren for always being a cheerleader and for reading those first, painful drafts; to Evie for joining the work early on and supplying invaluable assistance; to Susan, Sora, Enid, Doug, Patti, Wick, and the rest of my amazing colleagues in the LDC for providing the right words and assistance when I needed it; to my dissertation support group—Nancy, Ellie, Robb, Kim, and Barb; to Marty, Barb, and Phyllis who kept me centered and balanced; and to Andrew for getting me into this in the first place!

I have seen the faces and relived the narrations of the student participants at every turn of this project, and I thank them deeply for allowing me a glimpse of their rich lives and wisdom. I hope they feel that their time was well spent and that their trust was well-placed. I know my life was changed through my brief immersion in their world. And, for that opportunity, I thank the HEOP professionals and others at "Ivy University" who made this study possible and who were always interested in and supportive of this work. I would also like to acknowledge the Mark Diamond Research Fund of the Graduate School of Education at SUNY Buffalo for its support through a small grant that assisted in the funding of research materials.

Without the encouragement and expertise of Dr. Lois Weis, none of this would have been possible. Her faith in my abilities and her professionalism have been inspiring. I am deeply grateful. I was fortunate to have Dr.

Maxine Seller, Dr. Mwalimu Shujaa, and Dr. Harold Wechsler as invaluable committee members and sage teachers during my doctoral program. I thank these remarkable individuals for opening my eyes to new worlds.

Family has always been the heart of my life and, over the miles and through the months of minimal contact, I have always known you were there behind me. My love and thanks to Steve, Ann, John, Claire, Jessie, and the parental units, Bob, Eva, and Marilyn. Dad, I know you're up there, hands folded over your chest, shining your never-ending love over us all. This one was really for you!

RESILIENT SPIRITS

CHAPTER 1

Introduction

I'm Puerto Rican, Hispanic, Latin American. I don't know. I'm not PC [politically correct]. I don't know which one I am. I think I'm Hispanic. I could be a number of things....I don't know. Hispanic, I think of Spaniards. So, I think I'm Latina. I'm Latin American. Whatever! I check off Hispanic. I'm Puerto Rican.

–Tiana, a second generation immigrant

I learned to be around any type of people regardless. If I was the only Black kid in the university, it still wouldn't matter. You're here to get a college education. You can still preserve your culture and learn cultural identity, even though you just have to work ten times harder to do it, cause it's not handed to you.

–Damon, from upstate New York

Tiana and Damon are representative of the ever changing population served by higher education and that educators must continually work toward understanding. This book provides assistance in this effort by examining the processes of identity construction that socioeconomically and educationally disadvantaged students from diverse backgrounds undergo when they become part of the student body of an elite university. It reveals who some of these students are and how they are able to reconceptualize their marginality within the oppressive power systems that structure their lives, namely the at-large society of the United States and a more narrowly defined elite institution of higher education, which both continue to operate from distinctly Western, Anglo-European worldviews. The students in this study have chosen not to conform and assimilate into these systems in order to succeed, but instead to *strategically* resist these systems through both overt and covert oppositional behaviors.

Researchers (Cross & Strauss, 1999; Fordham & Ogbu, 1986) have studied **oppositional identity frames of reference** that Black youth develop when they conclude that their futures in White society are stagnant and meaningless. They often respond by actively and overtly opposing and rejecting anything that is a part of White culture. These behaviors can be seen in other subordinate groups in varying extremes and provide a means for the youths to survive. What my research indicates is that in order to survive in the elite White university system, the collective goal of these diverse students who have been admitted is to succeed within this power system, but not to be "broken in spirit" along the way. No longer choosing assimilation as the path to success, as generations before them have done, these students forge new paths by creating and employing "critical resistant navigational strategies" (Solorzano & Villalpando, 1998 p. 216) as they work their way through the systems that provide them with opportunities for upward mobility. These students exemplify the **resiliency** that Janie V. Ward (1999) identifies as a key factor in the success of Black youth overcoming "negative social environments." I've appropriated this concept of resilience to describe any youth facing barriers of racism or other forms of oppression because it captures perfectly the spirit of the students with whom I worked in this study.

The theory and context that structured this research revolve around four seminal questions that all entities in higher education grapple with concerning the changing composition of the student body. The following sections comprehensively discuss the significance of each of these questions. We begin by exploring the meaning behind the term "disadvantaged."

1. WHO ARE DISADVANTAGED STUDENTS WITHIN HIGHER EDUCATION?

One of the central purposes of undertaking this study was to expose and further understand the complexity of students enrolled in higher education at this point in time. I focus on the students who are viewed and classified as "disadvantaged" because my experience has been that most educators view these students monolithically and operate from stereotypical assumptions about what it means to be disadvantaged. Over a number of years of teaching at a selective and respected university, I observed the changing demographics of the student population that included more students from diverse and often impoverished backgrounds. As I followed their struggles at our institution, I wondered what happened for students like them who attended more elite universities. There are few ethnographic studies of the higher education population in general, let alone disadvantaged students in compensatory programs. Most of the existing ethnographic research of college students has focused on gender, race, or class dimensions to define disadvantage. Like other researchers, I approach research projects with assumptions and perspectives that are colored by my experiences with students. I also react to the literature that has attempted to explain why some students are disadvantaged and how our society defines disadvantage. Due to the current work being done by researchers and theorists within the sociology of education, my definition of disadvantage has been stretched beyond the dimensions of race, class, and gender

The complexity of identities among the college student population and the tremendous challenge that disadvantaged students face due to the vast cultural differences between their communities of residence and the elite communities of higher education are not widely understood. Poor and working class students from socioeconomically and educationally disadvantaged backgrounds, the focus of this study, are often portrayed within research literature, mass media events, and academic conversations as Black or African American, and they are usually compared to and contrasted with middle and upper class White students. This impression is further fueled by popular academic texts, such as *The Shape of the River* (1998) by two former Ivy League college presidents, William Bowen and Derek Bok, which received national attention for its exploration of race and affirmative action based college admissions, but which its authors admitted was limited by their focus on "black" students. They state in the preface: "One reason for focusing on black and white students in this study is that so much of the debate over race-sensitive admissions policies has centered on black-white comparisons" (p. xxvi). They also indicate that this decision was "practical" given the tremendous variations of cultures and challenges faced within groups of Hispanic, Native American, and Asian American matriculants. What is so often missing in all of these discussions is a consideration of how the dramatically changing ethnic and cultural compositions of our institutions are critical elements that we must come to better understand if our institutions are to adequately and equitably serve the needs of all members of our society. We cannot shy away from the complexity of studying these dynamics. This text is an intentional foray into this underexplored zone.

The diversity within the ranks of poor and working class students on college campuses far transcends the overworn notion of a Black/White student bifurcation, especially in **compensatory** programs that are the frequent catchments for non-White students from disadvantaged backgrounds. My research pushes beyond the Black and White stereotypically homogeneous student groupings and reveals the rich heterogeneity that is found within a student population of a New York State funded compensatory program, called the Higher Education Opportunity Program (HEOP), at an elite university. **Identity construction** is an individual and collective pursuit that coalesces around an orchestration of contextual elements that are experienced through the family, society, and within one's geographical, historical, and situational location. Therefore, the complexity and diversity of student populations, even within narrowly defined groupings, cannot be understood by the generic categorizations of Black, White, Hispanic, Asian, Native American, and "other." What often goes unconsidered are the ethnic, cultural, and historic variations within these groups that are glossed over and ignored by these sweeping (and bureaucratically convenient), generalized categories. The students within this particular compensatory program epitomize this complexity. These are the voices I seek to center in this book.

The term "disadvantaged" as it is commonly used in education and within the HEOP literature presents a problematic discourse and requires some careful positioning. Armand Altman's (1973) research of the HEOP population, one of the few and one of the earliest studies of this program, indicated that HEOP was born at a time when "disadvantaged" was often a vague, ambiguous codeword for Black. The HEOP language at that time defined educationally disadvantaged as "those whose academic achievement has been significantly depressed by debilitating environmental circumstances. As a result, such student's academic work is significantly below his capacity as determined by teachers, counselors, social agencies, and/or qualified persons" (quoted in Altman, 1973, p. 9). A conclusion that Altman reached from the three HEOP sites that he investigated was: "What is not said, and yet what seems to emerge more clearly each time the proposals [from the three research sites] are read is that black is equated with being educationally disadvantaged" (p. 11). A later study of compensatory programs (Alford, 1995) agrees that the targeted population of students from "socio-economically disadvantaged homes" was primarily Black, although Latinos are also mentioned. Problematic synonyms for disadvantaged are also employed in this study, those being "non-traditional" and "at risk." This discourse appears throughout the literature that deals with student populations who are deemed "disadvantaged." These terms usually imply that the students are unlikely to succeed in college because of some deficit, and that deficit is usually attributed to the students and their families, through their environmental and economic misfortune or incompetence. The compensatory programs then become tools for remediating the students and moving them into the mainstream of the respective college.

I want to make it clear from the outset that my definition of "disadvantaged" does not operate from the student deficit perspective. When I employ the term "**disadvantaged**," I work from the standpoint that this student cohort includes any individual who has been disadvantaged by the educational and economic system within the United States. This is not a student deficit model but an institutional model that places much of the responsibility and blame, if blame is called for, not on Black students and their families, but on institutions that lack the reflexivity and resources to respond to the needs of the populations they serve. The term "disadvantaged" within this book will be used as an indictment against these systems, not the students, either individually or collectively. I center the notion that many students are ill-served, i.e. "disadvantaged," by the systems in place in the United States, and the problem extends far beyond that of a Black/White, racially motivated power struggle. It is more that these systems do not operate around an understanding of the complexity of the cultural origins, differences, and needs within the groups that they serve. And, when they do understand, they often lack the competence and/or resources to meet the student needs.

The Higher Education Opportunity Program (HEOP) defines its student population, which it calls "disadvantaged," very specifically according to family economic limits and student educational achievement levels. In addition, it racially/ethnically categorizes these students within the categories of Black (Non-Hispanic), Native American, Asian, Hispanic (Puerto Rican and Other Hispanic), White (Non-Hispanic), and Other. The program also records information according to gender, age, and years in program. In its literature (Bureau of Higher Education, 1998) the program only identifies place of origin when it subdivides the category Hispanic to recognize Puerto Ricans. However, even then, Puerto Rican students have diverse cultural affiliations and perspectives that are overlooked by this limiting categorization. So, according to HEOP's parameters, disadvantaged students are from poor and working class families, the majority of whom come from monolithically defined and underrepresented racial/ethnic origins. The services of the program, beyond the financial benefits, provide for the support of the students, but through means that are often viewed as remedial or separatist. What students and professionals within higher education often read into this is that the students themselves are deficient and need to be changed in order to achieve in higher education. It is interesting to note that HEOP was conceived during the time (the late 1960s to 1970s) of great theorizing of students from a deficit perspective, which could account for the narrow categorization that persists in how the program defines its students.

This **student deficit model** can be traced back to a number of earlier theorists who focused on schools as sites whose functions were to reproduce the inequalities of class structures and social relations that were necessary within the unequal power distribution upon which capitalism was based (Althusser, 1971; Bowles & Gintis, 1976; Karabel & Halsey, 1977). Schools sorted and selected students who were viewed as passively and submissively accepting their assigned and differentiated roles in the social and economic hierarchy. Student identities were shaped by schools to fit their class destinies. While many of these early reproduction theorists focused on the structural imbalances that schools help to create and perpetuate economically and socially, always ensuring a base of disadvantaged workers, Pierre Bourdieu and Jean Claude Passeron (1977), further expanded and enlightened this discussion by injecting the concept of **cultural capital**, which I have found very useful in my research. The "best and brightest" were determined through possession of cultural attributes valued most highly by the dominant classes of a society. These included general background, knowledge, attitudes, and skills, including language, that were passed down by families through their class locations and were rewarded differentially in schools. By valuing most highly the cultural capital of the dominant middle and upper classes, these students met more success and were rewarded through their performance in the educational system. Upon graduation, these students were better credentialed to attain superior jobs, perpetuating the economic and social inequality that reproductionists highlight. The lower class students were taught to believe that their location in the social hierarchy was achieved due to their lack of ability, not due to the unequal stacking of educational outcomes. Again, the student was deficient, not the system.

The narrow focus of these theories, which usually explored only one aspect of the panoply of educational influences, overlooked the possibility of student resistance mediating what is represented to be a smooth and seamless reproduction of dominant ideologies. Missing in this body of work, was the exploration of the dynamic processes that occur within the "black box" of the school in order to accomplish the serious task of knowledge and value transmission. They focused on power and the ability of society to reproduce dominant and subordinate groups, economically, socially and/or culturally, but they only partially answered the question: How is it that working-class children often end up in working-class jobs and, conversely, upper-class children end up in positions that further their ability to produce wealth and status? While this work was ground breaking and provided the theoretical backbone for future research, these predictive theories have been displaced and decentered. I applaud their exposure of the complicity of schools in producing student outcomes, but disadvantaged students are far more complex than these "master narratives" reveal.

Sociological theory has evolved over the years, from research and literature that focused on student difference as a negative or a deficit, to positioning difference as something of value. **Critical theory** has pushed this perspective along and contends that there is a struggle for power being played out in the educational arena. As the power holders in society struggle to maintain domination over subordinate groups, critical theorists attempt to expose the inequities underlying the status quo and to equip exploited groups with the means to engage in the struggle on more even footing. In attempting to make education more empowering and less "painful," critical theories explore the meshing of economic, cultural, and political spheres with the dynamics of gender, race, and class (Apple & Weis, 1983; McCarthy, 1988). These theories advocate a joining of forces by people differentially oppressed (which I read as "disadvantaged") by any combination of gender, race, or class locations. The point is that oppressed people may not share similar consciousnesses or needs at the same point in time. However, by crossing gender, race, and/or class boundaries, collaborative groups can emancipate themselves from hegemonic forces, dissolve boundaries, and create new identities. Critical theory spawned important discourse concerning the inequitable distribution of education and the resultant effects on groups and individuals. The exposure of the contradictions of education held out the possibilities for changing existing power structures. What was lacking is how these groups would be able to come together across such deep societal boundaries.

From a **critical culturalist perspective**, race, class and gender must be treated as fluid, socially constructed elements within systems of oppression and processes of identity formation (Levinson & Holland, 1996). Taking the lead from theorists like Michael Apple (1979, 1981, 1982) and Henry Giroux (1981), critical culturalists began to explore the variable and dynamic "lived cultures" of individuals within student groups and how they interacted with each other and with the politics of schooling. Paul Willis's (1981) often quoted ethnographic study of England's high school "lads" is credited as the ground-breaking work of this genre because it revealed the concepts of student agency and resistance. Students, even those who were disadvantaged, came to be understood as three-dimensional individuals capable of making decisions based on their "situated knowledge," that which they had acquired through their varied backgrounds and experiences (akin to Bourdieu's cultural capital). Willis uncovered a "culture of resistance" within this male cohort, which was echoed for females in the work of Angela McRobbie (1978). As work in the critical culturalist genre progressed, students were no longer viewed as operating from predefined passive identities within monolithic class groupings who were acted upon by schools and society. Students were credited with the ability to act back upon oppression in complex and diverse ways.

An increasing number of ethnographies (for example, Connell et al, 1982; Fine, 1991; Fordham, 1993; MacLeod, 1987; Raissiguier, 1994; Weis, 1990; Wexler, 1992) responded to this flexing of critical theory, although the focus was generally on high school populations. Each study centers class, race, or gender, but their insights into student cultural production have been valuable to this research. While all of the preceding works have injected the sense of student agency, even among disadvantaged students, I want to highlight Jay MacLeod's 1995 expansion of *Ain't No Makin' It*. This study riveted my attention because it took two groups of disadvantaged high school students living in the "projects," the mostly White "Hallway Hangers" and the mostly Black "Brothers," and turned the programmed stereotype of these students upside down. Here, we saw a group of disaffected White youths who lived off the underground economy, who had few serious aspirations, and who were quick to reject the values of the dominant, business-driven society. In stark contrast was the group of Black students who took education seriously, lived morally upright lives for the most part (and especially in comparison to the Hallway Hangers), and bought into the dominant ideology of success as a result of hard work. Yet, in the end, despite some sincere efforts to realize the "American Dream," both groups were casualties of the system and seemed forever doomed to lead disillusioned lives of poverty in the projects. Like one participant said, "...there just ain't no makin' it!" MacLeod concludes that: "...this study points an accusing finger at one dominant dogma, itself a major obstacle to political change: the persistent belief that poverty is caused by the personal vices and cultural pathologies of the poor....The war on poverty has become the war on the poor" (p. 265). His work and the many others within this genre explain that even though students have some complicity with societal forces, disadvantagement occurs for reasons well beyond the simplistic notion of race. Whites are not always the advantaged, and Blacks are not always the disadvantaged. Class, gender, history, ethnicity, institutional systems of power, and a host of other factors mediate outcomes for groups and individuals.

Pushing beyond the boundaries that have been imposed by "the grand narratives" of early theories and society's preoccupation with static, scientifically determined definitions of identity, a number of theorists continue to ask critical questions about how dominant ideologies are reproduced and legitimized within our society, but with an eye on how people from any slice of life might be able to participate within social systems on more equal footing. They have shifted the gaze from male dominated, Eurocentric ideas, to different worldviews and perspectives. Hence, the rise in feminist voices (such as, Collins, 1990; Lather, 1991; Lorde, 1984; Sleeter, 1993) being heard from all corners of society, coming out from the marginalized spaces and into the fore. Feminisms (intentionally pluralized in an attempt to be more inclusive and acknowledge the multiple positions within gender centered work) of all types have arisen as a response to the traditions of patriarchy running consistently throughout the history of *man* and male dominance. The point is to decenter the male and open up the space for "others." Through this work, we have come to understand how women and "others" have been disadvantaged by patriarchal oppression.

In addition to the contributions of the feminisms, I have found the work of a contingent of African American writers valuable in developing an appreciation of alternate worldviews, much like the work of the feminists. A primary goal of these writers is to center African people and their interests and decenter European concerns (see, for example, Akoto, 1994; Asante, 1990; Gordon, 1994; Shujaa, 1994); in essence, they are turning the tables of domination in this country. Patricia Collins (1990) calls this developing a self-defined **"standpoint"** that is won only through self-conscious struggle, the constant rejection of being the imposed "other." They underscore the importance of race (understood to be an historically shaped category) and the presence of racism in the lived experiences of African American students.

Through **poststructural** theorizing, the feminisms and the multiplicity of worldviews (of which Afrocentrism is but one) are significant in enhancing an understanding of the complexity of student populations and the importance of the student perspective, which is the student's lived reality. Disadvantaged students are often working from worldviews that are in constant tension with the dominant worldview of the society they inhabit, and developing a "standpoint" is only done through purposeful work. While these theories are important efforts of consciousness-raising, they are short on research that explores the lived realities of these complex, multi-faceted students attempting to find their rightful place within the fabric of power overlaying their educational experiences. This research project is an effort to fill some of this void. Poststructural ideology is so fluid and ambiguous, that there are few hand-holds to guide and inform the researcher. But I find admirable their efforts to value all cultures, challenging us to find the means to disrupt oppressive, patriarchal models that have too long determined the course of education. They challenge us to cast aside stereotypical notions that our society has constructed around subjugated groups. When dealing with disadvantaged students, this task continues to perplex individuals within higher education, no matter how well meaning they may be.

2. WHAT IS HEOP AND HOW DOES IT IMPACT STUDENT SUCCESS?

In the previous section, I exposed how many research projects have explored why students *don't* succeed, often from the deficit model, leading some academicians to believe that elite institutions are not appropriate for disadvantaged students. My research stands these perspectives on their heads and poses the question: How is it that any disadvantaged students *do* succeed at elite institutions when the odds are so often stacked against them? The importance of programs like HEOP cannot be overstated, as this research will show. Educators would be wise to look to the experts who work within these programs for guidance and assistance in understanding student diversity, cultural difference, and how education can accommodate the various needs and experiences of a heterogeneous population. In addition, the space that programs like HEOP provide for students to engage in authentic identity work is critical to their success when there is a cultural mismatch between the student and the institution.

The Higher Education Opportunity Program (HEOP), the compensatory program that is the backdrop of this text, was one of four "equal opportunity" programs developed within New York State as a response to the Civil Rights movement during the 1960s. Student unrest and societal consciousness-raising regarding racism and sexism which were products of this time, engendered modifications of admissions policies and the restructuring of financial assistance as means to redress some of the perceived inequities within institutions of higher education. Proponents of democracy rushed to provide programs that would narrow the opportunity gap. HEOP was New York State's contribution to this effort for students wishing to enroll in independent, private institutions. It was authorized in 1969 by an amendment to the New York State Education Law (#6451) and was created as a partnership with institutions of higher education to supplement existing efforts to aid students who demonstrated potential to complete post-secondary programs, but who were economically and educationally disadvantaged (Alford, 1995; Altman, 1973; Bureau of Higher Education Opportunity Program, 1996; Ruppert, 1998; Smith, 1991; Trotman, 1998). However, as ErVin Gross (1990) pointed out in his study of HEOP administrators, these opportunity programs were viewed as "window dressing for the majority higher education systems" and were regarded as peripheral to the mainstream educational function. These attitudes placed HEOP in a precarious position, where its future was always up to the financial and political whims of the state bureaucrats.

This research will show that HEOP is a critical resource for students who are continually running into formidable barriers against success.

One major barrier is financial. Financial support for the HEOP students comes from the HEOP program which is supported by New York State (12.2 percent), the educational institution (37.6 percent), and Federal and other sources (50.2 percent). In addition to financial support, the colleges provide various supportive services for the students including mandatory prefreshman summer programs, remedial/developmental and supportive courses, tutoring, and counseling. However, in precarious economic times (which seem to be most of the time), HEOP's funding is constantly on the line. The federal and state governments, as well as the colleges, look for places to cut and these programs can appear costly and expendable. Despite the fact that HEOP has rallied support and lobbied for continued funding a number of times, the governments' contributions have decreased on a regular, annual basis (Bureau of Higher Education Opportunity Program, 1998). A tremendous amount of time during the semester is spent by the financial aid-dependent student in dealing with the bureaucratic financial systems and their reams of red-tape and errors. This is precious time away from their studies that other students without financial aid don't lose.

A second barrier is the nature of elite institutions. HEOP students attend private, independent institutions, and this particular study focuses on an elite university. **Elite institutions** are characterized by Robert Birnbaum (1991) as "...institutions with selective admissions policies, high tuition costs, middle and upper socioeconomic students, and high reputation. Such institutions apply a rich resource base to programs emphasizing general and liberal education...[and] are almost always nonpublic" (p. 118). By their very nature, they are designed to perpetuate an elitist culture, one filled with students who have been raised in the dominant culture to expect opportunity and success. Lisa Delpit (1988) unwraps what she terms the "culture of power" within classrooms at all levels of education. Her arguments are valuable for understanding the cultural conflicts that students from disadvantaged backgrounds meet when faced with an elite culture which is a stronghold "culture of power" in our society. Delpit advocates explicit instruction in the rules of the culture in power to those whose culture commands less power. She invokes the concept of "cultural capital," borrowed from Pierre Bourdieu (1977). This concept and context proved useful for this research, especially when exploring how students undertake the critical work of "becoming someone" within an academic culture that values certain types of cultural capital more than others. All students arrive with cultural capital, but, in agreement with Delpit, I submit that it is not the *quantity* of cultural capital as much as the perceived *quality* of that capital by the academic community at large, that differentiates the experiences of the students. Elite institutions have their own expectations of quality with which disadvantaged students need to come to terms.

An ethnographic study that further explains the cultural challenges that students face was Michael Moffatt's (1988) examination of a freshman class and the culture of the college population at Rutgers in the late 1970s and early 1980s. This study site was not an "elite" institution as it is commonly defined, but his research demonstrated deep racial tensions and contradictions, even among the more "liberal" and enlightened students. Many professed to value diversity in the student population, but many also found it difficult to adjust to cultural differences, especially when living in close proximity to each other. The student attitudes seemed class related, with the more liberal positions held by middle to upper class students, and the more racist attitudes generated by lower middle and working class students (an observation that lends credence to the assertion that community colleges, which often serve this population, may not be the best educational site for minority students). These racist tensions were attributed to the changing economic patterns that increased competition for jobs, especially those sought by the working class. At an elite institution, the competition may not appear to be so class driven, but it may in fact be stronger within this population because they view themselves as having more to lose. Resentment of disadvantaged students taking precious admissions slots and eventually competing with them for high caliber jobs may be even more significant for students at an elite university than at other institutions of higher education.

Despite these barriers, we know that many students in compensatory programs like HEOP do succeed and even at elite universities. A dissertation by Horace Smith (1991) was a quantitative, longitudinal study comparing HEOP students to "regular" students admitted to a four-year predominantly white university. Academic performance was judged based on grade point average, credits earned, rate of retention, and rate of graduation. The primary results revealed that HEOP students performed academically as well as non-minority students, they were retained and graduated at comparable levels, and the program had a significant effect on their success. In addition, minority students in HEOP earned more credits and maintained a higher GPA than minority students in the control group. The New York State Department of Education reports that 79.2 percent of HEOP students maintained grade point averages of 2.0 or better (on a 4.0 scale), and 28.1 percent had a 3.0 or better. A graduation rate of 54.4 percent was reported, which compared favorably with the national graduation statistic of 45 percent (Bureau of HEOP, 1998).

In order to show this type of success in the face of these barriers, students must be aware of the source of these challenges and able to make informed decisions about the most appropriate responses. Three concepts—hegemony, agency and praxis—help define this task. "**Hegemony**" refers to the Marxist concept of domination of one class over another through the employment of political and ideological coercion (Feinberg & Soltis, 1992, p. 50). Extending its dominant stronghold outside of the economic domain, it can be observed in interactions between the genders and races, as well as classes, when one faction assumes superiority over another. Hegemonic control is exerted in insidious ways as it is played out at a subconscious level within the academic culture. Therefore, counter-hegemonic awareness and the development of a "critical consciousness" become tasks for disadvantaged students at an elite university. Hegemonic awareness is prerequisite to the possibility of the second term, "**agency**," which connotes the individual's ability to "act back" and not be totally determined by societal structures. Agency enables resistance to hegemony (Giroux, 1983). The third critical term, "**praxis**," expands upon the concept of agency and is defined by Paolo Freire (1995/1970) as occurring "...only when the oppressed find the oppressor out and become involved in the organized struggle for their liberation...This discovery cannot be purely intellectual but must involve action; nor can it be limited to mere activism, but must include serious reflection..." (p. 47). Born from these central tenets, the critical culturalist perspective views cultural production as the vehicle for developing identity and agency within the structural constraints of societal institutions such as universities. This process illuminates what Bradley Levinson and Dorothy Holland (1996) call "the cultural production of the educated person" (p. 14), a process that needs to occur in order for disadvantaged students to make a space for themselves on campus, but which may not happen easily or quickly.

In order to undergo this cultural development, students from disadvantaged backgrounds need to find the means and space to exercise agency and develop a praxis. The means tend to focus on the importance of student coalitions, as explained in numerous studies. HEOP has the potential to create both the means and space to facilitate coalition building. Cameron McCarthy (1988) advocates for non-synchronous groupings in flexible and dynamic patterns which evoke agency and empowerment, and urges students to forge new alliances. This resonates with Audre Lorde's (1992) depiction of people as "walking coalitions," constructions of biology and society capable of individual and collective endeavor through the intersections of race, class, and gender. Warning against forming coalitions based solely on mutuality and empathy, Allsup (1995) states that bonds must "proceed from the political act and from the activity of solidarity. This nontranscendent coming to knowledge must enjoin the historical moments; that is, the intersection and interplay of race, gender, and class" (p. 284). Patricia Collins (1990) picks up this thread and formulates a "politics of empowerment." Her work centers Black women and develops a Black feminist standpoint. "By embracing a paradigm of race, class, and gender as interlocking systems of oppression, Black feminist thought reconceptualizes the social relations of domination and resistance" (p. 222). The empowerment sought through Black feminism does not seek to replace the dominant White male system with a Black female one. Instead it seeks to form an alternative conception of power based on more humanistic values. Collins allows that Black feminism is a "partial perspective" with no claims to absolute "truth," evoking shades of Donna Haraway's (1991) perspective when urging the creative couplings of subjugated "others." However, as Dorothy Holland and Margaret Eisenhart's (1990) ethnographic study reveals, it is often difficult for students (women, in this case) to become involved in supportive groups, let alone form empowering coalitions.

The creation of empowering space is seen as a shared responsibility between the school and the students, according to Bradley Levinson and Dorothy Holland (1996) :

> Schools also create a space for the formation of social relations among people of different classes, gender, castes, ethnic, and age groups which would be unlikely in other sites. Such relations may come to reconfigure previous alliances, allegiances, and sympathies. They may indeed be empowering. Thus, schools provide each generation with social and symbolic sites where new relations, new representations, and new knowledges can be formed, sometimes against, sometimes tangential to, sometimes coincident with, the interests of those holding power. (22)

While schools *may* choose to participate in this empowering activity, more likely it will emanate from the students as they create "**free spaces.**" Sara Evans and Harry Boyte's (1986) original conceptualization of free spaces was that they were "found" places in which to engage in democratic social movements promoting citizenship and change. However, the application that I propose diverges somewhat and I borrow a less specific interpretation that Evans and Boyte offer: "Put simply, free spaces are settings between private lives and large-scale institutions where ordinary citizens can act with dignity, independence, and vision" (p. 17). Some of the identity work undertaken by disadvantaged students in a foreign and/or confusing environment may best be accomplished away from what may be felt as the oppressive eyes of the university and the majority of its inhabitants. These free spaces may be similar to the "scaling down" that Richard Richardson and Elizabeth Skinner (1992) describe first-generation students at community colleges employing: "...most reported that it had still been important for them to reduce or 'scale down' the physical dimensions of college attendance—that is, to find places where they could study, meet friends, or seek support, spaces that provided some measure of 'comfortability'" (p. 37). My conception is also akin to that of Michelle Fine and Lois Weis's (1995) notion of "homesteading" among working class and poor young men and women. Spaces within communities were claimed by groups of these young adults as places of hope where recuperation and personal, as well as collective, identity work could flourish without the constraints of public surveillance.

These advancing feminisms and cultural theories that push boundaries and reconceptualize our understandings of power and politics, through a dialogue of inclusion, empowerment, and praxis constitute many current poststructural discussions (see, for example, Aronowitz & Giroux, 1991; Giroux, Lankshear, McLaren, & Peters, 1996; Sleeter & McLaren, 1995). Within this arena, the concepts of non-synchronous, fluid coalitions of student groups and the empowering possibilities of free spaces that enable students from poor and working class backgrounds to succeed within a constrained university environment, lend important dimensions to this research. The critical importance of HEOP in providing the means and space to form empowering coalitions, must be recognized and understood as an example of the type of responsible institutional planning and vision that enables diverse populations to achieve their educational goals.

3. WHO IS MERITORIOUS AND DESERVING OF ACCESS TO THE ELITE INSTITUTIONS OF HIGHER EDUCATION?

The faces on college campuses around the United States reflect a more diversified population than ever before as a consequence of admissions shifts stemming from the 1960s. Historically under-represented groups have been wooed and recruited to help fill slots that have gone unfilled in times of declining enrollments (Horowitz, 1987). This recent flurry of interest in diversifying our campuses has been prompted not only by the decline in numbers of the "traditional, white, male" college student, but by the political expediency of "correctness" and "equal opportunity" that has seized academic and occupational institutions in the past decade (Boyer, 1993; Levine, 1993). Affirmative action legislation and changing demographics have broadened our national awareness of the need for providing opportunity and more equal representation, although not without continuing controversy. The combination of these factors has led to increased numbers of economically and educationally "disadvantaged" students enrolling in institutions of higher education. But, there is cause to be concerned that, despite our increased awareness and the swelling numbers of "non-traditional" college students, the appearance of more opportunity is created while masking the continued inequality of this opportunity.

Affirmative action and other diversity efforts met with increasing resistance as the twentieth century came to a close. Although there appeared to be a race to embrace all members of the population, the results often smacked of tokenism and led to claims of reverse discrimination. The path toward providing equality of opportunity has always been a battle in this country, and the seeming appearance of improved opportunities for all groups has proved to be deceptive (Karabel & Halsey, 1977). Michael Apple (1993) warns:

> A new alliance has been formed, one that has increasing power in educational and social policy. This power bloc combines business with the New Right and with neoconservative intellectuals. Its interests lie not in increasing the life chances of women, people of color, or labor. Rather it aims at providing the educational conditions believed necessary both for increasing international competitiveness, profit, and discipline and for returning us to a romanticized past of the 'ideal' home, family, and school (p. 227).

At a time when the gap between the rich and poor in this country grows wider than at any point in our history (McClelland, 1996), our country is increasingly reluctant to provide more for those who have less. As the *Census 2000* (U.S. Census Bureau, 2001) indicates, there has been a rich population growth, augmented by changing immigration patterns, that brings with it increased needs that must be provided for, especially within the educational systems.

Laura Rendon (1998) identifies this current economic and educational struggle as a culture war and addresses two opposing viewpoints about access to higher education that frame this controversy. One side is based on **merit** and the "American Dream," that the individual succeeds or fails based upon universal standards that quantify the quality of effort. The standards that are recognized as "universal" are usually decided by the dominant White majority. The opposing view speaks to **social justice** issues from a collectivist perspective, based upon sharing wealth and power, and addressing inequities. The merit perspective views college entry as a competition that disregards prior inequities and promotes the "survival of the fittest" mentality among college students. The social justice standpoint purports to be more inclusive but through vaguely identified methods that leave critics edgy. Admissions procedures are not clearly articulated and the notion of "fairness" becomes easily distorted.

The *Chronicle of Higher Education* (Jaschik & Lederman, 1996) reported that in the mid-1990s, the use of racial and gender preferences in admissions to colleges, in the awarding of scholarships, in hiring, or for inclusion in state funded programs, was legally barred at the University of Texas, the University of Maryland, and the University of California, with several other states considering similar action. As a result, the numbers of students from under-represented groups declined at these institutions, and even the number of applications to these schools declined within these groups. However, even before the ban of racial and gender preferences, schools like the University of California at Berkeley were already grappling with the dilemma of how to balance merit versus equal opportunity. The numbers of overly qualified student applicants meant that thousands of students of all descriptions would be rejected, but of the large number of Blacks and Latino/as who qualified, their overall grade point averages were at the lower end of the accept-ance range, and Asian students competed with White students at the higher end of the range. Hence, Blacks and Latino/as were disadvan-taged by economic and educational systems that failed them long before they graduated from high school with dreams of making it in college (Rendon, 1998). Most of these students did not enter the college competition on equal footing with many Asian and White students. These leveled aspirations create fertile ground for the development of oppositional behavior (Cross & Strauss, 1999) among these groups who get left out despite their exemplary efforts to compete within the dominant system.

Although the courts are clearly retreating from mandating affirmative action, segments of society seem unwilling to return to strictly relying on narrowly defined "meritocratic" criteria, usually read as SAT scores, to place individuals in our institutions. How is merit to be defined? Many colleges and universities have responded to the recent legal battles by reclaiming the responsibility of social institutions to provide a diverse and democratic environment, especially when the goal is education. This can only be accomplished by considering many different factors during admissions deliberations, not only test scores and high school grades. An enrollment officer from the University of Rochester (Rochester, New York) responded to the legal decisions by stating: "The big losers are going to be the historically disadvantaged, underrepresented students on our campuses...But I would argue that everyone on our campuses would lose a great deal, also" (Jaschik & Lederman, 1996, p. A27).

With the anti-affirmative action mood of the nation, it is clear that access is viewed as a privilege and not a right. Countless times, I have heard the argument raised that not all students are appropriate candi-dates for selective institutions, regardless of their ability. If they can't afford these institutions, then they should look at community colleges and more affordable public universities. The argument is valid to a point, because these institutions exist for the express purpose of serving the diverse needs of the learning population. So, why do "disadvantaged" students need access to elite institutions of higher education?

In Armand Altman's (1973) early study of HEOP sites, his quantitative dissertation resulted in a recommendation that HEOP programs may best be suited to less prestigious colleges, perhaps two-year colleges. He stated: "A diploma from a more prestigious college may not quite be worth the four or five years of alienation, academic frustrations, and economic pressures experienced by a large percentage of the HEOP students" (p. 108). A number of researchers have followed with persuasive arguments that back up this conclusion. Most of the studies have come from community college populations and many have employed ethnographic methodology.

Dionne Jones and Betty Watson (1990) label disadvantaged students as "high-risk" students: minorities, those with inadequate academic preparation, the disabled, and those of low socioeconomic status. Their classification highlights the increased risk that these students run of not persisting to graduation due to a number of complex factors. These factors include, but are not exclusive of, insufficient educational preparation, ineffective instructional strategies, negative attitudes by instructors, inappropriate choice of majors, and lack of academic, financial and social support. A subgroup within this group of "disadvantaged" students could also be first-generation college students. Terri Mangione (1998) discovered in her search for working class college women participants for her dissertation that those students classified as first generation experienced the financial and experiential challenges that put students "at risk." Typically these students come from families that have less experience with higher education and can offer little financial support. Several of the community college studies focused on first generation college students, and this cohort appeared in my research, as well.

Howard London's (1989; 1992) work with first generation college students underscores the popularity of community colleges for first generation students. He explores the cultural challenges they experience as they break with the relationships from the past and enter another culture, anticipating access to upward mobility. This process is fraught with frustration as the students experience discontinuities in their lives, primarily due to the challenge of living within two cultures. Similar to Signithia Fordham (1997) and John Ogbu's (1988) arguments, these students risk ending up in "no man's land" with *two* cultures that won't accept them—one because they're acting "too smart" and the other because they don't bring the right kind of cultural capital (Bourdieu, 1977) to smoothly integrate into the culture of higher education. Their quest for something better presents "potential costs in personal and social dislocation" (1992, p. 10). One might assume that disadvantaged students in an elite university may experience even greater cultural discontinuity than at a community college.

While London explored the tensions *between* old and new cultures for first generation college students, Lois Weis (1992) examined the contradictions *within* a community college. This ethnographic project unearthed powerful tensions between groups of Black and White students, Black faculty and Black students from different socioeconomic classes, and between Black male and female students. The White students were a minority on the campus and they tended to distance themselves from Black students, toward whom many expressed racist attitudes. This research validated McCarthy's (1988) theory of nonsynchrony, demonstrating the differential experiences of students regardless of similar racial, social and gender affiliations. The creation of the "other" occurred *within* groups, as well as between them. Community college was not the perfect site for the serious students in their pursuit of opportunity.

However, several studies mentioned the increased comfort level disadvantaged students had at community colleges, versus universities. Julia Lara (1992) personally echoed London's observations about the challenges students experience in breaking away from familiar surroundings. She discovered that in leaving a community college and attending a university, she felt out of her element. The university students "were quite different from the working-class students I had met at the community college, who had been products of an urban public school system" (p. 68). She felt minority students were undervalued in classes and had a difficult time maintaining ethnic identities.

Laura Rendon (1992) realized that community colleges "served to ghettoize people of color" (p. 57) despite their image as a people's college. Community or junior colleges provided the foot in the door to higher education for many minority students and were the stepping stones to four-year colleges that were impossible to enter directly out of secondary school. But, Rendon also spoke of academic and culture shock when attending these schools. Her eventual transition to a four-year institution produced even greater ethnic and racial shock. Her family feared that she would become a stranger and, indeed, they had trouble understanding her work. Rendon provided a chilling summary of her experience in higher education: "To become academic success stories we must endure humiliation, reject old values and traditions, mistrust our experience, and disconnect with our past" (p.62). It is understandable that some potential students elect to bypass this experience. Wendy Luttrell (1996) interviewed adult women in a literacy program and heard, " I really wanted to go to college, but I would have been with students who were completely different from me…Even today I can't walk on a college campus without feeling a pit in my stomach and a lump in my throat" (p.104).

While not entirely comparable to an American community college, Catherine Raissiguier's (1994) study of young French women in a "lycee" provided similar insights into the ethnic, gender and class tensions between cultures and within institutions. She observed the ghettoization of women in the career tracking promoted through schools. Students, especially those of Algerian descent, felt marginalized by the mechanisms at play within the school. They felt undervalued and over-regulated. However, they found this institution a site that held potential for upward mobility and breaking with their cultural backgrounds, much along the same lines as London's first generation students. Therefore, they were willing to endure the oppression of the institution for the perceived rewards it held for their futures.

These studies tell us that no institution serves the needs of all people. But, what is clear is that no doctors, lawyers, and few CEOs have graduated only from a community college. This may have been a springboard for some, but the track record of success of transferability into four year institutions from two year colleges is not strong. Dionne Jones and Betty Watson (1990) discussed the increased risk of not persisting and the slower progression rates for students who transfer from a community college to a four-year institution (p. 13). And, as Shirley Mow and Michael Nettles (1990) and Cecilia Ottinger (1991) have pointed out, minority students are over represented in community colleges where students face increased chances of dropping out and not completing a bachelor's degree. Amaury Nora and Laura Rendon (1988) wrote about this effect especially for Hispanic students:

> A controversy presently exists that community colleges may have a negative effect on ethnic minorities, who represent their primary source of students (particularly Hispanic students), and that the colleges may actually serve to perpetuate race and class inequities in the American society (p. 126).

Minority community college students often accurately perceive that this education is "second best" and not the equivalent of "White education," and their effort and performance is often commensurate with this perception (Solomon, 1988). When students' desired educational outcomes are professional careers that require at least a four year diploma, the students' chances for success are greater if they can enroll directly into the institution and the program from which they intend to graduate.

In a study of two poor and working class urban communities of young men and women, ages 23 to 35, obviously older than the student population I've been discussing, yet from similar academic and economic backgrounds of disadvantage, Michelle Fine and Lois Weis (1998) documented several important facts concerning the economy and education among disadvantaged groups. First of all, from a number of previous studies, there is ample evidence that the most disadvantaged in our society benefit the most from education. Especially for welfare recipients, a college degree can make such a significant difference in their earning potential that they are able to live independently of government funded social support systems and become contributors rather than receivers. Second, in an effort to "do it right," these men and women strongly recognized the power of education and were enrolling in increasing numbers in GED programs and college, especially the women. Third, the economic pay-off of higher education is a reality for the disadvantaged sector of our population. However, across racial/ethnic and gender lines the relative gains in earning power are not equal. An African American woman with a four-year college degree who is employed full time will earn the equivalent of a White male high school dropout who is employed full time. This economic fact, the disparity in wages despite equal years of education, feeds a critical skepticism that poor and working class men, especially African American men, hold toward education. Their lower numbers in the workforce and in higher education partly reflect this ambivalence toward the pay-off of education. However, it is increasingly clear that it is imperative that the poor and working class make it through some type of advanced training beyond high school in order to find meaningful employment in this economy. The more the better, and the better the education, the greater the employment and life options.

Sylvia Hurtado and Karen Inkelas (1998) call attention to the deceptiveness of research findings that on the surface indicate vast improvements in the equity of college access because the numbers of underrepresented groups in higher education have jumped. They are concerned that attendance at *any* type of postsecondary institution is the definition being used for access. Their points are well-stated and deserve quoting in length:

> The broad definition of access to any postsecondary institution ignores the important fact that there is a hierarchy of resources and opportunities that come with attendance at different types of postsecondary institutions (Hearn, 1988) and these differ even at 4-year institutions that are further differentiated by selectivity status (Karen,

1991)....There is also evidence across studies that suggest as the higher education system expanded access to broader groups of applicants, much of the considerable enrollment growth occurred among the lowest tiers of the postsecondary system (e.g. Grubb, 1989, 1991)....On a limited scale, a qualitative study revealed how high SES parents position their children (middle-range academic performers) to attain access to the best colleges, utilizing a growth industry of services that can place low SES students without such assistance at a disadvantage (see McDonough, 1994). Thus, according to the broadest definition of access to any type of institution, we may be quickly approaching universal access and the picture for various groups can be portrayed as "good news." *However, most would now contend that this hardly represents equal access as students become aware of distinctions among postsecondary options, the system becomes more differentiated, and researchers reveal how different groups tend to pursue distinct postsecondary opportunities* [italics added] (p. 85).

In light of these strong arguments refuting a rosy picture for improved college access, I align myself with Laura Rendon's (1998) proposed definition for **access**:

> *Democratic access* ensures that all students, regardless of social background, race/ethnicity or gender, are provided a fair and equal opportunity to graduate from high school, enter the college of their choice, graduate from college, and enter the graduate or professional program of their choice (p. 64).

As Jay MacLeod (1995) concluded in his study, "...we have to struggle for a society that doesn't trample on the aspirations of its people" (p. 302). By consigning poor and working class students to certain types of postsecondary institutions, we are eliminating the opportunity for some of them to achieve their career and life dreams, and not because of insufficient ability or effort.

Therefore, programs like HEOP become the key to gaining access to the institutions of many poor and working class students' dreams. These programs are viewed by many as compensatory and stigmatizing, but given the meritocratic and capitalistic climate of the country, they are the best hope for these students at this time. And students in these programs understand this reality, as this research will show. They are willing to face the hardships of an elite university in order to achieve their goals. This project adds compelling support for Rendon's call for democratic access to institutions of higher education.

4. HOW DO STUDENTS NARRATE INTERCULTURAL TRANSITIONAL EXPERIENCES?

Leaving the predominantly urban, public school culture which most of the students in HEOP inhabit and entering an elite academic culture, sets in place a dramatic cultural shift. The transitional period is a time of limbo where the students must come to terms with the immediate changes. How students, and especially students in programs like HEOP, narrate their experiences during this time is virtually unexplored in research literature.

Despite the paucity of research specifically related to student populations like HEOP, the ethnographic studies of college populations are all instructive in their own ways. I have built this study from ideas gleaned from many different types of ethnographies and interpretivistic studies which all centered the human participants and their perspectives. The literature about community college students (for example: Lara, 1992; London, 1992; Luttrell, 1996; Rendon, 1992; Weis, 1992) contributed an understanding of the challenges these students face as many of them become the first college student within their family and peer groups, and how they negotiate the community college physical and cultural environments.

Gender based studies of higher education, although woefully few, have added perspective to my understanding of the gendered dimensions of college attendance. Primary among these would be Dorothy Holland and Margaret Eisenhart's (1990) longitudinal study of the identity formation of female students at two four-year institutions. The research looked at the lived experiences of these female students as they negotiated their way through a peer culture organized around gender relations. The study pointed to the irrelevance of the academic culture to female students and the importance of the peer group as a site of cultural transmission. There were internal divisions within the peer community and it was surmised that the standards that governed gender relations at the institutions were imposed on the female students, characteristic of patriarchal gender hierarchies. Black women experienced more oppression than White women on campuses, and therefore formulated different responses. Similar to Michelle Fine and Lois Weis's study (1998) of somewhat older women, Black women assumed more responsibility than White women for providing for their own future, especially in light of the lack of stable, reliable employment for African American males, due to historic and current racism. There was notable lack of involvement by all of these women students in groups that supported women (the difficulty of forming coalitions even based on similar needs). One conclusion about the women was that they, for the most part, accepted the "reality" of male privilege with little resistance. Recent dissertations by Susan Jones (1995), Terri Mangione (1998), and Laura Meyers (1996) also enrich our knowledge of women's identity formation on college campuses while working across race, class, and gender lines.

Within all of these ethnographic works, the construction of student identity was a critical component, as it is in my research. The way that each of these researchers conceptualizes identity is instructive, but for this project, I borrow from Lois Weis's study (1990) of White, working class youth: "... 'identity' can be defined as a sense of self in relation to others. Identity formation refers, therefore, to the processes through which people, either individually or collectively, come to see themselves in relation to others in particular ways" (p.3). The social construction of the self takes place dynamically over time, in a variety of settings, with different groups of people and experiences, and evolving from one's historical location. Instead of a unidimensional identity, individuals construct numerous identities based on race, ethnicity, gender, age, sexual preference, academic ability, career choice, religious belief, and numerous other factors (Tierney, 1993). Philip Wexler (1988), in exploring high school student culture, called the process of individual and collective identity formation "**identity work**," the work that students undertake to "become someone." The identity that is produced in the peer-influenced environment of school defines the individual, but results from a symbolic, collective socialization process. How students narrate their perceptions of this transformative process during their transition to college is the focus of this research.

The tremendous amount of research and ethnographic literature concerning student racial (usually Black and White) and gender difference in the elementary and secondary schools has spawned questions and concerns about educational equity in this country. However, what is lacking is the same level of concerted study of college students from a variety of racial and ethnic locations. Like a breath of fresh air, the occasional study flitted across the sociological landscape and piqued curiosity on my part. William Tierney's rare study of "The College Experience of Native Americans" (1993) and Felix Padilla's unveiling of *The Struggle of Latino/Latina University Students* (1997) were two of the unusual works that centered the voices of college students within underrepresented groups on our campuses. Tierney's project was to erase some of the socially constructed invisibility around Native American students, and Padilla strove to provide an emancipatory space for marginalized students. Only as my research progressed, did I truly appreciate the complexity of these types of studies and understand why so few exist. As I sought out ethnographic work on college students from a range of racial/ethnic locations, more pieces surfaced which will be employed later in this study, but there are remarkably few studies and theoretical works to guide the work of researchers of multicultural students, especially those who enter colleges already disadvantaged by societal systems and who, therefore, face a tenuous transitional period of adjustment. This study seeks to address this gap of knowledge and to increase our understanding of this diverse student population and their experiences.

CONCLUSION

There is a lengthy history of sociological research that has explored how our society defines and participates in the production of disadvantaged students. Much of this work, even today, operates from a deficit model which views the student, often urban and Black, as lacking cultural capital and in need of remediation. Through the evolution of the critical culturalist and poststructuralist perspectives, questions about dominant ideologies and the status boundaries that are societally imposed are forced to the front. I borrow heavily from these perspectives in defining disadvantaged students as those who have been economically and educationally exploited and oppressed by groups and institutions in the United States. I acknowledge the multi-faceted complexity of the students who make up this group and, through this research, I delve deeper than race, gender, and class to uncover and understand more of the cultural origins and experiences of these students, and how these affect their perceptions and experiences within higher education.

Despite the fact that students in compensatory programs in higher education come from backgrounds of disadvantagement, this is neither a project of pity nor blame. Many students in these programs succeed by exercising emancipatory agency and creativity in the face of hegemonic situations. The stories that they narrate sound a clarion call for action from institutions of higher education to expand access and opportunity to meet the needs of the citizenry. HEOP and similar programs can play critical roles in supporting these efforts and ensuring the success of disadvantaged students. A social justice praxis dictates that the dreams and aspirations of *all* of our children in this society, not just the elite, are important, and given equitable access to educational resources, all children can become valued contributors to our country. We are all stakeholders.

The familial context and academic history of the HEOP students is explored in Chapters 2 and 3. Chapter 2 defines the breaks in the student group along three lines, coinciding with their history of immigration. Earlier family experiences develop three collective identities—the Pleasers, the Searchers, and the Skeptics—that are useful in understanding the college experiences that these students narrate. Their individual identities can be traced through these early years. Chapter 3 reveals the influence of the pre-college academic experiences within urban public school systems. Through an examination of the similarities and differences in experience for the three groups, we better understand how these students were positioned for entry into higher education.

In the remaining chapters, the students narrate their transitional collegiate experiences beginning with their first glimpse of the campus. Chapter 4 analyzes the academic college experiences and integration of the HEOP students during the mandatory summer program and fall semester. They were learning more than academics and this becomes the story of breaking the academic code at Ivy University and developing survival strategies. We hear how they worked to turn their marginalized positions within the academic culture into locations of strength. Chapter 5 peers into the social environment surrounding the students as they attempted to create a home away from home, to integrate socially into this space. Their use of time and space outside of the academic venue is revealed to be a negotiation between competing demands that they fight to balance. The fragile development of peer relationships within the social and academic space is the focus of Chapter 6. The presence of stigmatizing situations on a daily basis mandated strategic responses from the students which will be viewed through the frame of William Cross and Linda Strauss's (1998) theory of identity functions. Chapter 7 illustrates how the students were active agents in their pursuit of success on this campus. They coped with high levels of stress and mobilized around political responses to institutionalized oppression that contributed to their stress, all the while relying on the support of the one resource on campus that was responsive to their needs—the HEOP office.

Chapter 8 pulls these strands together and offers conclusions and implications derived from the lived experiences of these HEOP students at an elite university. The salient factors of identity construction expressed by this group of disadvantaged students as they make their transition to an elite university provide important perspectives that can assist individuals working to make higher education more responsive to ever-changing parameters.

CHAPTER 2

The HEOP Students:

Life Histories of Searching for the Dream

I don't really like that term, American Dream. I think people from all over the world have the same goals, and it's just that you're in one country or another.

–Clarissa, first generation immigrant from Guyana

The Higher Education Opportunity Program (HEOP) population is a "rich" group to study because it represents one of the most diverse groups at "Ivy University," an elite institution in upstate New York. The students share a common economic background, but represent a number of different racial, ethnic, and cultural groups and both genders. Because of this diversity and the complexity of adequately researching the interplay of these dynamics, I chose to limit this study to predominantly incoming freshman HEOP students.

In preparation for working with a group of students from diverse backgrounds, I focused on the challenges that the differences of gender, race, and ethnicity might pose for students from a subordinate economic class that would contrast sharply with the dominant group on campus. When I finally started working with the students themselves, I quickly realized that this complex group fractured along lines that were beyond gender, class, race and even ethnicity. I started picking apart the issues and events that had placed these students in disadvantaged situations, and I tried to avoid the pitfalls of essentializing these groups, as Michael Omi and Howard Winant (1994) warn: "Obviously, a key problem with essentialism is its denial, or flattening, of differences within a particular racially defined group" (p. 72), or within any group formed around fluidly constructed and changing constructs, including ethnicity, gender, or class. Over time, the students coalesced around three groupings defined by the factual length of time the students have lived in the United States. These groups only became apparent after interviewing the students and learning their life histories which had positioned them to pursue a degree at Ivy University.

The three groups that I identified, and which will be thoroughly discussed in the following chapters, were the "**Pleasers**," the "**Searchers**," and the "**Skeptics**." The "Pleasers" were the students who were first generation immigrants, born outside of the continental United States and who had immigrated to this country sometime before college. One of the outstanding characteristics of students within this group was their attempt to please primarily their parents, then their community, their school, and, finally, themselves. The second group, the "Searchers," were the second generation immigrant students, those whose parents immigrated to the United States sometime before the students were born. These students have always been citizens of the United States but have lived bicultural lives straddling their parents' culture(s) of origin and the dominant White culture within this country. Their search for identity between and within two or more cultures was a defining characteristic. The third group was the "Skeptics," those students who were multigenerationally United States citizens, but who have been historically disenfranchised by the dominant White society. Generations of oppression have led to a skepticism about their opportunities within the US system.

In examining the life histories of these students, aspects of their inside, internal identities as distinct from the outside, external identities became apparent. There is usually less negotiation and tension between these two aspects of identity when the students already shared many identity dimensions that matched the dominant culture (Jones, 1995). In order to better understand the identities that the HEOP students brought with them to college, this chapter explores the externalities that structured the development of the inner core of the students' identity. Through their narrations, it became clear that they did not share many of Ivy University's predominantly White identity dimensions. How they negotiated these differences will form the substance of following chapters.

THE RESEARCH COHORT

Twenty-three students formed the research cohort. Of these, sixteen were incoming freshmen, three were second year, one was third year, and three were fourth year students at Ivy University. Sixteen females and seven males participated. Nine of these students were first generation immigrants, the "Pleasers"; seven were second generation immigrants, the "Searchers"; and seven were the "Skeptics,"non-immigrant, multigenerational citizens of the United States. (For more detail about the student participants and the research methodology, see Goodwin, 2001.)

Fifteen of the 23 HEOP students were from New York City where at least a quarter of the population is foreign born (Youssef, 1992, p. 68-70). New York City has been a major destination for Caribbean immigrants since the 1970s, the borough of Brooklyn attracting almost 40% of them (p. 69). Of the seven students who hailed from Brooklyn, five of them were from Latin America. Four of the students and families lived in the borough of the Bronx, which attracts 16% of the immigrant population of New York City, mainly Europeans and Caribbeans (p. 70). One student resided in Queens, one in Manhattan, and one each on Staten Island and Long Island. While each borough of the city is ethnically diverse, many of the boroughs are inhabited by significant populations of specific nationalities which make them attractive for incoming immigrants who seek to maintain ethnic affiliations.

The patterns of settlement for the sixteen first and second generation immigrant families followed some predictable paths. However, the port of entry to the United States has many exits, not just New York City. Three of the students were from Vietnamese families who arrived under refugee status and were, therefore, subject to federal resettlement policies. The policies attempted to disperse the population throughout the country to avoid the concentrations that cities like New York City experienced as an "immigrant magnet." By settling smaller clusters of refugees in areas spread out across the country, the government hoped to ease the refugees' transition and lessen their impact on localities (Seller, 1988, p. 305; Portes, 1995, pp. 263-264). These three families were resettled in large communities in upstate New York. But whether from New York City or upstate New York, these students came from urban areas, most of them densely populated.

Within the broad categories that HEOP uses to define its population by racial and ethnic characteristics, eleven were Black, five Hispanic, four Asian, and three "Other." The "Other" students defined themselves as a "walking United Nations," "mixed," and "not White, not Black, not 100% Latin." Because the names that are used to describe the social constructs of race and ethnicity get so entangled and confused, I want to clarify the terminology that I employ throughout this text. I use the term **Black** to refer to those students who have identified themselves as Black, African, or African-American because it is, as Beverly Tatum (1997) points out, more inclusive. A number of HEOP students defined themselves as Black and noted that they were *not* African or American. I use **White** to refer to Anglo-Europeans or Caucasians. There are limitations to the use of either Black or White as descriptors for groups of people, especially because the terms of color deny the extreme variations of cultures and origins for the people within these groupings. But there are issues of power, racism, and oppression that need to be noted and that often get played out in our society along these artificial lines of color. Throughout this text, I capitalize Black and White to designate them as markers of cultural, social groupings, not colors.

Likewise, we enter a verbal maze when trying to find the language to describe the group that is categorized as "Hispanic." This panethnic label reveals little of the cultural diversity and national origins that these families represent. Many scholars have struggled with terminology to describe the multiple groups that inhabit the United States, as well as the Caribbean, Latin American, and South American countries. The task is complex because the groups are not racially homogeneous due to tumultuous histories of occupation, involuntary immigration, border wars, and internal warfare. The terms Hispanic and Latino do not mark racial or ethnic groups, but indicate culturally connected backgrounds. As Edna Acosta-Belen and Carlos Santiago (1998) point out:

> Hispanics, as they are identified by government agencies, or Latinos, as they generally prefer to be called, all have been lumped together under a collective label that tends to eclipse the many different nationalities, cultural experiences, and histories shared by the individual groups (p. 31).

These writers urge us to avoid the narrow and hegemonic perspectives that suppress and exclude the variety of cultural forms that exist in all societies. Ilan Stavans in *The Hispanic Condition* (1995) attempts to do this by sorting out the names used by various factions to describe these geographically and historically related groups of people:

> What are we: Hispanics, *hispanos*, Latinos (and Latinas), Latins, *iberoamericanos*, Spanish, Spanish-speaking people, Hispanic Americans (vis-a-vis the Latin Americans from across the Rio Grande), mestizos (and *mestizas*); or simply, Mexican-Americans, Cuban-Americans, Dominican-Americans, Puerto Ricans on the Mainland, and so forth?... The United States, a mosaic of races and culture, always needs to speak of its social quilt in generally stereotypical ways....[I]n printed media, on television, out in the streets, in the privacy of their homes, people hesitate between a couple of favorites: *Hispanic* and *Latino* (p. 24).

For the sake of consistency, I will adopt, with a slight modification, the following terminology that Stavans offers: "...I herewith suggest using *Latinos* to refer to those citizens from the Spanish-speaking world living *in* the United States and *Hispanics* to refer to those living elsewhere" (p.27). This is in agreement with the terminology accepted by

Acosta-Belen and Santiago (above), as well as the other authors of chapters within the text, *The Latino Studies Reader* (1998), in which their chapter was located. Recognizing that Latinas may take umbrage at being excluded within the male referent, Latino, my intention is not to ignore the continuous political struggle for recognition and voice in which females engage. Hence, the more cumbersome but inclusive **Latino/a** will be employed when referring to families that reside in the United States.

In summary, the 23 students who participated in this research can be described as predominantly urban, predominantly (16 first or second generation)immigrants, largely female (16 females and 7 males), and racially/ ethnically mixed (11 Black, 5 Latino/a, 4 Asian, 3 "Other"). After painting these students with such broad and, some would say, stereotypical strokes, we now turn to the more focused examination of the lived experiences of these three groups.

THE PLEASERS: FIRST GENERATION IMMIGRANTS

The early identities of the HEOP students were shaped by the influences of the parental histories and cultures. For the Pleasers, their childhoods were lived elsewhere, in a variety of countries and cultures other than the United States. The students relayed portions of their early lives that elucidated the roles that families, traditions, ethnicities, neighborhoods, and economics played in the formation of their identities. The families hailed from a variety of countries: the Dominican Republic, Ghana, Guyana, Jamaica, Thailand, Trinidad, and three from Vietnam. Three of the students identified themselves as Black, three as Asian, one as Hispanic, and one as a "walking United Nations." Five were female and four were male. This section weaves the major similarities that were noted, those revolving around issues of the American Dream, the need for a secure environment, the value placed on education, the disparity for parents between levels of education/skill and status of work, the importance of family, and the importance of traditions, with the most evident areas of difference between immigration patterns of refugees and non-refugees, their experience with the English language, American citizenship, national/racial/ethnic identities, and their family histories.

Coming to America for the Dream

These first generation immigrant students brought more to the United States than just their personal possessions. Far more valuable were their histories and life experiences coalescing around bittersweet memories of home: binding ties to family left behind; to teachers and friends who had been strong figures in their childhoods; and, to the sense of belonging to a homogeneous community that was one's starting place, one's home. These "sweet" memories were tempered by the bitter experiences of separation from parents due to prison or immigration, economic deprivation, fading opportunities for advancement, and sacrifice on the part of all family members. With great anticipation, some of it anxious and some of it eager, these students brought these identities to their new country which would become home. Their task was to learn to be bicultural, become enough of a United States' American to make a niche for themselves, yet never forget the part that was forged elsewhere.

These students were no strangers to hard work and dreams; they were not afraid of either. They brought with them what they hoped would be the "right" cultural and academic capital to enable them to participate in the "American Dream." Some of them came with facility in English and some came with the barrier of language as their first hurdle. But they were not short on intelligence or hope, and all believed that America would offer them opportunity and a new start. Jennifer Hochschild's (1995) work, *Facing Up to the American Dream*, thoroughly examines the paradox of the **American Dream** and identifies the major tenets which underlie this ideology. "The ideology promises that everyone, regardless of ascription or background, may reasonably seek success through actions and traits under their own control. True success, however, must be associated with virtue" (p. 4).

Overwhelmingly, the students and their families came to the United States to pursue the "American Dream," however that may be conceived. The words they used over and over were "a better opportunity." To these families, there is a dream, whether it is called a "Vietnamese Dream" or a "Jamaican Dream" or a more generic "Latin American Dream"; the important point is that immigration occurs because there is an urgent reason for change. And, in any change, the optimistic perspective is that it will be change for the better. These immigrant families were ready to base their dreams on the terms set by Hochschild's definition of the American Dream (1995, pp. 18-24). They sought success and they were willing to work for it; they did not just expect that it would be handed to them as they "passed go" or the custom's checkpoint. They prayed that their background and immigrant status would not hamper their ability to achieve a better life. And they were "virtuous" people, willing to learn and follow the standards and rules that the United States set for achieving success. John Ogbu (1991) and Marcelo Suarez-Orozco (1991) have pointed out that immigrant families hold a "positive **dual frame of reference**" which enables them to compare two countries of residence and feel optimistic that the United States holds more opportunity for them. They see the potential for upward mobility, the possibility that with hard work and education their children will rise beyond the marginal jobs to which the parents are condemned. However, through her research with Dominican immigrants, Patricia Pessar (1997) points out that this dream doesn't match the reality they discover:

> As we shall see, for many of these people, both the "Dominican dream" of a rapid and successful return back home and the "American dream" of going from rags to riches remain elusive. They struggle, instead, with a deteriorating New York economy, over-crowding, limited education and skills, high incidences of female-headed households, and racial and ethnic discrimination (p. 131).

Even though the situations that compelled these families to immigrate to the United States were different, the quest for improved opportunity was certainly the shared goal, and they tolerated the accommodations that had to be made. Three families came as refugees from Vietnam, those of Luc, Tran, and Mai, with the nuclear family intact. They were part of the "third wave" of Vietnamese diaspora (Centrie, 2000). Each family sought a place to escape the memories of war and the imprisonment of the fathers, and a place that would not constrain their children's futures as an act of political revenge. All of these families were settled in upper New York State. The remaining six families resided in New York City and experienced different settlement patterns from the refugees. What was similar, however, was the quest for more opportunity for the children to become successful. One student, Clarissa from Guyana, arrived with her nuclear family, her mother. However, the remaining five families came at staggered times. One or both parents came ahead to "test the waters" of employment opportunity and to develop a viable life in this country before bringing the rest of the family over. These students from Ghana, Trinidad, Thailand, Jamaica, and the Dominican Republic, were usually left in the care of relatives, often the grandmother, until the parents had managed to save enough money for the "papers" and could send for the children. Patricia Pessar (1997)has noted that leaving children behind while parents secured jobs and enough income to sponsor the children's migration was a common, yet problematic pattern for Dominican immigrants. An exception to leaving children with relatives was Veronika from Ghana. Her father left when she was six and her mother followed when she was 14, leaving six children to care for themselves for two years, subsisting on the monthly packets of money sent by the parents, which was rarely enough. Veronika stated that "...there were times when I went to school with nothing to eat 'cause there was no food in the house. You'd see everybody with their lunches, and I'm just sitting there, trying to ask people for food." These families illustrate a widespread pattern of children left behind in sometimes questionable living arrangements in the homelands for a period of time.

The patterns of settlement for the families echoed the need for ethnic affiliation that continued beyond immigration. Most of these families resided in areas that had large populations that resembled them and provided an opportunity to form ethnic communities that may have helped buffer the assault of new cultural and societal demands. Maxine Seller (1988) identifies ethnic communities as groups of people who unite around common national origin, language, religion and, perhaps, physical characteristics. She explains that these commonalities are sought out due to internal needs of the incoming group members, as well as perceived external pressures from the dominant and established groups. The ethnic community shares memories, as well as aspirations for the future, that can help reinforce lifestyles and values (pp. 3-6). Through the maintenance of an ethnic identity, the community may also delay or soften some of the issues of immigration, among them the feeling of being the "other."

Accommodations to Location

Setting foot in a new culture, the United States, forced the immigrant families to undergo various transformations when the "old" traditions collided head-on into the pressures of the "new" society. The challenges of identity construction within this dual frame of reference were immense. Language loomed large as one of the major hurdles for many immigrants. Some of the Pleasers were fortunate to come to the United States with a well-developed ability with the English language, surpassing the skill of some of those who were born and raised on these shores. Four of the students felt comfortable with English, although two were self-conscious that their accents, word choices, and phrasing would betray their foreign roots. These concerns were unproblematic; if anything, they allowed them to interact more with others in the process of explaining where they were from and their customs. However, for the non-English speakers, it was another story. These students related, over and over, stories of miscommunications that left them and their families feeling truly outside the mainstream of American society. Charles Hirschman (1996) maintains that:

> Immigrants—the first generation—are handicapped by their newcomer status and rarely expected to achieve socioeconomic parity with the native population. Learning a new language, the lack of recognition of educational qualifications from a different system, and native prejudice and hostility toward those with foreign accents and cultures are major obstacles for immigrants (p. 56).

Lack of language proficiency presented problems in schooling (to be discussed in Chapter 3) and in employment opportunities for the parents. Students were enlisted by parents as translators in several cases.

Just the legalities of immigration positioned the immigrants as "others" until they became citizens. For the refugee families, that meant that after one year in the United States they could adjust their status and become permanent residents. For non-refugee immigrant families, the wait was five years before they could apply for citizenship. This presented a complication for Roberto, an immigrant from Jamaica, who ended up waiting an extra two years for the approval of his citizenship request. In the meantime, he had to forego admission to his first choice college. And Veronika, from Ghana, would not be eligible to apply for citizenship until her second year in college. So, the national identity of these students was not necessarily American.

Even when citizenship had been secured, there was a determination to not be identified solely as American. Three of these students preferred the racial/ethnic identity of Black over African America because, as Veronika stated: "I am not American in any way and so African-American does not work for me." Clarissa described her grandparents as "mixed" and indicated that, "we have members of the family that are everything." Two of the Vietnamese students and one from Thailand preferred "Asian" as their racial/ethnic identity, while Mai, a Vietnamese female, indicated "Asian-American." Paolo, from Trinidad, and Ileana, from the Dominican Republic, gave the most complex responses when asked about their racial or ethnic identity:

> *Paolo*: None....No, I consider myself a walking United Nations....I'm racially mixed; like, extremely racially mixed.

> *   *   *   *   *

> *Ileana*: That would be hard. Maybe Hispanic as a whole because I'm one quarter Dominican, one quarter Japanese, one quarter Puerto Rican, one eighth Haitian, and one eighth German.

Most of these students described a freedom in their homelands to wander and explore within the safe confines of their vigilant communities. This was one of the sacrifices the Pleasers made for the "privilege" of immigrating to the United States. The families moved into areas that bore no resemblance to "back home," and the questionable environment of the unknown instilled protective constraints in parents who once felt little need for them. Four of the students, from Vietnam, Guyana, Dominican Republic, and Jamaica, complained that their parents tightened the leash. The diversity of the new neighborhoods exposed the families to influences from all over the world, and not necessarily the influences they sought for their children. Where the previous neighborhoods had been fairly homogeneous and known entities, these neighborhoods stood taller, compressed greater numbers of people within its spaces, and sheltered languages and customs that were different and sometimes dangerous. The fact that the immigrant families were viewed as different, as well, added to the fear of the new environment. Many of the students described a lack of community that was as significant a change for them as the more diverse, bustling communities experienced by those who lived in New York City. Some of these families were positioned within areas that harbored an ethnic enclave that they affiliated with, but all around were "others" who had little in common with them other than the space they shared. Most of the parents assumed a protective stance that felt stifling to these students.

Work and Money

Most of the Pleasers spoke of the stress of economic upheaval in their countries that prompted their family's emigration. However, it is interesting to note that while two of the Pleasers felt that their economic status had improved in the United States, the majority felt that things were just as tight, if not tighter than when they lived in their native countries. Some felt that the situation was worse when they first moved to the United States. Parents had to work longer and harder to provide for their families. On top of other financial strains, the New York City students lived in one of the most expensive cities in this country in terms of cost of living.

For some families, the move resulted in **downward status mobility**. In other words, their economic situations in the United States placed them in less socially respected positions than in their own countries. In their own countries, their education levels were respectable. Most of the fathers had completed some college before immigrating, although their wives had significantly less education. Of the Pleasers who thought they knew the educational history of their fathers, all five of them had some college experience, one of them achieving a master's degree. In contrast, four of the mothers had completed twelfth grade or less, and two of these mothers finished college. A number of parents had been teachers in their homelands. In most cases, both parents were employed in the United States but in low paying, unskilled factory or health care positions. Several of the parents had suffered health problems that forced them into unemployment and/or debt. Two of the fathers returned to their homelands (Ghana and the Dominican Republic) during the course of this research. Patricia Pessar (1997) commented about the rebound effect for Dominicans:

> A final point in Dominicans' discourse on immigration may surprise native-born Americans accustomed to the notion that immigrants come to settle. I refer to the fact that many intend to return home in order to best enjoy their hard-fought gains in social and economic standing. In their words, in New York *"hay trabajo pero no hay vida"*("there is work, but there is no life") (p.131).

The most remarkable success story was the mother of Panyos, from Thailand. She immigrated with only a fourth grade education, but through her longevity and diligence with her job as a gem sorter, she had become so skilled that her employer offered her incentives to stay. Language was not a barrier in this line of work.

Despite the financial strains that these families felt, many of the Pleasers were not regularly employed in high school. The first generation immigrant parents made education the top priority and discouraged their children from regular employment. Luc, from Vietnam, worked about ten hours a week at a fast food restaurant in order to supplement the family's income and, more importantly, to gain English skills. Tran, also from Vietnam, worked about eight hours a week at a hospital as part of a school program. Several other students had minor, part-time jobs, but nothing that would interfere with school. As part of their protective stance, parents of the Pleasers protected their children from the streets of their neighborhoods and the rigors of low wage employment. However, in doing so, they further isolated their children from situations that would place them in greater interaction with their new culture, which delayed the full impact of immigration.

Families and Traditions

Of interest in this group of nine students was that seven had parents who were a couple, although this needs to be loosely defined in light of some of them living apart for extended periods of time during the periods of staggered immigration. The two divorced couples were divorced before the mothers immigrated with the children. This number is notably high for the HEOP population with whom I worked, and certainly considerably higher than in the population at large where divorce rates are touted at over 50% of all couples who marry.

However, family relationships became complicated, especially with parents who were absent from their children's lives for a significant period of time. Most of the Pleasers spoke of strict parents (Mai, from

Vietnam, indicated that *all* Asian parents are strict) who sheltered them from the realities of life. Despite the physical and emotional abuse which the students described as acceptable in their cultures, but which would be considered criminal abuse in the United States, most of these students described their relationships with their families as close and meaningful. But in the dialectics of any relationship, closeness in some aspects of the family bond does not translate into unproblematic relations. Paolo, from Trinidad, described his family as "corrupt" and "screwed up." Without going into detail, he stated that he was physically and emotionally abused as a child, and he recalls a lot of anger and name calling in the home. Veronika, from Ghana, expressed her closeness with her mother, but shared the frustration she felt about a family who couldn't communicate and a father who was absent for a critical number of years and didn't really know her (and who returned to Ghana during her freshman year in college). Roberto, from Jamaica, had a working relationship with his mother but qualified it: "My mom is like my only family. We're close, but we're not as close as those TV families. I can talk to her, but she's not always there for me to talk to her..." After sharing that his father was very strict and beat him until about age 14, Tran, from Vietnam, described his family as "...very internal emotional....They know what you're doing, they know what you are going to, they know how you feel, but they don't say it out." Cracks in family unity added further complications to the formation of identity during the early years of life and affected the students' ability to develop relationships of depth and trust, which some students later commented on when discussing friendships and romantic relationships.

For many of the Pleasers, extended family provided a safety net. A number of these students had lived with their relatives for years while their parents were in the United States. Many of them were deeply influenced by relatives who became their role models. Most Pleasers spoke of the strong connections with their extended families and the difficulty of leaving them behind.

Because the Pleasers lived for years in different cultures, all of them far older and with more established traditions than the United States, I expected that their lives would continue to be immersed in a number of meaningful traditions carried over from the homeland. When I asked them about traditions that they celebrated with their families, most of them shook their heads and said, "none." Probing this, many observed some aspects of Christmas, mostly the gifts and excitement of the season. Further questioning brought to light a variety of religious traditions, some of which continued to be observed in the new home, but many of which had tapered off to almost non-existence. Luc (Vietnam) and Panyos (Thailand) went to a Buddhist temple on occasion, usually major holy days. Roberto (Jamaica), Paolo (Trinidad), and Ileana (Dominican Republic) were raised in the Catholic faith, but none of them, at the time of the interviews, attended church. None of these five students spoke of deep commitment to their beliefs. Tran (Vietnam), who was Catholic, indicated that he prayed every night. After explaining his family's celebration of the Chinese New Year, he described his devotion to the celebration of Christmas, reflecting a bicultural observance of holidays. Mai's (Vietnam) family was polytheistic which she defined as, "...we respect every God. We believe in Jesus and Buddha....We celebrate Christmas and the day Buddha was born. We have a lot of holidays." Craig Centrie (2000) observed: "As recent arrivals, the Vietnamese have a connection to traditional Confucianist and Taoist values, such as respect for education, teachers, and elders, as well as a drive to do well for their families and community" (p. 68). Although the students did not speak of these belief systems (other than Mai), they were evident in what the students shared about their families and their behaviors. Of the two students who were Protestants, and who both indicated that they attended church, one indicated that it was just a perfunctory obligation, while the other was faithful in attending several church functions a week. In puzzling through the reasons for the seemingly weak cultural traditions that these students exhibited, the most probable explanation was that these students all came from families who were working hard to just survive and had little time and few resources to devote to the development of family and cultural traditions. Family bonds were stretched by parental absences which made traditions difficult to develop, even when the cultural traditions may have thrived in the neighborhood outside their doors. And then there is the guarded nature of one's inner identity, that may not easily share the depth of one's most intimate beliefs.

THE SEARCHERS: SECOND GENERATION IMMIGRANTS

The Searchers were born and raised in the United States, but by parents who were immigrants and whose cultures of origin set the tone within the family circles. More than the first generation immigrant students, these individuals bring a cultural background of dual allegiance. Through their parents and extended families, they are surrounded with cultural impressions of the parental homeland. But their experiences as native born Americans temper their need to affiliate deeply with the parental culture. Instead, they have formed identities within the culture that they have lived every day of their lives, that of a citizen of the United States.

These students' families reflect the "mosaic" of Latino/a cultures to which Stavans (1995) earlier alluded with genealogies from Puerto Rico, El Salvador, Cuba, Peru, and Ecuador. Diverging from this Latino/a pattern, but adding to the complexity of this group, are families from Grenada and Taiwan. Two of the young women have parental roots in Puerto Rico. Although Puerto Rico is a commonwealth, a protectorate of the United States, and, therefore, their parents were not true immigrants when they migrated to the mainland, I place these students with the second generation immigrant families because their parents were born outside of the continental United States, and their cultural background in Puerto Rico made the transition to the mainland US as fracturing as the experiences of many immigrants. They are also viewed by sectors within the dominant, "established" United States' society as outsiders, despite the status of Puerto Rico as a US protectorate. In fact, they may face more oppression through prejudicial attitudes than many immigrant groups. Antonia Darder and Rodolfo Torres (1998) raise this point: "Although formally US citizens since 1917, albeit with limited political rights, the benefits accruing to Puerto Ricans as a result of such status have been minimal when compared to more recently arrived Latino groups such as Cuban Americans" (p. 15). Their larger argument highlights the blame placed on poor and working class Latino/as for "...poor urban conditions, soaring welfare rates, and the deteriorating national economy" (p. 14). Puerto Rican migrants are not exempt from the anti-immigrant sentiments being echoed across the US. Therefore, these students of Puerto Rican heritage face similar issues to those of other second generation immigrant students.

Despite being predominantly Latino/a, the individuals in this group identify themselves in a variety of ways. Four are Latina, one is Black, one is "mixed" (mother from Taiwan), and one is "living...not White, not black, not 100% Latin" (parents from Puerto Rico). Six of the seven students are female. Six were born and raised in New York City and one in Florida. In many cases, these students have never visited their parents' homelands, so they live their cultural heritage vicariously, some more, some less, through their parents.

The Dream

The Searchers are the children of first generation immigrant parents who came to this country seeking opportunities that were non-existent for them in their countries of birth, much like the parents of the Pleasers. The often unrealized dreams of the parents are transferred to the children upon whom the burden of success now rests. The lives that these second generation immigrant students narrated allow a glimpse of how they have been groomed through these early years to take up the task of becoming successful both in the eyes of their families and within their own minds, which are not necessarily shared visions.

In a home with parents who were first generation immigrants, the identity of the children is impacted by the cultural heritage of the parents that is interpreted, translated, and modified through the next generation. In studying recent immigrant adaptation, Charles Hirschman (1996) describes a "**standard intergenerational process model**" for second generation immigrant children:

> The second generation, the children of immigrants, are socialized and educated both in mainstream society (usually the public schools) and in their ethnic homes and neighborhoods. From the former, the children of immigrants gain the skills necessary for equal participation in the American occupational structure; from the latter, many internalize the immigrant belief that America is a land of opportunity for those with perseverance and determination (p. 56).

The second generation immigrant students in this study often reflected cultural influences from their home environments that were rooted in the immigrant faith in the possibility of achieving this American dream. Martine (parents from El Salvador and Cuba) addressed this most clearly:

> Yeh, I love this country. Some people are born here but say they love Dominica to me. And I say, "How can you say that after what this country has given you, what it's providing for you?" I take nothing for granted, because I've seen my father especially, and my mother comes from a country that's been at war for like 13 years. Both my countries are like horrible.

It is interesting to note that while Martine extolled the virtues of America, the country of her birth, she continued to call both Cuba and El Salvador "*my* countries."

More indirectly, but certainly demonstrating an appreciation for the improved opportunities provided in the United States, Alicia criticized the opportunities for women in Peru (her parents' native country), as contrasted to the United States. Her mother defied custom to achieve a doctorate but was not allowed to work in Peru because she had a child. She also spoke of the austere expectations for serious students in Peru. Their lives were devoted to academic pursuits. "There's no TV, no friends, no socializing, no network. You study and that's it." However, Alicia's mother arrived in the United States speaking little English and, because of this, was shut out of employment opportunities commensurate with her educational attainment. For her the dream was not fully achieved, although she was allowed to work, but as a taxi driver, which certainly did not utilize her pharmacological training. So, while America may have provided opportunities that were unavailable in their native lands, most of the parents quickly understood that it was not the "land of milk and honey," either.

Work and Money

Like the Pleasers, none of the Searcher families experienced a smooth transition into positions of economic upward mobility even though that was the dream of immigration. For a few, their status levels declined after immigrating. Two of the young women indicated that one of their parents came from families who were fairly well off financially in their homelands. Family rifts had forced the parents to emigrate and experience a drop in their economic positions. When asked about their family's financial situation, four of the Searchers responded that money has always been an issue in their households. They observed how their parents always made things work despite the lack of money and steady employment, but they felt guilty asking for money after seeing how hard their parents worked and the personal sacrifices they made. When asked if money was tight, Tiana (Puerto Rico) stated, "Way tighter, which is hard, because I need money, also. And to ask them for money, I know I'm taking away from something else they need to do."

Even though the education levels that the Searchers' parents brought to the United States varied tremendously, most of them ended up in low skilled service sector jobs, much like the Pleasers' parents. Three sets of parents had some college experience, with one couple each having earned doctorates. This couple now drives taxi cabs in New York City, and the other two couples hold secretarial and bus driving jobs. Several of the parents had achieved only a junior high school education and were part of the unskilled janitorial and housekeeping service sector. Those who completed high school were no better off. However, several fathers became self-employed owners of a tire shop, a beverage store, and real estate, although they continued to struggle for financial security. Even in this light, self-employment could be viewed as making it further than any of the parents of the Pleasers. However, like the Pleasers' parents, none of these families found lucrative jobs awaiting them on arrival to the United States. They worked hard in low level jobs to survive, and their dreams of financial security have, for the most part, been deferred to their children.

Several of these families experienced financial decline when the parents divorced. Jason, (mother from Taiwan and White father), talked about his mother having a difficult time managing money, and his father was not contributing child support consistently. The foreclosure of their house when his mother hurt her back compounded the embarrassment that Jason voiced about their lack of money:

> A lot of times [it was embarrassing] because the school that I went to, a lot of the kids were very well off. My mom tried to give us the best clothes and a new baseball bat. I think that's why we got into a lot of financial problems. I don't know. It's still like a kind of stigma attached to myself, even now. If I don't have any money in my pocket...

As in Jason's family, several parents suffered health problems that threw them into financial crisis when, as a result, they had to change to lower-paying jobs or they became unemployed.

Unlike most of the Pleasers, the Searchers worked for pay during high school. Most of the jobs were typical after school jobs at retail stores, although Marie (Ecuador) worked in her father's tire shop everyday after school. The students indicated that they needed to work to help their families and to pay for extra school activities. Tiana (Puerto Rico) worked the most, 30 hours a week at a fish shop even though her high school program limited her to 18 hours of work a week. As she said, "I needed money to live on."

Families and Traditions

Family relationships for the second generation immigrant students indicated more tensions and fractures than those of the first generation immigrant students. Four of these families were headed by parents who were still married to each other. However, for the other three families, the effects of divorce played out in increased economic hardships like Jason explained in the previous section. Divorce made it that much harder for these families who already held low-wage positions to hold things together. More difficult than just the financial repercussions, were the changes in family structure. Tiana (Puerto Rico) and Yasmin (Puerto Rico) ended up living with their grandmothers. When asked to describe her family, Yasmin revealed deep resentment toward her parents:

> I want to say dysfunctional, but I don't know in what sense. The only thing, nobody in my family killed anybody...They [Yasmin's parents] had my two brothers in the Bronx. After a couple of years, they moved to Puerto Rico and then they moved to Miami where they had my sister. And then they moved to California. My mom got pregnant for me and they moved back here. And then they split...they left my brothers

and my sister there with my grandmother and she took care of us....I disown my dad. My mother, I kind of disowned her, too. They were very irresponsible to do what they did. They got married very young and they couldn't be together after my oldest brother, but, yet, they had three more kids and there was even a 10 year break between my oldest brother and my oldest sister....

Four of the young women in this group commented on the strictness of their parents, an issue in common with most of the Pleasers. Martine (El Salvador and Cuba) described her parents as: "Very strict. I don't know if this is the right word, but demanding." She and Marie (Ecuador) indicated that their parents were very cautious about where they went and with whom. There was a strong concern about the safety of being out on the streets in New York City. Laila's (Grenada) parents were also very protective of their daughter which she attributed to her unique childhood:

I was the middle child of three children and my older brother and my younger brother, they both had autism. They never put pressure on me, my parents. They encouraged me, as long as I did my best. They never pressured me. They would say, "You are the only well child." But, they were very protective. I didn't get many opportunities to go to the movies with my friends, especially when I was young.... Being West Indian parents, they have certain values and certain things they want upheld.

Tiana (Puerto Rico) had been an only child for 10 years and described her mother as overly protective, similar to the experiences of the other young women in this Latina cohort. She stayed inside and played by herself most of the time. These young women observed that they were regimented more closely by their parents than many of their peers. This tendency to protect females is often attributed to male family members, but, in Tiana's case, it was her mother who created the repressive environment. Michelle Fine and Lois Weis (1998), in their study of poor or working-class young adults, commented on this protective tendency: "[W]e repeatedly heard about maternal maneuvers of what we might consider *strategic agoraphobia;* mothers incubating babies and children within their apartments and homes much more intensively than in the past" (p. 197). This effort toward "good parenting" was clearly evident among most of the first generation immigrant parents, including those of the Pleasers and the Searchers. The students chafed under this close monitoring, but understood the source of their parents' concerns.

While several of these students assumed considerable household responsibility, especially for their siblings, none of them complained that parental expectations were unfair or overwhelming. Alicia (Peru), like Laila (Grenada) and Yasmin (Puerto Rico), shouldered a great deal of the caretaking of her siblings. Her parents had such erratic work schedules as taxi drivers that Alicia was often late to school because one of her many jobs was to drop her siblings off at their school. She called herself the "virgin mother" who protected her siblings when her parents fought.

Relationships with extended family were difficult for students whose relatives lived in homelands they had never visited. Several, like Martine (El Salvador and Cuba), indicated that they had no extended family in the United States. Martine's remaining family in Cuba had been out of touch since the late 70s, and she rarely saw her aunt and cousins in El Salvador. For those few who had extended family living nearby, the relationships were usually described as close and united. And Tiana and Yasmin (both Puerto Rico) spoke of solid love and respect for the grandmothers with whom they lived. However, Jason (Taiwan) discovered that divorce separated him not only from his father, but from his father's family, and he had seen his grandmother from Taiwan only once. Several students described rifts between the parents and grandparents, resulting in estranged relations with relatives living in other countries. Relationships with extended family fell into unique patterns for each of these students. However, there was much more variation among the Searchers than the Pleasers, especially with the loss of contact between significant members of the family, sometimes by choice and sometimes through the natural attrition of time and distance.

The Searchers demonstrated an apparent resignation or preference to separate from the parental homelands, which may explain the lack of interest most of these students also expressed in cultural traditions. This group narrated more discontinuity than continuity in terms of traditions that bind families. Like the first generation immigrant students, these Searchers and their families were not subscribing to many of the traditions of their homelands. When asked if their families had any special traditions or rituals that they followed, the majority of the students responded that they gathered for at least one holiday a year, usually Thanksgiving. Laila's (Grenada) response seemed indicative of the attitudes these students shared toward traditional holidays: "I guess you can consider we have very regular *American* [my emphasis] traditions." It is conceivable that the students participated in more ethnically based celebrations or traditions, but they did not consciously associate these with traditions or holidays, thinking only that the American celebrations, or as Jason (Taiwan and White) called them, "...*normal* holidays," counted in this country. Jason's family did celebrate "normal" holidays, but he was upset that this was mostly a residue from his father's cultural domination of the family. He had only recently begun to appreciate his Taiwanese background. The economic status of these students from immigrant backgrounds, the Pleasers and the Searchers, made traditions and rituals luxuries that they had little opportunity to cultivate. Marie (Ecuador) explained: "We don't have time to make up traditions. We have to basically work."

Among the Searchers, religious traditions were also undergoing "Americanization" and retooling to suit the individual versus the collective identity. Yasmin (Puerto Rico) was the only one who spoke strongly about her Catholic faith. Comments from the other students indicated a distancing from the religious traditions of parental homelands. Tiana (Puerto Rico) explained that she "church-hopped," seeking the right "atmosphere." The mothers in this group, like the Pleasers, seemed more inclined to participate in church than fathers, but even they were not regular attendees. Most of the students had not rejected religion, but they had observed the weakening of its importance in their parents' lives and had questioned its place in theirs. Tiana, Martine (El Salvador and Cuba), Alicia (Peru), and Marie (Ecuador) were actively engaged in choosing their own religious involvement which seemed to have little to do with their parents' cultural/ethnic backgrounds. The influence of a collective identity around these traditions did not appear as strong as the students' desires to create their own meaningful traditions around Americanized versions of holidays and family configurations, as well as religious affiliation.

Narrations of Location

Of the three groups in this study, the Searchers narrated the most conflict and complexity when attempting to describe themselves in any way. Their identities seemed the most in flux. Ruben Rumbaut (1996) studied the formation of ethnic identity among children of immigrants and observed that second generation immigrant children often identify themselves as American, whereas first generation immigrants usually assume an ancestral or national-origin identity (although the Pleasers were an exception to this observation). In between, lie individuals who are in the process of making the transition between these two poles and who tend to identify themselves as hyphenated Americans (p.167). These Searchers, all second generation immigrants, reflected the entire range of ethnic identities. However, they did not seem as eager to lose their ancestral identities as Rumbaut observed in his research. When asked in which racial or ethnic group they located themselves, Laila (Grenada) immediately chose the hyphenated African-American, Marie (Ecuador) indicated Hispanic, and Alicia (Peru) said Latin. Tiana's opening quotation for Chapter 1, is reflected in these other responses which are quoted at length because they capture well the internal identity struggle that represents this group:

> *Yasmin* (Puerto Rico): Living! Minority not qualitatively, but quantitatively. Not White, not Black, not 100% Latin. Mixed. Some people call me White, when there's only a Black/White comparison. Others say like you're Spanish, like you're Puerto Rican, therefore Black. Others, you're American. [Later, when discussing her friends:] ...I'm Puerto Rican.

> *   *   *   *   *

> *Jason* (Taiwan and White): Um, mixed. I can't really put it...Asian-German, Asian-White. I don't really like doing that...you know, since I'm half Asian and half Caucasian, it's kind of like split up my life....I always look at it, I brought out my Caucasian side and I hated my Asian side. I always hated it. I was always embarrassed about, somebody would say, "Did you watch that movie where somebody was a chink, blah, blah?" I'd think, that's me. But then, at the same time, some of those forces pulled me in certain directions without me knowing it. Maybe I just think too much about it.

> *   *   *   *   *

> *Martine* (El Salvador and Cuba): Latino. Spanish. Yeh, it depends on who I'm with. Certain people don't like the term Hispanic. I really, honestly don't care. Call me Spanish. Call me Hispanic. Spanish is really not correct, but I don't care...

> *LG*: Why do you define yourself in these groups?

> *Martine*: Because everybody seems to have defined me in it. It is my culture and my background, even though I'd rather just say I'm American. I honestly consider myself more American than anything else.

Two of the women preferred "American," although they voiced many optional identities. Most of these students were undergoing to the same "name" dilemma that Stavans (1995) identified earlier. They ran through the gamut of identifiers that they have used and that others have ascribed to them. There are interesting mixes of racial identifiers: Black, White, and Caucasian; with national/ethnic identifiers: Hispanic, Latin, Puerto Rican, and Spanish, just as we saw in the Pleasers. For many of the Searchers, their ethnic identities are still being formed, based on their ancestry, but also through societal messages that quickly reduce identities for convenience, but with little thought or justification. They have not neatly aligned themselves in the three categories that Rumbaut identified. Even in the transition between national affiliation, there is little tendency for this group to hyphenate their identities.

Another point of discussion concerning how these students identify themselves, is the influence of societal expectations that limits their choice of identifiers. Patricia Fernandez Kelly and Richard Schauffler (1996) explain that: "Among vulnerable groups, the ability to shift ethnic identity often provides a defense from stigma and an incentive to defy leveling pressures. How they define themselves depends on the context" (p. 50). Some terms that groups and individuals find offensive or slang (for example, "Chicano") are avoided, while other identifiers are selected when speaking with people who understand little about cultural/ethnic differences. The term, Latino, is generally understood to mean someone from a Spanish speaking background, although it obfuscates the true heritage of the person. Yasmin (Puerto Rico) and Martine (El Salvador and Cuba) indicated that others have defined them, and they sometimes choose to accept these identifiers, and, at other times, reject them. None of these students voiced a preference that was based on their parents' perspective. If anything, Martine narrated a regret over her father's strong cultural identification:

> My father has dedicated a lot of his life to politics, because [of] Cuba and communism. Since he was against the revolution, he's always hoping....like communism has had a big effect on my life because he's not always there because he concentrates on that. In a way, it's like communism took him away from me. That's the way I see it.

The bottom line is that few of these students felt comfortable enough, or chose at this stage in their identity development, to call themselves American, nor strictly assume the ethnic identity of their parents.

The Searchers, unlike the Pleasers, were subjected to the fall-out from their parents having already survived and adapted to the US environment. These students, for the most part, were born in the communities in which they grew up, six of the seven in New York City. They viewed their neighborhoods through the eyes of a native, not an immigrant. While their parents may have retained an immigrant fear of the urban streets, most of these students dispelled the commonly held notion that New York City is rife with crime and is an unsafe place to live. Even though some of the Searchers' neighborhoods were dangerous enough that the parents limited their children's exposure to them, the students, for the most part, were accepting of the neighborhoods in which they had spent their lives. Several had witnessed a positive change in their neighborhoods and attributed it to more of a police presence, and, beyond that, the students seemed to give them little thought. The Pleasers were far more observant and critical, both positively and negatively, having another country as a base for comparison. While they appreciated the opportunity to be in the United States, they recognized a distinct change in their personal freedom and in their ability to use public space. They expressed an awareness of feeling like outsiders which the Searchers didn't experience. To the contrary, they viewed themselves as part of a changing community that ebbed and flowed with the times.

THE SKEPTICS: INVOLUNTARY IMMIGRANTS

The Skeptics grew up in families who had been a part of the American fabric for generations, yet they were marginalized from the mainstream due to economics, race, and societal prejudices. While the Pleasers and Searchers are recent immigrants whose families voluntarily chose to immigrate to the United States, the Skeptics are descendants of **involuntary immigrants**, many of their ancestors arriving in this hemisphere as slaves (Ogbu, 1991). These students inhabit a unique, historically determined location. While they are citizens of the United States, years of overt and covert discrimination by, and forced subordination to, the dominant White, Anglo-European majority, has placed them in the position of being minorities on most campuses with unique needs and interests, somewhat like immigrant students, yet in many ways very different.

The seven Skeptics all defined themselves as Black or African-American. Three of them were from New York City, and the remaining four were raised in urban areas of upstate New York. Five were female and two were male. With these descriptors, this group sounds the most homogeneous of the three. However, just as with the other two groups, these individuals did not form a monolithic collective. Their narrations show a number of lines of fracture.

The Dream

Among the Skeptics, the American Dream only surfaced in their conversations during a focus group when I asked specifically about their interpretations of the American Dream:

> *Stacey:* I went to high school with a lot of foreigners and the fourth of
> July is a great day to me. I don't know where I get all this patriotism

from, but I happen to like being an American most of the time and I guess I'm kind of proud to be American. The American Dream, on the other hand, I don't know about that. I suppose it depends on which American you're talking to and where they are in their lives. So, I think it varies from person to person, because you can be American and be from somewhere else. So, it just depends on which American.

Sybill: I think a lot of the American Dream is a white picket fence, six figure salary. But to me, my dream is just happiness and whatever that makes me. A lot of people get caught up on the materialistic things. It's sad.

Nicole: [Americans value] money and getting ahead. Status.

None of these students openly embraced the concept of an American Dream, but through their goals and aspirations that will become evident in later chapters, they still indicated a belief that it is possible to achieve dreams. The dreams just may not look like everyone else's.

This lack of verbal attention to the national myth of dreams and opportunities for success may best be explained by John Ogbu's work with voluntary and involuntary immigrant cultural models (1991). For the Skeptics, the explanation for their location within the poor and working class is not based primarily on voluntary immigration status, like it is for the Pleasers and Searchers. The families of the Skeptics have experienced generations of discrimination which make them skeptical that their situations will improve significantly. Ogbu calls this a "negative dual frame of reference with respect to status mobility. Unlike immigrants, they do not see their situation as temporary; on the contrary, they tend to interpret the discrimination against them as permanent and institutionalized" (p. 14). The voluntary immigrants see societal barriers as temporary, the positive dual frame of reference that things truly are better in the US, and that education is the key to the folk theory of getting ahead. They can blame many of their problems on the fact that they are still "foreigners" and "different" and that they will eventually climb over these hurdles. On the other hand, for the involuntary immigrants, their cultural differences with the dominant society are symbols of identity and self-worth they strive to maintain, in effect erecting ever higher hurdles between them and equitable opportunities for achieving success in the dominant society. They have been around this track so long with discriminatory stumbling blocks erected at every turn, that they no longer collectively buy into the dominant White version of the American Dream.

Work and Money

The Skeptics' parents' experiences with the disparity between educational and employment levels lend further credence to the myth of the American Dream for these families. While the lack of skill with the English language might have held back some of the immigrant parents in their ability to compete in the job market, none of the parents of the Skeptics faced this dilemma. All of these parents had been in the United States for generations, many of them descendants of involuntary slave immigrants. However, these parents were also consigned to low-skill and low-wage jobs remarkably similar to those of the immigrant parents.

Unlike the voluntary immigrant parents, all of these parents had completed high school, and twelve of the fourteen had gone on to college programs of some type. Many of them had been forced to drop in and out of higher education, but five of them had completed at least a bachelor's degree. Despite these achievements and this interest in education, many of them held jobs surprisingly similar to those of the immigrant parents, and several were unemployed. Low skilled jobs like janitor and bus driver were intermixed in this group with potentially better paying jobs like bank accountants, social workers, counselors, and phlebotomists (both a mother and a father). However, the permanence of the jobs, the availability of full time versus part time, and the inclusion of important benefits, seemed to be ever changing variables. Like the immigrants, the major factors contributing to this education-employment gap that the students identified were divorce and health problems. Any event that changed the delicate balance of these families' lives threw them into very precarious economic straits. There were no resources on which to fall back.

Most of the Skeptics indicated that their families had always struggled financially. The only exception was James who felt that their finances only became an issue when his parents divorced, compounded by both his father's health problems that prevented child support payments and his mother's loss of a lucrative job. Damon's parents (both with college degrees) chose to sacrifice better paying jobs for the community outreach organization that they ran. Several of these students commented on their utilities being shut off when bills piled up, and the debt seemed to be getting worse. One of these young women, Teresa, reflected on her family's difficulties: "They're looking at their situation and they're thinking that all the doors are closed, you know, and there's no way out of this situation. I mean, they've just given up, basically." Two other young women were involved with their fathers in disputes over their lack of child support, especially for educational expenses.

Like the Searchers, most of the Skeptics worked in high school out of necessity. Some of them continued to work the same jobs after they entered college. Stacey, the only student who had not worked, regretted that she had not had the opportunity to hold a job in high school like so many of her friends. Home responsibilities after school, educational programs in the summer, and volunteer work left her no time for a job.

Families and Traditions

Six of the seven families in the Skeptic's cohort were headed by a single mother. With the exception of Teresa's father who had passed away, all of these parents were divorced. Damon's parents were the only intact couple. Five of these mothers experienced serious health problems which further compounded the financial insecurity of being a single mother.

Among these students, the descriptors of their families often expressed the closeness that many of the immigrant students voiced. James was an only child and described that situation positively:

> I got a lot of attention from my father and my mother. I guess from being an only child, they really flooded me with a lot of attention and stuff, especially my father. He was one to take me out to the movies, plays, and play with me and all that stuff. My mother, too. And I think after my parents got divorced, I got really close with my mother. She's basically my best friend. I can really talk to her and tell her things that most people probably wouldn't tell their parents.

Damon had five siblings and Sybill had three, but they described their families in similar glowing terms. Both of them stated that their families were "close knit." All three of these students spoke of their families with great respect.

Among the other four students, the families were described with less enthusiasm. Many of these students bore the major responsibility for the family, doing almost everything except work full time. Stacey narrated one of the more extreme situations. Her divorced parents both had serious drug problems and left their children in the care of the grandparents. When asked to describe her family, Stacey's description reflected the chaos of her childhood:

> CRAZY! I mean, some of them are mentally disturbed, certified mentally disturbed people. Some of them need to be certified, but there are others, not my whole family. Just most of the people on my mom's side [are crazy]. Like I have some aunts and a couple of cousins that I would say are turning out to be like not even normal, but nice, well-rounded

> people. The rest of them, I think most of their lives are going to be
> spent in the projects....That's sort of like the mentality they have.

Because she was the oldest girl, Stacey ended up doing most of the cooking and cleaning for all ten of her relatives who lived together and also
cared for her two younger sisters, to the point that they referred to her
as "mother."

All of the Skeptics spoke of extended family who were major influences in their lives as they were growing up. Unlike the other two
groups, all of these students spent a great deal of recreational time with
their cousins. Some of the extended families were remarkably large and
continued to live near each other.

The Skeptics' responses about whether they observed any traditions
with their families ranged from Nicole's simple response of "nope," to
James' effusive descriptions of celebrating everything from birthdays to
each Christian and nationally recognized holiday. The other Skeptics
indicated that they also observed these special days with their families
and special meals. Church was central to many of the religious holidays
for four of the young women. The only student to mention anything
unique was Damon, who spent some time explaining the Kwanzaa
traditions, which have a spiritual African foundation.

Six of the seven students in the Skeptic cohort felt that the Christian
religions had been central influences in their lives. For Stacey, religion
was one of the few constants in her life:

> Church was one thing that was stable. My belief in God and that he
> really does intend life to get a little better sometime is a really big
> thing....You know, it can't get much worse because I can't take much
> more and he's never going to put too much on there....But, sometimes
> when I feel I'm all alone, you're never alone. Always here [God].

Narrations of Location

When responding to where these students located themselves racially
and/or ethnically, the Skeptics preferred the hyphenated identity of
"African-American," although half of them accepted either "Black" or
"African-American" interchangeably. Whether Black or African-
American, it was clear that the Skeptics maintained an identity that set
them apart from being just "American." As John Ogbu (1991) points
out: "Involuntary minorities perceive their cultural frame of reference
not merely as different from but as in opposition to the cultural frame
of reference of their dominant-group 'oppressors.' ...[T]hey interpret
these differences *as symbols of identity to be maintained*" (p. 15). While

these students voiced no loud opposition to the dominant group, they were consciously maintaining aspects of their identities that marked their difference from White dominant society.

Unlike the other two groups, four of the Skeptics were from upstate New York. While their cities were considerably smaller than New York City, most of the students resided in the urban centers of these communities. They described their childhood neighborhoods with fondness, but two of them noted a decline in quality of their neighborhoods as they grew up. The remaining three lived in New York City and narrated different childhood experiences. Several of them had witnessed high levels of crime around their schools and apartments. Of all the HEOP students in this study, Stacey was witness and victim to the most crime. She described two serious attacks on individuals on her street and several of the male relatives in her family sexually abused her for a number of years. Unlike the Pleasers and Searchers, the Skeptics had not noted improved levels of police presence to deter crime, nor did they indicate overly protective parents who limited their exposure to what they perceived to be negative elements in their environment.

CONCLUSION

This chapter focused on the twenty-three research participants whose life histories clustered into three groups determined by the length of time they had lived in the United States. Working from John Ogbu's (1991) description of voluntary and involuntary immigrants, these groups were identified as: 1) the "Pleasers," first generation voluntary immigrants; 2) the "Searchers," second generation voluntary immigrants; and 3) the "Skeptics," involuntary immigrants whose families were multigenerational citizens. Within these groups, the chapter explored the students' unique cultural heritages and how their early identities were shaped by the influences of the parental histories and cultures, the United States' culture expressed through the urban experience, and relationships with family and friends. There was an active interdependency among and between the multiple aspects of inner and outer identities and the forces from within and without that continuously shaped and refined the essence of these students.

Far from the assimilation models of years ago, these twenty-three students were struggling to establish their own identities, not "American" as defined by the American Dream and mainstream society, and not purely ancestral as determined by their collective cultural histories. At varying stages of development, these students were striving to establish hybrid identities of their own choosing. In matters such as these that touch close to the inner core of one's identity, it was often difficult for students to sort out, verbalize, and even bring to consciousness how they thought or felt about some aspects of their lives and histories. What comes through clearly though, is that this is not a group of disadvantaged students who can be essentialized and monolithically defined and categorized. Even within the three groupings that I have chosen, these students constantly defy easy collective identities.

In the next chapter, these complex identities are played out within the greatest leveling institution of American society, the public schools. Of particular interest is how these critical early experiences within the family and the neighborhood, in concert with the schools, position the HEOP students for the college experience.

CHAPTER 3

Structured Expectations:
Precollege Academic and Social Experiences

I hated high school work-wise. I don't know why, but I always wanted to go to college. Yes, I know why. It's because it was the next step; that's what you need to succeed.

—Vanessa, from upstate New York

Through the school years, the students narrated active movement through a number of transitional phases. These phases were marked by movement away from parents and away from familial traditions for some, movement through structured expectations of the educational system, and movement toward higher education. The parents and students, some more successfully than others, strategically fought their way through urban school systems to achieve the quality of education and respect that would position the students to take advantage of opportunities for upward mobility. The three groups, the Pleasers, the Searchers, and the Skeptics, described these moves with some overarching commonalities but also with some distinct differences.

In this chapter, pre-college academic experiences are dissected under the lenses of parental and student involvement, the schools' accommodations to individual students, the academic focus of these groups of students, and their college goals, how they arrived at the decision to attend Ivy University. The Higher Educational Opportunity Program (HEOP) entered the students' lives for the first time and played a decisive role in this critical stage of their transitional development. Of primary interest is how these students were positioned through their educational opportunities to enter an elite university. The path diverged in a number of directions, especially between groups, but led all of these students to Ivy University.

THE PLEASERS

Accommodating Schools

For the first generation immigrants, the Pleasers, one of the most stabilizing forces in their lives seemed to have been the school in their homelands. This was surprising given the amount of abuse most of the students suffered at the hands of their teachers. The students clearly articulated that what we consider abuse in the United States is not abuse in other countries:

> *Roberto* (Jamaica): What you call abuse here is not abuse. A parent can, as long as they don't kill their child. It's okay for them to do whatever they want to do....You could go home and tell your mother that the teacher hit you and it's like your mother won't get upset. You must have done something wrong for the teacher to hit you.

It was also surprising that six of the nine Pleasers indicated that they liked or loved going to school because a number of these students went to schools that had virtually no resources, that were overcrowded, and that were run like military camps. The threat of abuse was common and there would be no sympathy from parents, because they usually reinforced the teacher's discipline at home. Many of the students spoke of the regimenting aspects of school: the wearing of uniforms, the conformity of the content and the mode of didactic dissemination of knowledge, the rigid tracking that determined one's educational trajectory and hopes for higher education at a very early age, the lengthy hours of class, and long rides to reach a school that provided adequate education. Despite all of these restrictive elements, most of the students felt that they worked hard and learned well. They had a measure of respect for the teachers. From the way the students talked, school was one guaranteed continuity in a life filled with discontinuities. It was something that was constant, never changing and an opportunity to be with friends. It was also viewed as a chance for a future, although within very limited parameters.

Upon entering schools in the United States, the experience took on different dimensions. Most of the Pleasers were in secondary schools at the time of their immigration and attended urban public high schools, either in upper New York State or in New York City (NYC). Veronika (Ghana) was the only Pleaser who attended a private high school, a small Catholic school also in NYC.

Although the first generation immigrant parents succeeded in controlling their children's exposure to many of the cultural influences of their new country, one space that parents could not manage and make safe for their children was the school. Some tried to exert some level of control by enrolling their children in private schools, but only temporarily. Many of these parents were unable to participate in their children's education in this country, whether due to language barriers, lack of opportunity because they were always working, or intimidation by an imposing structure with which they had no experience. So, in these spaces of education and peer interaction, the students were now faced with the prospect and the necessity of becoming bicultural. Antonia Darder (1998) discusses this process in terms of developing:

> ...a hybridized state. This is to say that their [subordinate cultural group] histories of forced interaction with the dominant culture have required consistent forms of adaptional behaviors which have, in many instances, eroded, restructured, and reconstructed the language system, cultural beliefs, and social traditions of these groups (p. 130).

Schools became the test sites for the dreams that these students and their families brought from their corners of the world.

Immigrant children new to this country were accommodated in a variety of ways by the schools they entered. Throughout the stories the Pleasers told, there was constant pressure to conform to a perceived norm, created and recreated in school after school. Margaret Gibson (1991) comments about valuing immigrant students' cultures instead of changing them:

> The minority cultures and identities are themselves a strong source of capital and a resource that schools would do well to recognize and support....A policy of *additive acculturation* would help students distinguish the acquisition of academic skills and proficiency in the ways of the wider society from their own social identification with a particular ethnic group (p. 375).

The most obvious push by the schools was to learn English, the way that Americans speak it.

Language became the site of some of the students' first contests with the school system. Those students with limited English proficiency were placed down in class level and/or taught in either bilingual or English for Speakers of Other Languages (ESOL) classrooms. These students included Luc, Tran, and Mai (all Vietnamese), Panyos (Thailand), and Ileana

(Dominican Republic). These students each had unique experiences as a result of these specialized programs, but often they spoke of negative consequences. Ileana was misplaced in regular ninth grade classes for a few days. Correcting the error, she was taught totally in Spanish in what was called a bilingual class. After a year and a half and still knowing little English, her teacher transferred her to the honors program, claiming she was too smart to be in bilingual education.

Schools have plans to accommodate non-English speaking students, but there are tremendous variations in the types of programs that are available, and none of these students spoke about how the diversity they brought to the school was celebrated. The accurate placement of students into the most appropriate program is problematic, but it is so critical to the students' well-being at this vulnerable moment in their lives that it deserves top priority. Several of the Pleasers wanted to return to their native countries rather than endure the school experience. Tran (Vietnamese and placed back three grade levels) shared feelings that were voiced by the others:

> You're just sitting there looking at them, and they're looking back at you, and you don't understand what they're talking about. You can't talk to anybody around you. Everybody was like different. I just wished that I could go back to Vietnam right away. I didn't want to stay there any longer. I just wanted to get up and go.

When resources are always tight and politics are always present, school districts may claim to have few options. Marcelo Suarez-Orozco (1991) in his study of Central American immigrant students and their school experiences, discovered these factors and more:

> So rapid was their English acquisition that teachers at both school sites reported that school counselors systematically held students in English as a Second Language (ESL) classes and lower-level bilingual classes much longer than was necessary due to lack of space in the regular English classes. This was part of a systematic pattern of subtle discrimination that emerged in the course of fieldwork. The powerless immigrant children were not a priority; they were assigned to lower-level classes, even when they had successfully completed the same classes in their country of origin (pp. 43–44).

What the Pleasers experienced confirms Suarez-Orozco's findings. The process of "subtle discrimination" and othering takes place even within the schools with the best intentions. Veronika arrived in the United States from Ghana speaking "proper" English, but she was still placed back two years in high school in order to learn US history. Maria Matute-Bianchi (1991) also took issue with school programs that assumed a cultural homogeneity among student groups, such as immigrants, and observed that:

> ...simplistic educational solutions are proposed to fit stereotypic categories of students: ESL for the non-English speaker, multicultural education for the "culturally deprived," and special programs for the "at risk," the migrants and learning handicapped. The response has been to create categorical programs for categorical students, with the expectation if not fervent hope that we can change the students to fit the "regular" school program (p. 243).

Even when schools claim to have the students' best interests at heart and to use resources wisely, the effects of some of the programs do not seem to be well thought out. Several students talked about the isolation of these programs. Luc (Vietnam), the only student in her ESOL class for an entire year, offered some poignant (and unaltered) comments about this isolating experience:

> In high school, I don't have anybody, because nobody could understand me anyway. When they asked me something, I just stood there and smiled. And sometime, I think they laughed at me, but then I smile again. That's the reason nobody [pause]...They talk to me, but since I didn't understand them, they get tired....Because right now I'm still mad, you know. I say, nobody wanted to be friend with me.

Ileana (Dominican Republic) ended up in a bilingual class that sounded like an appropriate intermediary step but did not serve her well. In a paper she wrote for one of her college summer classes, she explained her "self-imposed" isolation:

> As an immigrant, I can only speak about my own experiences. I was part of the bilingual program for two years and not only did I not learn English, but I used to segregate myself from the rest of the school. I did not learn English because they used to teach me all the classes in Spanish and only one class of English. Also, while in this program, I only wanted to be around people that were Spanish speakers. I started to learn English when I was transferred to a regular program where classes were taught in English. The bilingual program does not work because it creates a small world for the students. In this "world," they feel they are in their own country and do not see the necessity to learn English.

In addition to these concerns about isolation, be it voluntary or involuntary, the Pleasers shared concern about two things: boredom, and having to prove themselves to their teachers. Most students commented on how the schools were less strict and tradition-bound than their native schools, and how they were bored because school was easier. Just sitting quiet in class often earned an "A." These students were often accused of "kissing up" because they had learned from early ages how to behave, as Roberto (Jamaica) indicated:

> I didn't have to put as much work into it, because I knew that if I didn't give it my all, the teacher wasn't going to do anything to me. It's kind of like the fear of getting into trouble in Jamaica that pushes you to do well. But here, it's like, not to put it bluntly, but the teachers could care less....I'd be in the classroom bored all day...I guess you could say I kissed up a lot. That's what my friends would describe it as, but I don't think so....But I did that because I wanted my teachers to know that I was smart.

Ironically, the Pleasers' other concern about having to prove oneself stemmed from lack of language proficiency as well as assumptions teachers made about the ability of students coming from school systems that were assumed to provide inferior education, exactly the reverse of what most of these students said when comparing their homeland schools with their US schools.

When one literally has no voice with which to communicate, it's difficult for others to see the potential within. These students relished the opportunity in the interviews to give voice to their experiences. Locked out because of language, the lack of parental advocacy, or programs that fit poorly, immigrant students do form a powerless contingent, a mute group of students whose needs are often met inadequately, but they rarely complain in school about these things. They are the Pleasers.

No matter how resource poor a school might have been, each of the Pleasers found at least one teacher who reached out to them. Many credited their ESOL teachers with easing their academic strife and making them feel connected to school. They commented on these teachers being nothing like their teachers back home; they cared and were willing to stay after school to help them. Panyos (Thailand) claimed that a turning point for him was when one of his eleventh grade teachers assertively encouraged him to participate more in school activities. This act snowballed into the creation of a tutoring club that won Panyos awards at New York City Hall and CBS studios, an invitation to address the United Nations, and a $5,000 scholarship from a New York City paper. "I owe all this to my teacher....She saw something in me different from others; she helped bring it out." Panyos ended up the salutatorian of his graduating class. The students who didn't have strong relationships with teachers made connections with advisors. The teachers and advisors provided academic advice and placement, and helped them get through the system and into college.

The Pleasers benefitted from a cultural model held by immigrants that John Ogbu (1991) describes as leading to optimistic attitudes and strategies that enhance their educational success. Parents stress the importance of education as the instrument for status mobility. Another point in their favor was that immigrant students were often viewed as "desirable students" by their teachers, which Suarez-Orozco (1991) documented when he talked with teachers of Central American immigrant students:

> These teachers noted that immigrant students expended more effort, studied harder and often received better grades than other minority students. Teachers reported, too, that immigrant students were much more respectful and "nicer to have around" than either Anglo or other minority students (p. 43).

The Pleasers' teachers and advisors did nothing extraordinary, but they were able to see in these students their tremendous potential, talents, and gifts. They assisted each student in becoming somebody, a critical step in the formation of identity—feeling that others believed in them, and found value and worth in who they were. As a result, these students started believing in themselves, too.

Academic Focus

The Pleasers did not find academic success just by being quiet and "kissing up," nor were they just fortunate to find a mentor who could smooth the way for them. In addition to a combination of these things, the Pleasers positioned themselves for success. They didn't shirk hard work. Three of these students were in the National Honor Society, one became salutatorian, and one was valedictorian. Most of them were involved in honors classes, AP courses, and a wide range of activities that made their college applications stand out. However, some schools offered no, or only two, AP courses. Most students were involved in supplementary programs after school, during the summer, or on weekends, such as community college courses, programs at universities, and other workshops. Science and math programs were favored over all disciplines, which was beneficial for these students, especially those who lacked English proficiency. However, several students felt that these areas had been emphasized to the detriment of language, writing, and the humanities, in which they wished they'd had more work before college.

In addition to showing high academic achievement, most of the Pleasers, despite language and cultural barriers, formed academically beneficial friendships. Their friends shared their academic seriousness and most were also college-bound and at the top of their classes. Several students commented on the enriching sharing of cultures, such as Mai (Vietnam) describes: "I like my friends. Even though I didn't speak English at that time, they tried to talk to me and teach me how to pronounce right. They teach me a lot about American culture, and I taught them Vietnamese culture." However, Luc (Vietnam) and Ileana (Dominican Republic) felt socially ostracized. Luc's situation was not by choice, but Ileana carefully constructed her isolation and associated exclusively with her cousin. One reason she did this was because other students weren't receptive to her and made fun of her struggles with the language, as in Luc's experience. But the main reason seemed to be the stereotype that Ileana believed about these students who were also Dominican. Ileana stated that they were not her type because many were on welfare and their behavior made Hispanic people "look awful." She effectively distanced herself from students she perceived to share some of her ethnic history, but who were different in their values and aspirations. Both of these young women were unable to make a peer group connection.

College Plans

The Pleasers' academic experiences had been strong enough to earn them admission to a four year college or university where they could continue to pursue the dreams that had brought their families to this country. Three of these students had not envisioned college in their futures until they were in the US and were influenced by the students around them who seemed to automatically expect to go on to college. However, Paolo (Trinidad) didn't plan on college even as he worked his way through high school taking honors courses. He stated that he started the process of applying just because his advisor encouraged him to do so, and "...in the process of applying, I got into it, but at first I wasn't." Not many people around him, except a few of his friends, were considering college.

The remaining six Pleasers had definite plans for college, and rather particular disciplines, but they were often clueless about the college application process. Their choices of majors and college often reflected their parents' desires. Ileana (Dominican Republic) always wanted to be an engineer, or more accurately, her father always wanted her to be an engineer. He discouraged all other interests. However, she explained that "...the last semester of high school, I decided that I didn't want to be an engineer, but an economics major....He was like, 'why are you making me spend my money for something, economics, that's not related to science?' That's not worth it." Ivy University offered both majors, so it was a suitable college for father and daughter. An interesting three-way dialectic of college decision making was expressed by Panyos (Thailand) who described his experience:

> Yeh, I want to be a teacher, because my teacher said you can be a good teacher. My mom told me to be whatever I want, "Do whatever you like." She said, "You came all the way here to be a teacher?" What's wrong with that? They make a pretty decent amount of money. "Yeh, I know, but you can go further than that." This is my mom talking. That's why I came here [Ivy University]; they want me to be an engineer. They don't care what kind.

Like the other Pleasers, Panyos decided to attend Ivy University because it would appease his parents, toward whom he felt deep responsibility, and it would allow him the opportunity to earn a prestigious college degree. So, although college decisions were often compromises, they were not viewed as sacrifices in the Pleasers' eyes.

While families tried to be supportive and encouraging, the persons most involved in helping the Pleasers with this potentially life altering college decision were school advisors and teachers. Luc's ESOL teacher encouraged her to enroll in a community college, acquire more English experience and college credits, and then transfer to a four year university. For many, teachers and advisors knew about Ivy University and the scholarships available. They steered the students toward college visits and application. If not through advisors or teachers, the students learned about Ivy University through relatives or through the recruitment efforts of the HEOP personnel from Ivy University, who showed up at some of the high schools in the spring of their senior year.

Even though dreams, passions, and people influenced the college choices that the Pleasers made, the bottom line in the decision process came down to money. When asked what factors influenced them to attend Ivy University, the final decision was "money." Clarissa (Guyana) was torn between two schools and let the finances make the decision for her:

> My decision was I had to go to college; there was no choice in that. What school I went to, my mom pretty much left it up to me to choose what I was interested in....This was the only school upstate that I visited. I thought I liked it and my decision was kind of last minute. I said the school that gives me the best financial package I would go to....I

went to open the mailbox and I got a better offer from here, and this
is like the day before everything was due. So, I said, okay, I decided I'd
come here.

THE SEARCHERS

Accommodating Schools

The Searchers did not share as complicated early educational histories as the Pleasers because they lacked the immigration component. The
schools the Searchers attended were also primarily public, but ranged
across a large spectrum of types. Four students attended urban NYC
schools, whose graduating class sizes were often significantly smaller
than when they began. Alicia (Peru) was admitted through examination
to a specialized NYC art high school. Tiana (Puerto Rico) attended "better" NYC public schools up until high school when she earned entrance
into a transfer program that placed her as a boarder at a highly rated
public high school in a neighboring state. And Yasmin (Puerto Rico)
went to a smaller, but "better," public high school in Florida. Notably,
three of the Searchers volunteered information about safety issues in and
around their high schools, whereas the Pleasers attended similar high
schools, but did not raise these concerns. These students cited behaviors
at their "tough" schools that ranged from swearing, to petty theft, to girl
fights, to gangs and knife fights.

Parents of second generation immigrant children were generally not
as reluctant or as unable to participate in their education as those of the
Pleasers. The stories about schooling related parental interventions and
negotiations to position their children in advantageous academic settings. They, like the Pleaser parents, held the vision of education as providing the means for social and economic upward mobility. The Searcher
parents, however, had the advantage of more experience with American
systems and, for the most part, they were able to intercede on their children's behalf.

Several students spoke forthrightly about somewhat questionable tac-
tics that were used to gain entrance to certain schools. These strategies involved using relatives' addresses to attend better schools in
other districts. Tiana (Puerto Rico) claims that in order to get into a
better elementary school, which she called a "real smarty-pants
school," her mom justified a change based on her good grades. "My
mom did a lot of hustling to get me in there."

Parents intervened in less questionable ways that also demonstrated a
level of assertiveness with the educational system. Marie's (Ecuador)
mother expended a lot of energy maintaining a level of involvement in

her children's education: "[M]y mother, like she was more interested. My father worked, so she would come and talk to the teachers. She didn't speak English; she just spoke Spanish, so it was kind of hard to talk to the professors. She would try. She would get a translator to tell her how we were doing." Jason's (Taiwan)mom actively interceded to prevent her son from being placed in a "special program" which would have removed him from regular classrooms.

Not all parents felt the confidence or the need to be as involved in the schooling process. Laila's (Grenada) parents were not able to help with her homework, but she always felt that the expectation was that she would do well in academics:

> [B]ecause of coming from West Islanders, your child is supposed to be doing good, but they don't really know how the American system goes. So, if they [the teachers] say, this child is supposed to be doing such and such in school, they knew I had to be doing good in school, but they didn't know what I was supposed to be doing in school....I would say to my parents, "Look, I got a 90 average"' They would say, "That's nice." I don't think they really knew what that meant.

Most Searchers echoed these parent expectations. Alicia (Peru) found them difficult: "Coming from immigrant parents, it's really hard. I've talked to a lot of people who have immigrant parents. It's really tough....So, it's a lot of stress on you." However, these high expectations combined with an awareness of the educational system, allowed most of these parents to position their children in more advantageous educational settings, something that did not happen for the first generation immigrant parents.

Even though the Searchers had been born in the United States, two of them, Alicia (Peru) and Martine (El Salvador and Cuba), entered school speaking only Spanish. However, their advantage over the Pleasers were that they were younger when they entered the school system and they had been surrounded by an English speaking society from birth. Therefore, for them, language did not present the hurdle that it had for some of the immigrant students when they entered the school system. Language acquisition at this early age came easily, and what the schools provided for the transition, one a regular class and the other a bilingual class, worked well for these two young women.

The Searchers were not as vocal as the Pleasers about most aspects of their education, but they voiced a critical awareness of the more social aspects of schooling that they had experienced. As protective as most parents tried to be, especially of the young women, part of their social education was developing strategic responses to racial and class charged situations.

Laila (Grenada): [C]hildren can be cruel. When I was younger, I didn't have better features, long hair or anything like that. I think I had a Afro or something. The kids would tease me about my jerry-curls. And if you're not wearing the proper attire, reject shoes or something like that, they'd make fun of me. I think that helped me because now I don't take it personal. I used to come home in tears. But, I always had friends.

*   *   *   *   *

Yasmin (Puerto Rico):...Yeh, but I kind of noticed who hung out with who [in middle school]. It was kind of obvious all the Spanish people hung out together, all the Black people hung out with each other. It was kind of by music than by race. It wasn't just Black people, some White people....[In high school] my grandmother would drop me off at the bus stop and I would go with people who lived in this area. Some people would call it a Spanish ghetto, but I don't think it was the ghetto, cause it wasn't that bad. There were gangs and stuff there, but I didn't feel intimidated because these were people I knew and were my friends.

*   *   *   *   *

Marie (Ecuador): There were all types, many Hispanics in my school. There were also Muslims.... Junior high was pretty rough. There used to be bullies, but I was never involved. I was very conservative and I always tried to give respect to everyone. So, I just ignored them or walked away....There was so many of them, so you couldn't do anything. So, you always had to watch your back and be careful. Try not to have any problems....[E]specially in high school, it was so common for girls to get pregnant, smoking and everything. I was in a bio-med course, so all the kids were smart and knew not to get involved with problem things.

Contact with teachers was not nearly as prominent in the narrations of the Searchers as it was with the Pleasers, although several students had valuable relationships with their teachers. Jason (Taiwan and White) experienced both the highs and lows of teacher relationships:

I can remember my accounting professor like senior year on my first day. He like didn't have a book for me and he said, "You probably won't use it anyway, just like your brother." Something like that. How could he even dare say something like that to me. He didn't even know me....My older brother was pretty much a trouble maker and a lot of teachers carry those stereotypes, too.

Jason realized between his junior and senior year that he was perpetuating the image that his teachers expected based on his brother. He realized he was "...into a lot of stupid things with a lot of bad people.... That's when I realized that I needed to get away from these people." At this point, he cleaned up his life and was fortunate that his math teacher came to his rescue and helped him "straighten out" and work through the college application system that led him to a fresh start in a new location. Some of the Searchers found the teacher support and encouragement they needed in high school. However, most of these students did not seek out nor find noteworthy relationships with their teachers. On the whole, this group seemed more independent and in search of their own direction, politely listening to family and school officials, but not placing much stock in external guidance.

Academic Focus

Although their school narrations seemed to emphasize the social over the academic, it was clear from their achievements that the Searchers were academically skilled students. For most of them, the school experience involved some negotiation for quality schools and higher tracks of learning. The most common observation that the students made about public schooling at the upper levels was their involvement in honors or advanced classes. Many stressed the number of math and science courses they had completed, and the number of AP credits they earned. Alicia (Peru) was always talented with art and by the time high school came around, she had an impressive art portfolio and was admitted to the public art high school. By far, the most unusual school experience was Tiana's (Puerto Rico). From her "smarty pants" elementary school, she was accepted into an advanced junior high school. From this, she was accepted into a program called "A Better Chance" (ABC), which she described:

> It's a non-profit organization which sends talented minority youths to suburban upper middle-class areas....Once you get accepted to the program, you have to apply to certain boarding schools...[Y]ou go to the top public schools of the country and you live in a dorm house and go to the public school....I went to [City] High School which is top 10 or top 5 in the country...And so, for 10th grade, I moved to [the city] to go to boarding school.

Tiana had little to say about her high school classes, other than she usually did very well, with the exception of a "C" in AP English. That got her grounded by her residence directors.

The Searchers did achieve at fairly high levels academically within the schools that they attended. However, as a group they do not appear to have been as stellar as the Pleasers who were often top of their classes. Also, the Searchers did not seem to have the same level of involvement with school activities and teachers that the Pleasers indicated. Of the Searchers, Laila (Grenada) and Yasmin (Puerto Rico) sounded the most active. Laila was ranked 7th in her class and she was girl leader of an honors group, a leader in the science club, a volunteer in a tutoring program, and a participant in several school clubs. Yasmin was a member of the National Honor Society and in the top 6% of her class. She assumed a leadership position in a Caribbean community service organization and was involved with some sports. Even though the students were not as heavily involved in school activities as the Pleasers, they assumed a lot of home responsibilities and usually worked for pay at the same time.

The Searchers spoke about the social aspects of their school years with more openness than the Pleasers. Two of the Searchers were the only students in this study who indicated involvement with drugs. As it turned out, Tiana (Puerto Rico) worked her long hours at the fish shop after school partly because she needed money to keep up with the friends she made at her boarding school. There she lived between two worlds, the girls in her boarding home who were minorities in the ABC program, and the high school girls from town. She describes the difference:

> I had the girls in the house and then I had my "other" friends....they were clean-cut druggies. They did school. They did everything they had to do. But they did partake in their drugs. And I was just fascinated. How do you do all these weird drugs? Like they were taking like tab and acid and all this weird stuff....But the girls in the house were all clean-cut, straight edge girls. I was the least because I drank. Oh, goodness, they were so dry, which is fine. You know, it doesn't make you any better or any less of a person if you drink...

On top of drinking, Tiana stated that she used to smoke marijuana a lot, until she had a really bad high. Tiana occasionally skipped school with her "other" friends, whom she called "all American, teen-age kids." Despite the drugs and "release" time from school, Tiana indicated that she and her friends did well academically.

Before Jason (Taiwan and White) got legitimate jobs, he and his older brother sold drugs. His older brother and his brother's friends got him involved, and Jason started hanging out with "thuggish" people. He offered some insightful comments about the effects of drugs:

> I changed a lot as a person. Especially marijuana, it has a tendency to
> make you feel like the people close to you aren't. You build like this
> wall against them....something internally, I just lost myself, and then I
> began to recover myself. I stopped hanging out, stopped smoking and
> dealing with drugs. A lot of my closest friends, they left me and that
> was really tough. I always thought that my friends would be there for
> me, but it wasn't like that.

Jason cleaned himself up, and by senior year he still had a few good
friends and was hoping to find a way to get into a college. He managed
to do well academically, despite the distraction with drugs.

The rest of the Searchers described eclectic groups of friends, but
most of them shared an academic focus. These students sounded like
they socialized more than the Pleasers, but not to the point of distraction from their academics. They and most of their friends did well
academically.

College Plans

In addition to being determined to go to college, most of the
Searchers had specific career aspirations. Laila (Grenada) shared an
interesting personal observation:

> I knew I had to be something educational. If I had a gift, I would have
> recognized it a long time ago, like some people with singing said, "I've
> been singing since I was four years old," and they knew. So, I said, well,
> maybe my gift is in school. Some people go to college and say college
> is not for me. But, I knew I would do something educational.

Several of the students felt pressured by their parents into making college choices, but not to the same extent as the Pleasers. Marie (Ecuador)
was one of the few who spoke about the pressures of being a first generation college student: "...so there was always pressure that I could do
good, because my parents couldn't....My hopes were like I always wanted to get my parents out of the neighborhood. When I can afford it, I
want to buy them a house." Most of the career dreams centered around
professional careers in medicine, engineering, law, business, politics, and
anthropology. One student's greatest fear was boredom: "I don't want
to be a desk jockey," and another just wanted to be happy: "Now I care
about being happy....I wanted life to be fast forwarded to like 50, where
I'll have my kids and they'll be at their jobs, and I already finished the
working part and I'm with my dogs....Yeh, I just want the good stuff.
Fifty and 60, when you retire and you get to travel with your husband."
An interesting variation of the American Dream!

The parents of the Searchers were influential in some cases, but had little effect in others. Some students found role models in their parents and aspired to careers that would reward their hard work. Others found negative role models who inspired them. Laila (Grenada) found incentive by: "I think looking at people around me. It's so often that you see teenage pregnancies, gang violence, and something like that. That's not something I want to be." Alicia (Peru) talked about her parents being "anti-role models." She learned a lot about what she didn't want to be by observing them: "I don't want to be passive like my mom, ill-tempered like my father, a religious freak like my grandparents on my father's side. But then, I still want to believe and be hopeful....I want to be strong, but I don't want to be dependent. I never met anybody that I really want to be like."

Most of these students felt that they were on their own with college decisions and that there was not much support from home. Jason (Taiwan and White) stated, "I wanted a lot of options. I was really excited about my future, especially because I realized there wasn't much to hang on to back home." Yasmin (Puerto Rico) also assumed full responsibility for her college search:

> At times, like when I told my grandmother I was going to college, she didn't really believe me, or influence me. She'd say, "Now you know, we don't have money for that." I was like, don't worry, scholarships. My mother said, "You should go to Miami Dade. Everybody goes there." It's a community college. After all the work that I have done, she wanted me to go there! And be with the same people who couldn't even read or write a paper. She insulted me.

Most of the Searchers were strongly motivated to attend college and to gain a professional degree that would allow them to pursue financial comfort and happiness. However, they, like the Pleasers, chose Ivy University primarily because it offered them the best financial package. Alicia (Peru), like several other students, was also accepted to other universities, but couldn't turn down a full scholarship: "So, this school was more convenient for my father to pay off and this school is pretty good. It's a good institution. So, it didn't have exactly what I wanted like humanities and social sciences, but I guess I could still live with it. It's not going to kill me." Just as for many of the Pleasers, Ivy University became the convenient school for compromise because it offered a range of degree programs that appealed to both students and parents, and because the financial packet was the strongest of the accepting colleges. What several Searchers found alluring, beyond the academic choices and the financial aid, was the HEOP staff. Several of the students had visited campus and "loved" the HEOP staff they had met. Jason decided to attend Ivy University "...because it was the best option, not just in terms of financial aid, but also in terms of academic opportunities. I wouldn't get the support from other schools that I would get here....having people there [HEOP] to watch over me, which is good."

THE SKEPTICS

Accommodating Schools

The Skeptics' schools were also public for the most part but, again, quite different one from the other. Two of the Skeptics were the only students in this entire HEOP cohort who indicated a preschool experience. Four of the students attended urban high schools, three in upper New York State and one in NYC. One student was in a specialized program that bused her to a predominantly White high school on the fringes of NYC where she could pursue math and science. Another attended a specialized NYC public science and math high school to which he had won admittance. Sybill was the sole private school graduate of the Skeptics, having attended an exclusive girls' school set in an urban area of upper New York State. Her admission was also secured by examination, and scholarships enabled her to enroll. Private schools were not even an option for most of the HEOP families. The cost and logistics made them out of the question.

Like the Searchers, violence was a problem in several of the high schools. James attended the prestigious specialized high school that was located right across from some projects. At the bus stop, the students were harassed and frequently robbed. Stacey complained about students who were violently disruptive in her resource-poor NYC high school classes. Damon, in upstate New York, explained that his was a "violent school" and that there were a lot of fights between the Hispanics and African Americans. He had seen bottles broken over heads and a boy's mouth split open by a razor he'd concealed there to cut someone. He got punched in the mouth before he got a chance to use it. Teresa's school in the same city had the worst reputation in the city in terms of academics and discipline problems. The heightened security of metal detectors at all doors had eliminated most of the gun and knife problems. But students indicated that school security officers were useless; they usually advised the students to just give their money to anyone trying to rob them.

While the parents of the Skeptics had more familiarity with the educational systems than all of the immigrant parents, this didn't always parlay into greater school involvement. One student felt her family had influenced her education negatively, and Vanessa found less support than she wished:

> My mom always told me to do homework. She never like helped me with my homework or anything like that. I always wanted her to do that. You know, how you see on TV or you hear from other people, "My mom sits down and helps me with my homework." But it was never like that. She wanted me to do well, but she never helped me. She only got so far in high school and a little bit of college.... I always thought because she didn't get that far in her education, that was why we were so poor. So I always wanted to be really successful and make money.

Both of these young women stated that their parents' lack of encouragement or involvement instilled in them a greater desire to succeed in higher education. Another student's parents were literally out of the picture during her school years and her grandmother had little time to do more than offer verbal encouragement. When parents were unable to advocate for their children, for whatever reason, these students' needs were marginalized within the school system in similar fashion to those immigrant students whose parents were silenced by the language barrier.

The parents of three of the Skeptics were far more involved in the educational systems and intervened at critical periods to enhance their children's opportunities. James's mother rescued her son from being placed in a "special class" because his fourth grade teacher said he was talking too much and disrupting the class. Damon's mother and father dealt with a second grade teacher who he described as: "...unbearable. She told me I would be nothing more than a janitor....It wasn't a racial thing because she said it to Black kids and everybody. Equal opportunity hater." Damon realized, "If I didn't have the support from home, I'd probably end up being a horrible student and having a complex my whole life." Sybill's mother arranged for her admission to an elite private girls' school because she was "...being picked on for being smart" at her public junior high school.

The Skeptics were distinguished by their schools as "different" primarily due to their academic ability, but also for other attributes. The Pleasers and Searchers who were second language learners were often tracked in special language classes until they were brought up to speed. The Skeptics were also tracked, but usually in various types of courses that would set them on the road to college. This seeming advantage often had some downsides.

In a private school, Sybill was in a rarified atmosphere with the vast majority of students bound for colleges, and prestigious ones at that.

Sybill commented that: "I just like the fact that my intelligence was favored." However, she found that being only one of four Black students in her grade made her stand out for things other than her intellect. She was the first Black person with whom many of her classmates had close contact. It was not just the students who made her feel different: "A lot of the faculty and administrators didn't understand me or my heritage, my culture. They made a lot of assumptions. They would make remarks that I don't think were mean-spirited, but just ignorance; [they] didn't know any better."

In transferring from a school in Georgia to an upstate NY school, Vanessa felt temporarily "derailed" from the "fast track:"

> It was such a different environment. Student's didn't want to talk which was really hard for me. The culture shock, the whole work load, the students would curse; I couldn't believe it. I would still say like, "Yes, ma'am; no ma'am."...Everyone was really different. The people down South seemed so much friendlier....In Georgia, I used to be so much smarter than I was in [my new city]....I think up north schools, they go through so much more.

Vanessa found that her accent made her stand out, and her difficulty making the cultural transition between the two sections of the same country was somewhat similar to that of the immigrant students. Nicole was in the specialized program and she also described some transitional challenges:

> And I was in a program called Gateway, and that was basically for minority students who were interested in pursuing math and science related fields....It took me an hour to get to high school, and then on top of that, I didn't know anybody neither. So, my first couple of months in high school were really rough just because I didn't know anybody.

Stacey, who lost out on the opportunity to attend a specialized high school because she backed out of taking the entrance exam, spent over an hour each way commuting to her zoned public high school, which she found lacking: "On the most basic level, the materials we get to use, they were really bad. They really need to do something. I mean, books were like copyrighted in 1960." She took all of the most advanced courses they offered and still had a hard time filling her schedule her senior year. Teresa also observed that her school lacked adequate educational materials, but she found it more noteworthy that she and other athletes were a privileged class of students in the school, hearkening back to Bruce

Carrington's (1982) arguments in "Sports as a Sidetrack" that schools catering to Black students do less to encourage academic than athletic achievement, thus maintaining an unequal power structure in which Black workers are destined to remain in low paid, menial labor.

Interestingly, the students who had the best high school experiences were the two who had the earliest struggles. Damon attended an urban high school that had an "academy of excellence." He was placed in advanced classes that challenged him and he loved his school and class: "I did well and I always say that college can be like high school times ten. I had so much fun in high school; it was great!" James attended a large but prestigious public high school in NYC specializing in science and technology where he took challenging and rewarding classes. Both of these young men voiced pride in and loyalty to their schools.

However, within the schools, the students offered little praise for attempts toward cultural appreciation or Gibson's (1991) "additive acculturation." All of these students were survivors of these systems and most would have been considered top performers in their schools. One can only speculate how much the educational experiences could have been enhanced if these students had been encouraged or even allowed to share their wealth of genealogical history and culture.

The Skeptics had a lot to say about various teachers that they had over the course of their education. However, few of them, if any, seemed to form the influentially close relationships that the Pleasers experienced. The Skeptics' narrations careened back-and-forth between positive and negative experiences. James had an elementary school teacher who pulled his ear "every time I was bad," and another who recommended him for the "special" class. But in high school, he seemed content with the quality of the teachers even though there was no one who really stood out. Damon had the miserable early experience with his teacher who told him he'd be a janitor, not a leader when he grew up. After that, he was highly complimentary of many of his teachers. Twice he was voted by the teachers to receive a special award because, "They said I was caring and got along with my peer group as well as my teachers. I helped guide and shape the lives of students in my school." Damon commented that, "Having great teachers, I guess I was blessed."

Sybill also reported problems early in her education. She was distractable in class and was always in trouble. In middle school, she was still in trouble:

> Yeh, I had problems with the teachers because they treated us like idiots so I would vocalize, "I don't appreciate this. I don't like this," and they thought I was being smart mouthed. I hadn't learned, at that

point, to refine what I want to say in a politically correct manner, so I just spoke my mind.

She reported more positive interaction with her high school teachers, but one teacher, in particular, was so difficult to get along with that it made her think deeply about her identity: "That was a lot of stress. It made me view myself as a Black woman, in a small very close-knit group....I think it made me smarter, made me think more, maybe less trusting, more cynical." She felt that the teachers showed a general lack of appreciation toward and awareness of other cultures.

Teresa had little respect for a number of the teachers at her urban high school and responded that several of them "had lost their minds." However, she had several strong attachments, one to a teacher who happened to be a minister and the mother of a friend, and who taught a class on current issues that Teresa found stimulating. The other was a job coach who connected the students with part-time jobs that would utilize their business training and taught them career awareness.

Stacey's quietness in class was viewed as a problem by her teachers, but was partially due to her reluctance to always be the only one with an answer: "I think I got put into classes with some of like the dumbest people on earth. And it was just like, I hated raising my hand because I always knew the answer and they'd get mad at me for knowing the answer, like it was my fault." However, Stacey felt that several of her teachers had been outstanding, especially one who purchased school materials to bring her AP chemistry class up to speed with other schools. While the Skeptics appreciated committed and knowledgeable teachers, they were often more cynical toward teachers and did not describe a beneficial rapport like that of the Pleasers.

Academic Focus

While the Skeptics did well academically, like the Searchers, they were not as highly rated by their schools as the Pleasers. Many of these students ended up in the top 10% of their classes and took honors and AP classes, but there were no valedictorians, salutatorians, or members of the National Honor Society. However, there were some remarkable achievements. The Skeptics took advantage of many opportunities to participate in their schools, be it through sports, clubs, or student government. Damon and Teresa came to the fore as leaders within their schools and were the most active of the Skeptics. Damon was voted "Most Likely to Succeed," elected homecoming king, involved in student government, served as a mediator for his peers, created and planned community youth programs, volunteered to teach young people

Spanish, served on the New York State Governor's Youth Leadership Council, and made various presentations around the community, state and country regarding youth leadership. Damon described himself as an activist, and felt responsible to his high school peers: "People said, 'You're the man.' You have to live up to them." In addition to his activities, Damon completed the most challenging courses his school had to offer.

Teresa became senior class president, participated in various sports, was mistress of ceremony for her school choir, was part of a youth apprentice program for students in the business program, but she had no chance to complete any AP courses because her school did not offer them. She commented on the poor academic preparation her high school provided:

> I didn't know that going to a high school that was below standards was really going to affect me in life until I got to college and realized that I'm totally unprepared for what's going on around me. And I have to make it on my own wits. I mean, I don't have any experience from high school. I think I didn't know it at the time. I didn't know it until I got here that I went to one of the worst high schools in the world. I don't know anything and it's not because I didn't pay attention. It's because it was never taught to me.

The Skeptics were the most involved in athletics of the three groups. They also reported involvement in some clubs, science enrichment courses, science fairs (receiving some awards), and community service.

These students were academically inquisitive and willing to work to make a difference. Their schools did not always make it easy for them to become involved in constructive enrichment activities. The lack of honors or AP classes constrained them academically, and holding many extracurricular activities after school forced hard choices when work at home or for pay was imperative. Nicole was the only student who reflected on her *lack* of effort in high school, despite having completed two AP courses:

> I guess high school, I don't remember sitting down and actually doing my work and studying. I really don't remember doing any of that, and I guess I really didn't know how to do that....Yeh, now I think if I would have put in effort, I could have been a genius! [Laughs.]

The Skeptics identified the most eclectic friendship groups, some academically focused friends mixed with less academically ambitious friends. Some ended up in prestigious colleges, others in jail. Some of the friends were casualties of the school system before graduation. Nicole was grateful that she had been transferred out of the zoned school that many of her neighborhood friends attended because, "I see how a lot of them ended up, and I'm just happy I didn't go there cause I don't know what could have happened, if I would have followed the same track or whatever. So." Several of the students with academically focused friendship groups described them all as "nerds."

College Plans

From very early in childhood, the Skeptics had planned to continue on to college. They had dreams of careers that often veered into radically new areas as they grew up. Science and math figured prominently in their academic preparations and their future job trajectories, although this group had the widest range of career interests. Some, like Stacey and Nicole, just dreamed of getting away. The careers that were on their minds as they left high school were medicine, forensic science, law, journalism, counseling, psychology, teaching, drama, and politics. Several of the students felt that math and science had been "pushed" on them in high school:

> *Nicole:* ...like my big thing was going away to college. I had to go away to college. And, uhm, I just wanted to be, I guess, you know, like married with two kids, great career....Well, when I was in high school, I thought I wanted to be a doctor. I think the program I was in just tried to push that on us, though. I don't think that was really what I wanted to be....They always had like just doctors come talk to us....I guess why I wanted to be a doctor was because they just like pushed it in our face.

*   *   *   *   *

> *Teresa:* People pump up the math and science so much, but English is important, too. And if you can't communicate with people, you're not going to be able to get that formula across or that theory across, so English should come first. You have to know how to read and write adequately in the world cause the way college English classes are taught, these kids coming from this school [her high school] going to college are going to be totally and completely lost. Everybody does not have the motivation of myself and my other friends who came from this school to say, "We're going to beat the odds."

Damon always felt his destiny was college. His family consistently reinforced the importance of academics:

> They [his parents] always said education is important, so they prepared
> me for it, as if I was going to college. But when it came to the ultimate
> decision, they didn't tell me where to apply. My house is just like this
> frequency, you know. You don't even have to say that; that's just the
> way it is. It's kind of like with the president serving two terms. You just
> know, the precedent is set. With older brothers and sisters going to col-
> lege, you go to college.

Damon only joking slightly shared that his career aspiration was to be
president of the United States. One of his high school teachers tried
to dissuade him from politics because it's such a scandalous profes-
sion these days. However, Damon was only more determined: "It's a
dirty field. I guess I'd like to clean it up."

The Skeptics took even less direction from parents and teachers
than the Searchers. Damon, James, and Sybill's choices were supported by their parents, but they were not strongly influential in making
these choices. The four remaining students never mentioned any
direction or guidance in career plans from parents or teachers. In fact,
several shared how their parents had been anti-role models, negative
in influence. This was a very independent group who may not have
finalized their life plans before they entered college, but they were
making their own decisions.

When discussing their reasons for attending Ivy University, the
Skeptics gave the most thoughtful responses. Affordability through
financial aid was mentioned by a few students, but it was not stated
to be the guiding factor that it was for the Pleasers and Searchers. It
was usually mentioned in addition to other considerations. These
included: attending college fairs in high school where recruiters from
Ivy University were motivational; campus visits during a minority
student week-end in the spring, or on their own; and the location—
for some it was attractive because it was near to home and for others
the attraction was its distance from home. Teresa had the most unusual reason for this as her college choice. Her high school grade point
average was too high to allow her admittance into several local colleges through HEOP, so she was referred to Ivy University by other
colleges, because it was more selective with students and it was
allowed to accept students into the program with higher averages.
Teresa had never considered this college because she thought it was a
"school for doctors" and she didn't want to be a doctor. Her mother
suggested she attend a community college and work, and Teresa was
as offended as Yasmin (a Searcher) had been when her grandmother
had suggested something similar. Teresa explained:

I said, "I can't do that." I'm sorry to tell you, but I could not bring myself to go to [community college]. I'm not saying it's bad, but I'm too intelligent to go to a community college. I mean, a person with a 3.78 cum does not go to a community college. It just doesn't happen.

FINDING HEOP

Into this critical time and space in these students' lives, the milestone transition time between high school and college and adult life, the HEOP counselors at Ivy University stepped carefully but determinedly. Their job in the spring was to visit high schools and provide information about Ivy University and, more specifically, the support that HEOP can provide. A number of schools, especially in New York City, were targeted for recruitment because they had a history of being sources of students who matched Ivy University and HEOP's admissions criteria. Hence, a large number of the HEOP students came from the metropolitan New York City area to attend college in a significantly smaller city in upper New York State.

The financial assistance offered by HEOP was a prime determinant of these students' attendance at Ivy University, whether stated or not. Also influential were the reputation of the institution and the particular program of study, the recommendation of teachers or friends/ acquaintances, and the positive impression the students formed through recruitment efforts of the HEOP staff. I was surprised that many of the students were unaware of HEOP before they completed their applications to Ivy University. Many of them indicated that they checked the box on the Ivy University application because it was an opportunity for more financial aid (although they were unaware of what the program entailed) or the university sent them a notification that they were eligible for HEOP and asked if they were interested. These students would not have been able to attend Ivy University if it had not been for the financial support of HEOP, yet this program is not widely understood or promoted. I wonder how many high school students might look differently on their chances for college and be more serious in their high school efforts if they were aware from early on that this program existed and that they could qualify.

CONCLUSION

Chapter Two explored how the growing up years in the nexus of family and neighborhood had influenced the formation of the students' identities, culturally and socially, and the impact that immigration, both voluntary and involuntary, had on these family dynamics. Chapter Three examined the role that schools played in this time of identity formation working in concert with the families. Each of the groups, the Pleasers (first generation immigrant students), the Searchers (second generation immigrant students), and the Skeptics (involuntary immigrant students) faced unique challenges in the school systems, but responded with some similarities.

All of these students completed high school knowing that they were going on to college. Teachers and school counselors, more than parents, assisted the students in deciding which college and which major suited their goals. HEOP staff from Ivy University recruited at several of the New York City high schools, but many of the students learned about the program only after applying for admission. Money was the bottom line for most students in the choice of which college to attend. In all cases, the students received the best financial package(or one that was equal to other offers) from Ivy University. In order to participate in HEOP, these students had to meet the stringent economic and educational guidelines of the state program. This meant that none of these students would have qualified for admission to Ivy University if they were not coming in under HEOP. In most cases, their SAT scores were lower than the cut-off number for admission, despite the fact that many of these students finished within the top 10% of their high school classes.

Even though they were not positioned at the top of the acceptance pool for college, the students approached their entry to college with enthusiasm and with lofty goals and aspirations. They prepared themselves for another rupture in their security blanket. For the Pleasers, many of them would be leaving their geographic home, again, and all of them were faced with making adjustments to a new culture, again. For the Searchers and the Skeptics, most of them looked forward to leaving their familiar neighborhoods and embarking on a new experience "somewhere else." They found Ivy University an appealing location with friendly HEOP staff to welcome them.

College experiences shape so many aspects of identity that students usually step into this critical space of identity construction gingerly, after much careful thought and tedious planning. It was, therefore, interesting to hear most of the students describe their choice of colleges, after some college visitations, as coming down to the school that offered the best financial package. Given the realities of the HEOP families' financial situations, this was a necessary consideration. But, equally important should be the opportunity to continue the journey of self development that has only just begun. And whether one can achieve the type of environment that nurtures this quest at the college that can and does offer the best financial package is a question worth posing. The reasons for attending Ivy University seemed to be externally imposed and not directly related to the students' internal drives, which may be difficult for them to express or bring to a conscious level. The economic wooing of the students by universities competing to lure the most able of the urban poor, compounded by the families setting their sights on professional degrees that buy status and upward mobility, made some students compromise their original dreams and desires. Some of the HEOP students spent a considerable amount of time identifying the most appropriate major and career goals. Some of them were fortunate to find the support of a teacher or school counselor, and some had parents who directed or inspired them into certain disciplines. Although money was a primary concern, both in terms of college affordability and future earnings, the Searchers and Skeptics especially were seeking some measure of self-satisfaction as an outcome of their years of education. They wanted to end up with the opportunity for financial security, but also with a career and lifestyle that was personally attractive. Both the Searchers and Skeptics seemed more willing than the Pleasers to distance themselves from their parents and the perceived need to sacrifice their own interests in order to show respect for their parents.

The search for an appropriate major and career path led many of the students through a number of choices, often beginning with medicine. By the time they had chosen Ivy University as their college destination, most had refined their search to some other area of science and research or business. Several of the students noted that their schools or parents had forced math and science and medicine on them, which had created an oppositional response in them. They entered college looking for more of the humanities or social sciences. Whatever their entering aspirations, the students felt that Ivy University would offer them the opportunities to earn credentials that would be valued in the American society and in the eyes of their families. They turned to college with optimism.

CHAPTER 4

Academics at Ivy University:
Becoming College Students

I realized that it wasn't like high school any more. It required a lot more potential, a lot of hard work put into it. University is not a joke.

–Tran, a first generation Vietnamese immigrant

It was July and the first day of the prefreshman summer program that the Higher Education Opportunity Program (HEOP) organizes each summer for the incoming freshmen students. I arrived early and was the first person in the room. It was also the first day of my official research and I was eager to begin. I took a seat in the back row of the large auditorium with elevated rows of seats. Suddenly, the double doors at the back of the room were flung open. Two young women scanned the room and, seeing me, called out, "Hi!", giggled, and then slammed the doors shut as they turned and ran back down the hall. Soon the room was filled with more than forty students, many as exuberant as the two young women, and about ten faculty and staff members. The summer session had officially begun.

For the next three and a half weeks, I became the fly on the wall in the classes these students attended and on the campus they inhabited. I was a rather conspicuous fly, because I was visibly much older than all of the students and whiter, both in coloring and culture, than most of them. All the students knew was that I was a researcher who would be observing their classes. For the most part, they were content to allow me to shadow them without too much concern. Occasionally, I overheard them speaking quietly among themselves trying to figure out why I would want to spend my summer in their classes. On two occasions, students did approach me and ask about my research of their program. But, for most of the program, I sat and quietly observed, knowing little about these students, and filling my notebook with recorded impressions of what seemed important in these early weeks of college. It was only later, in the fall, in personal interviews, that I confirmed what I observed early on—that this was a remarkably diverse group of students, far more than I would have imagined from reading about the program and far more complex culturally than the Black/White dichotomy that most people associate with compensatory programs. Just who these students were became an amazing story.

Fall semester, as I sat and listened to them tell about their successes and challenges within the academic sphere of college, I found the student stories fascinating. Their ability to face each day with optimism and hope, in the face of some monumental challenges, made me understand more deeply the meaning of resilience, a concept attracting recent attention by researchers (see, for example: Davidson, 1997; Ward, 1999, 2000). Some of the narrations indicated that the students were finding ways to successfully navigate the new terrain, but other students were stubbing their toes on the rigors of classes for which they had little preparation in high school, on the unapproachableness of some faculty, on the diverse and sometimes ineffective teaching styles of professors, and on the novelty of having time that they needed to manage, that was not automatically managed for them by family or school. In puzzling over this ability to be resilient in the light of what some might find insurmountable challenges, I eventually came to understand what they had really been sharing with me. These students were all engaged in what I have called **strategic instrumentalism.** They were developing skills and devising strategies in order to achieve their set goals without "selling out" and assimilating into the academic culture that privileged dominant White ways of learning. Therefore, these strategies that the students were creating and employing had aspects of resistance to the culture around them, even though this resistance and opposition was not overt and sometimes not even a conscious effort. Furthermore, these oppositional means to an end could be *strategic*, in that they furthered the achievement of the students' academic goals, or they could be *nonstrategic*, in that they became counterproductive to goal achievement and were, in fact, self-defeating.

This chapter explores the HEOP students' adjustments to, and impressions of, the academic side of Ivy University. In their narrations of their academic transitions, the students share their perceptions of the campus itself. They describe the immediate adjustments forced upon them as they negotiated the curriculum and developed relationships with faculty, while trying to understand the cultural climate of Ivy University. These were complicated tasks. However, the Pleasers, the first generation immigrant students, had already experienced a major life transition where they were out of their element in a new environment. For the Searchers, the second generation immigrant students, and the Skeptics, the historically disenfranchised native born students, this magnitude of change was a new experience that required skills that hadn't yet been called into play. The identities that these students brought to campus, in varying degrees of development, would be thoroughly tested and would be critically engaged in developing their survival strategies, which collectively I call strategic instrumentalism.

THE VALUE OF THE SUMMER PROGRAM

Despite the challenging academic activities in which the students engaged in high school and their top academic achievement (explored in Chapter 3), their SAT scores made them ineligible for regular admission to Ivy University. HEOP was their ticket in. Ivy University allowed HEOP students to score slightly higher on the SAT than the HEOP at other colleges that were not as selective. However, their scores were not high enough to meet admissions standards for the majors to which they were applying at Ivy University. Most of these students reported SATs in the 1000 total range, well below the 1200+ average of most students at the university. The students realized that they would be at a disadvantage on this campus, but they had done well academically, to this point, and they hoped that they would successfully adjust to Ivy University.

Realizing that HEOP students face unique challenges in making the adjustment to college, a prefreshman summer program is mandatory at all private institutions that participate in HEOP. This program is intended to integrate preparatory academic skills with social bonding experiences that will enhance the students' connections with peers and selected faculty and staff. Ivy University operates a three and a half week program in July which includes the twenty plus incoming HEOP students and about an equal number of students who do not qualify for HEOP (many are from outside of New York State), but who appear to have similar backgrounds and who may also benefit from the summer program. The summer program stresses academic and social strategies designed to ease the adjustment to the demands of college. The program is not only for racial and ethnic minority students, but because HEOP's population is overwhelmingly composed of underrepresented students, it has all the outward appearances of a minority summer program. Programs of this type are not without controversy.

An article in the *Chronicle of Higher Education* explored how selective and mostly private universities were considering eliminating, or radically changing, their summer programs that focused on minority populations (Gose, 1998). A number of benefits of these summer programs were contrasted with the questions and concerns that were forcing institutions to take another look at the value of these programs. The benefits included the forging of friendships with other minority students, getting a foot up on negotiating the campus and its systems, building "a strong sense of commitment to the community of students of color" (p. A68), developing classroom savvy, and encouraging discussion around issues of oppression that might be experienced within both the campus and the wider community. The negative side raised issues about these programs often being viewed as remedial by the institution and by the participating students, creating divisions between minority and White students, stereotyping students in such a way that it inhibits honest discussion about race, and serving as "indoctrination" sessions. However, one assumption that was stated in the article that fuels these arguments was that many of the incoming students in these programs are now from middle-class backgrounds and no longer need a pre-college experience. Clearly, for HEOP, this is not the case. The director of HEOP at Ivy University had strong opinions about this:

> I shudder to think what their experiences would be like without coming to a program like this....It just seems like minority students see this as an opportunity not for remedial development in any way, so they apply in larger numbers. But, we've heard the feedback: it's counter-productive to have this isolated experience when that's not what we're really trying to do...It happens to some degree. If you have a hostile community out there, they're [the HEOP students] going to cling together. I don't really have a problem with it.

Many researchers and writers (such as, Cross, 1995; Cross & Strauss, 1998; Fine & Weis, 1998; London; 1992; Tatum, 1997) have expounded upon the need for people from underrepresented groups to have spaces, such as these summer programs, in which to form supportive relationships and build the resiliency that will be needed to resist marginalization within an institution that may perceive them as a threat to "tradition."

UNFAMILIAR SURROUNDINGS

Upon gaining admission to Ivy University, the HEOP students prepared for a major transition in their lives. They had varying amounts of information to assist them with their mental preparations. Some had visited the campus during the spring semester, either during an invitational minority week-end for potential Ivy University students or upon the recommendation of a teacher. Others knew little about the campus and surrounding community until the day they were delivered to campus for the mandatory summer program for HEOP students. Many of their friends were preparing for experiences at different colleges and they shared trepidations and expectations. Families were proud that their children were going to attend an institution with a strong reputation and held out high hopes for their children's success.

At the time the students arrived, at the height of summer, the grounds were meticulously manicured and planted. Flower gardens were tucked in spaces between permanent plantings of shrubs and trees, providing a display of color and natural beauty. Benches were interspersed around the campus to invite students to take advantage of the garden displays. The large quadrangle in front of the impressive library was verdant green and attracted clusters of students and professors when the weather was fair. The Greek Revival architecture loomed large and impressive and cast long shadows of tradition. Outside of the repair work and construction noise that is inevitable on a campus in the summer, the campus felt like a green and natural oasis of calm that engendered an academic focus. Even within the classrooms, the ivy covering the outside walls crept in through the windows, bringing the outside in. This environment was an abrupt and surreal contrast to the urban environment and pace of New York City from where so many HEOP students came.

A number of the students, but especially the Pleasers who came from a dual frame of reference, commented on the physical attractiveness of the campus that made them feel welcome from the beginning. When asked what they found appealing about Ivy University, I heard comments like, "...the environment, really the environment. The knee-jerk expected environment. The landscaping....I just like walking around campus," and, "The ivy going up some of the buildings, the grass with an occasional pathway, the statue of the guy who founded it. I love it!" Its location far from home also contributed to its physical attractiveness: "I like the atmosphere. It's beautiful. I like where it's located. It's far from home [New York City], but it's not that far."

The students spoke in fairly glowing terms about the beauty of the campus, even though they found it isolated. Some found the quiet isolation of the campus a benefit because: "It gives me time to think, though, to explore myself." However, others, especially the Searchers, were more critical and found it annoyingly difficult to get off campus unless they begged a ride from someone with a car or took infrequent buses. Many of these students were used to the bustle of big cities and the relative ease of public transportation. There were also comments about the campus being smaller than anticipated, both smaller in size and in number of minority students, and smaller-minded in terms of the rumors and gossip that were quickly spread in this environment. Jason, a Searcher, found the student environment a let down: "But it really wasn't like a normal college experience like first semester. Basically I was just like, 'I don't want to be here....You know, these people, I can't relate to; I can't understand them. I really don't want to go and attempt to understand them.'...It wasn't something that I enjoyed." So, while the campus was physically attractive, the students quickly observed changes in pace, in easy access to the community, and in peer relationships that left them feeling somewhat ill at ease.

A more subtle aspect of the climate of Ivy University arose in my interviews with faculty, staff, and administrative assistants, when the majority of them discussed what I would call an "identity crisis" that enmeshed Ivy University: how to become an Ivy League caliber institution? The university identity crisis had recently involved a reorganization plan that admitted fewer students who, therefore, had higher academic credentials. The freshmen students were not aware of the plan and its ramifications, but they certainly felt the fall-out in the rigor of their courses which led to their consensus that Ivy University was an academically rigorous institution. In fact, Tiana (a Searcher) observed that Ivy University "...will be making Ivy soon if they keep it up. Before I graduate, it will be an Ivy."

The central question for the university seemed to be how to carve a niche in higher education during this time of rapidly changing student demographics which reflected society's increased diversity and push for advanced education. As the following excerpts from interviews with various layers of university personnel show, the institution was struggling with how to maintain its elitism, and even increase it, in this period of time when it was politically incorrect to be perceived as exclusionary:

> *Graduate Teaching Assistant*: And that's part of the whole thing that cracks me up about here. It's elitist, but it's elitist to the point where they want to be like Harvard, Cornell, be Ivy League. You're not Ivy League. Develop your own character, your own image....Seriously, I hear this all the time: "This was my second choice cause I didn't get in Cornell."... You know, this should be people's first choice. You know, "I'm proud of [Ivy University] and it was my first choice."

*   *   *   *   *

> *Dean of Students*: We are perhaps more homogeneous than we used to be...We eliminated from the pool a lot of students for whom [Ivy University] meant a real struggle if they were to be successful here. Because, you know, when we reduced our enrollment and reduced the size of the freshman class...we didn't really lock people out randomly. We said, we're going to cut it off in the bottom and take the top 900 to the extent that we can and that's how it's worked....We've been able to upgrade some of the things that we ask for in the English series....Now, with all of that, I worry about the extent to which the HEOP population benefits in the same way as does the general popu-

lation....These are special admits, period. It's not just because of the economic grounds. So, that has been a concern and I think, quite honestly, I can't say how that has worked out.

*   *   *   *   *

Chemistry Professor: Most of my colleagues [professors] say exactly the same thing. Ever since the [reorganization] there's that whole empty group; they're gone. Literally, we struggled for the last ten years with people who had no business being at [Ivy University]. They weren't interested in what we had to offer, and they weren't prepared to participate and, frankly, I didn't have any idea what to do with them. And, further, I wasn't terribly interested in figuring out what to do with them. If they wanted to be here and have what we had to offer them, well then that's a very different job for me...

*   *   *   *   *

History Professor: The [reorganization] is an expression of the current administration, and the idea is to have, in their dreams, students like the Princeton undergraduates who are bright, White, rich, who don't need a lot of financial aid or academic support.

These comments from university personnel illustrate the range of attitudes that surrounded the students in this environment. There were indications that this reorganization was a weeding out process and students like those in HEOP were no longer welcome. Some of the faculty found this step to be more cost effective, as well as making their lives as professors less complex. It seemed to be implied that many of the students like those in HEOP did not readily assimilate into the Ivy University culture and were, therefore, not the model students the faculty sought. There was confusion about how to deal with students who did not fit their narrow definition of what their students should be, or what they had been. Reluctance to adapt to a changing population, especially one that might be offering some resistance to the status quo within the classroom, became apparent. So, not only were the HEOP students dealing with their own transitions to college, they also had to contend with a university in transition, undergoing an identity crisis at a greater magnitude than their own. The academic implications were strongly felt by the students, even though they were unaware of the level of turmoil within the institutional politics.

Student comments were reflective of this academically charged atmosphere. All of the students felt they were working hard: "This is definitely the school where you have to become a hard worker," and

"It's living up to its name of having the highest workload. The work is very difficult." Even Yasmin (a Searcher) who had an easy first semester stated: "I think they aim high and expect high, but they treat you like nothing if you don't make it....The class of '99 is supposed to be the last dumb class [due to the reorganization plan]. I feel like the students here are getting smarter every year."

THE PREFRESHMAN SUMMER ACADEMIC PROGRAM: TRANSITIONING TO ACADEMIC LIFE

Each student took the full complement of classes that were offered during the summer program: writing, math, academic skills, computer skills, and a pivotal four-credit course about health and society. Within a short time, I discerned three fairly distinct programmatic goals and outcomes taking shape around the curricular and extracurricular experiences that were created for these students. These goals and outcomes were, to some extent, the "hidden curriculum" (Apple & Beyer, 1988; Bourdieu, 1977) of the program, although aspects of these goals could be found in HEOP literature. The first goal was to teach and learn the academic "code" of being a student at Ivy University by developing academic survival skills and strategies. The second goal was to engage the students in "consciousness" raising educational experiences. Finally, the most clearly articulated goal was to build bonding experiences between the students, and between the students and the university. The first two goals are more academically focused and will be discussed in this chapter. The third goal, building relationships between the students, will be thoroughly explored in Chapters 5 and 6.

The Academic Code

A variety of courses, staffed by a diverse group of instructors, introduced the students to college life and to new ways of thinking and learning. For the most part, graduate students taught the writing, math, academic skills, and computer classes. A few faculty members were involved in the math and computer courses, and a full time faculty member taught the content course which dealt with health and society. The instructors were carefully chosen. Their high caliber, both in their expertise and in their enthusiasm for their disciplines and teaching, would be difficult to replicate and could mislead the students into false expectations regarding the quality of the rest of the faculty.

The variety of courses exposed the students to diverse class formats. One of the expressed purposes of the health and society class was to allow the students to sample the large lecture format that they would find commonplace in the early years of college. The seasoned professor delivered lectures three days a week and was a dynamic speaker who held the students' interest and piqued their curiosity to the point that many would ask questions in class and stay after class to talk with him. The health and society course was especially appealing to the students interested in medicine. Mai (a Pleaser) felt the experience "...helped me understand how classes really are, especially in health and society. When we were in there, I get used to the lecture that helped to see how class is like....I think he was a very good lecturer and he did try to involve the students now-and-then." Some of the students found the lecture format challenging: "It was lecture. I like participating in class. Like raising my hand, like talking, I like being involved in what is going on." The hour and a half was a long time for some of them to sit and listen. The students also experienced smaller recitation sections of 20 students for this class, once a week, and led by a graduate student teaching assistant.

The writing course had even smaller classes of 10 which provided opportunity for discussion and interactive learning. Developing college level writing skills was the expressed purpose of the writing classes. In four sessions a week, the classes explored rhetorical strategies that were employed in the two common articles and developed the background for strong argumentative writing. Each student also received three half-hour tutoring sessions with different writing instructors during the course. The writing course addressed a need that was expressed by many students whose major concern was English. Ileana (a Pleaser) was amazed at the progress she made. "I learned how to write better. Because I am writing papers now that, like, wow, am I writing this?" Some felt that even more writing could have been included. However, Alicia (a Searcher) felt that the writing class was a "joke" because it was so unlike the English course requirements she experienced during her first semester.

As I became better acquainted with the academic histories of the students, I was concerned that reading skills were not addressed. The turn-around time was very tight for assignments, and some of the numerous readings for the health and society course came from professional journals that were written at challenging levels. Veronika (a Pleaser) explained her reading strategy:

> There was too much reading. So, we'd get into groups and we'd all read one paragraph after [another] paragraph and that helped a bit....There was really a lot of reading and, like most of them, I just skimmed through them. Like for the first week, I read everything through, but this is just four credits. I only have to pass....so I would skim through it and made sure I knew what the overall idea was, but it wasn't like I was paying attention to every single detail.

Mai (a Pleaser) confided that "...also, I have a hard time to read, so it take[s] me longer than the regular student....I understand it, but...it's hard." Aware that some of these students were not exposed to the most demanding academic preparation and that many of them spoke English as their second language, it was puzzling that there was no consideration given to strategic reading, a critical part of learning the academic code. However, teaching reading skills and strategies is often viewed as "remedial" work and Ivy University did not provide anything that resembled this.

The remaining three courses, math, computer, and academic skills, received few comments when the students spoke about the summer courses. When they were mentioned, the comments were often negative. Some disliked the math course for such reasons as the teacher did not individualize the course enough, the students were "out of control," and it didn't cover enough. While Clarissa (a Pleaser) didn't "despise" it, she commented that, " I think they need to work on that math class a little more to help us more. Because they did some stuff, but they could have covered more." Similar comments about the lack of useful applications of strategies were made about the academic skills course which divided the students into three sections that met once a week. In addition, the instructors integrated study skill strategies with the health and society lecture section for part of one lecture period each week. Topics that were covered included transitioning from high school to college, time management, stress management, working with professors and students, concentration, learning styles, motivation, reading, notetaking, test taking and research issues. The students developed a critical eye early on about which strategies and resources would be instrumental to their needs and which would not.

In addition to exposing the students to a variety of class formats and academic skills and strategies, there were workshops once a week to explain how to navigate the academic system at Ivy University. These sessions familiarized the students with the variety of disciplines offered on the campus and with the core requirements that students must complete for graduation. The students met various deans and department administrators and learned about the three disciplinary divisions: natural science and engineering, social science, and humanities. They heard about clusters of courses, multidisciplinary combinations, double majors, and grade requirements. The director of the career center spoke about the choice of a major and the need for flexibility. The assistant director of academic support explained the resources that were available to the students and how and when to access them.

The three and a half weeks were packed with classes, tutoring and counseling sessions, homework for every class, and various social activities. The students had mixed comments about the effectiveness of the various academic components. Despite the occasional criticisms, while observing the classes, it was clear that a number of students were actively engaged in the topics, the readings, and even the lecture format. However, as the courses wore on, many of the students around me in the back rows of the large lecture hall were closing their eyes more frequently during lectures and chatting to each other about how they hadn't finished the readings. The initial burst of motivation was difficult to maintain for students who were up most of the night completing assignments and engaging in social distractions.

A negative aspect that just about every student mentioned was the lack of time. First of all, the program was so tightly orchestrated that they became exhausted by the time the last week rolled around and a number of papers and other assignments all came due. Many of the students found reading articles every night challenging. But even more significant was that many felt that three and a half weeks was inadequate to crack the academic code of higher education. Sybill (a third year Skeptic), who was a program assistant for the summer session, observed that: "The students really didn't have a chance to learn time management and study skills, which is very important, I think. Timing is important because it seems like you have so much more time, but really you don't." As much as they felt the work was demanding, the students also realized the value of this preparation. They would have liked more opportunity to develop and refine their writing and math skills, and to space out the assignments and prepare them with more care. On reflection, two Skeptics, who took identical courses, both liked the program but voiced diametrically opposed *perceptions* of the rigor:

> *Teresa:* It was just what I expected it to be. I expected it to be hands on and jump right in the college thing. This is what's going to happen to you, so deal with it. I think the program is good because it over-exaggerates the experience by about 10 times. The stuff we did over the summer is like totally more difficult than what I'm doing now.

*   *   *   *   *

> *Damon:* Professor [Smith] put it best when he said it was like a training course. Getting ready for the real world. I'm in the real world now which is 10 times worse. My senior year was my easiest year....I was not real primed for college then. [The summer program] got me ready, otherwise I would still be in my senior mode.

Even though the students seemed grateful for this initiation to academics, some instructors questioned the value of this summer instruction. One of the study skills instructors who continued to work with many of the HEOP students in the learning center in the fall observed:

> You talk about the [summer program] as being the transitional thing, but I really think it's kind of a false set-up, because once the year actually begins, it's very different. Even the way we talk about preparing them for classes and all of that. I mean, it all really depends on what they take and how that actually works for them. It seems like we're sort of saying, well it might be like this and you need to do this, but it's not until they're actually in there that it hits them and that's the thing I think often happens. Students will say later, "I wish I had listened to you, what you had said then." Or, "I don't remember what you guys had talked about, but now is when I really need that help."

Consciousness Raising

In observing all of these classes during the three and a half weeks, I began to feel that Paolo Freire (1973) would have been pleased with the "emancipatory" curriculum and critical pedagogy that some of these instructors assembled for the students. There was a distinct effort evident in the design of the curriculum to raise the consciousness of the students through the selection of topics and articles that posed critical questions about dimensions of power and hegemony in the American society. Some students were not as ready for this as others.

Topics in the health and society class dealt with socioeconomic class issues surrounding health care and research. Students became engaged with the material at a surprisingly deep level, and there was evidence that many students had not had the opportunity to critically explore the structural conditions of health care in this society. They were amazed by the statistics and conclusions emanating from the lengthy readings they completed from health journals and selections from textbooks. The recitations elicited personal experiences from the students regarding their health care situations. These were interactive sessions where students seemed hungry to share experiences. A number of students spoke about the disadvantages of HMOs and how profit oriented they were. They explained the difficulty of obtaining and keeping adequate health insurance and of the burden to their families when buying student health insurance at Ivy University. The point was made that there seemed to be plenty of money on campus to invest in the most up-to-date labs and equipment, but not much concern was evidenced about the financial struggles that students experienced on that campus.

Not all students welcomed this opportunity to explore disparities in societal systems. Martine (a Searcher) struggled with the course because of the controversial nature of the issues that were raised:

> I hate health. I hate medicine. It's not my calling....It's a good course because I learned how to take notes from a lecture. He was a good professor. He did keep you in there as in listening. It wasn't like he was boring... Somebody was sharing and they brought up race. I was thinking about sharing and money and the next thing I was thinking about was the whole race and the money. I started thinking about only bad things about my own government, which is something that I really love. I started thinking racist ideas and that's not the way I am. It bothered me that the school would bring it up....It was too much about race. Especially when you stick a lot of minority students that have had problems with money and then you bring up race.

The writing instructors taught seemingly complementary emancipatory classes that also captured the students' attention. Two articles that raised questions about bilingualism and racial representation in advertising formed the core curriculum from which the writing assignments were developed. The instructors explained that controversial topics were selected to provide an opportunity for critical reading, reflection, and discussion. Janie Ward (1999; 2000) urges educating youth to recognize racism and discrimination, and to develop strategies of opposition that empower them to become more resilient in the face of negative social situations. Through these articles and the ensuing discussion, the instructors began a conversation around these issues. The class periods themselves were interactive, with students discussing interpretations of the articles and raising questions that were freely discussed by the class members. There was a lot of work in small groups and at the blackboards. Students were actively engaged in all of the classes that I observed, and appeared to be keeping up with the assignments. Ileana (a Pleaser) enjoyed the articles that were chosen: "I liked them because it was basically about issues, like minority. I really like to debate a lot, and it was really controversial issues. I like more the second one that talked about how are minority represented in commercials and the media." But, again, in contrast, Martine found that the writing class also focused too much on issues of race:

> English was good, but honestly, this school is very racist and this English class proved it. There was not one thing not going on in that class that had to do with race. I knew I was a minority, but they took it to another level. They made a certain hatred come out. For example,

they would talk about commercials. It's like you're looking too deep
for commercials. I was never brought up to feel like a minority. I can
relate to everybody, but in class everything had to do with race and you
just bring up this anger....Making English the official language, you're
bringing up a touchy subject. I understand that's going to happen, but
people took it to different levels. Or, maybe, I just didn't want to take
it to that level.

I was sitting in on Martine's English class the day they discussed the
representation of minorities in commercials and most of the students
seemed to enjoy engaging in the lively discussion about current adver-
tisements and the lack of, or misrepresentation of, minorities.

These courses raised current sociological issues about oppressive systems of dominance and hegemony. For many of the students this was the
first time the door had been opened for honest discussion of sensitive
topics that obviously touched some nerves of the students. While welcomed by many, these students could have benefitted from more specific guidance in recognizing and understanding systems of power in our
society and in imagining possibilities for interrupting and reinventing
power structures. This summer program is an opportunity to teach dominant power codes to students from subordinate power groups (Delpit,
1988; Ward, 2000) and to expose students to poststructural feminist
models (for example, Collins, 1990; Haraway, 1991; Lather, 1991;
Sleeter, 1993) that decenter hegemonic powers and explore the creation
of shared power within and between collaborative groups. Or this could
be a time to study racial identity development models (for example,
Cross, 1995; Marcia, 1966; Tatum, 1997) that could enhance the
awareness these students have toward their individual and collective
identities. This teaching is daring, risky, and open to more criticism from
neoconservatives that these summer programs are forums for "indoctrination" (Gose, 1998). But the students have lived within these power
systems, often without having them named, and they show a hunger for
open discussion of what they have already experienced and what they
may expect to experience in the college environment. These discussions
could also aid them in the strategic instrumentalism that they started to
develop as the real work of the academic year began.

Bonding

The third goal, creating a collective bond between the HEOP students
and to the university, will be taken up with more detail in Chapter 5.
This goal was articulated and achieved with more clarity than the other
two goals, the teaching of the academic code and consciousness-raising.

However, the students made it clear that little bonding occurred in the academic classes themselves.

THE FALL CURRICULUM

The summer introduction to the seriousness of college expectations helped prepare most of the students for the reality of college work. However, upon their return to campus in the fall, they immediately noticed that the academic world had been ratcheted up a few notches in difficulty. Maneuvering the foreign terrain of college courses required strategies that the students may not have had to use before to succeed. Certainly, they had little experience other than the summer in dealing with the unique teaching styles of tenured professors who are experts in their fields. A HEOP counselor discussed this and other transitions:

> I think for some of them the challenge is making the transition from high school to college and all that comes with being on a college campus. Living situations are different; you're obviously not at home; the food is obviously different; the teachers are different and how you interact with the teachers is different, at least that's what we try to help them understand in terms of the strategies for learning. So, I think that's a challenge for them, basically that transition. You are a student but you're at equal levels with your professor and yet they still do have the power to give you that grade.

Strategic Instrumentalism

The students found themselves immersed in a culture that required social and academic skills that were difficult to envision and to learn until one was living in this setting all day, everyday, for months on end. They were prepared over the summer to "hit the ground running" in the fall, but the ground felt a little less even than it had before, and the run slowed to a hesitant walk in some cases. During this transitional time, the HEOP students began to devise a system of *strategic instrumentalism*, developing strategies that enhanced their ability to succeed and achieve their set (and, for some, ever changing) goals while, at the same time, resisting assimilation into the elite academic culture and maintaining a cultural identity of their choosing. I identified four areas of strategy development that contained aspects of both positive **strategic resistance**, accomplishing the tasks of strategic instrumentalism, and **non-strategic resistance** that were counterproductive and self-defeating, in some cases.

Acquiring Academic Capital

Having been initiated into the academic "code" over the summer, the students now set to work to build more solid and strategic academic capital, those skills and strategies that would allow them to compete on more equal footing with students from more "advantaged" backgrounds. For some, this was an extension of what had begun in rigorous high school courses. For others, this necessitated critical assessment of courses and how to acquire the core language and study skills to assist them in achieving their academic goals. They often took what was offered them and then modified it to suit their own purposes.

If the students had completed challenging courses in high school in the subjects they were required to take their first semester, mostly introductory math, science, and composition courses, they indicated that the courses went well, even too easily for them. Ileana (a Pleaser) stopped attending her calculus class, and only went to recitations and worked from her textbook. "I don't learn anything in my calculus class...the thing is that I took AP [Advanced Placement] calculus back in high school, so that's why I know the things that are going on right now." James (a Skeptic) identified chemistry as his least favorite class for the same reason; he'd been a chemistry major in high school and the introductory course was a required but repetitious review. On the other hand, Veronika (a Pleaser) indicated that chemistry was her favorite class, despite the high teacher expectations because, "...like last year I took it and that was my worse class. But this year, maybe it's because I took it last year, so I gained like this understanding, but it's really helping me this year. So, this year, I like to read through stuff and I understand everything. It just happens. I don't have to put in a lot of effort." Students who attended high schools that provided AP classes in a number of subjects and offered a variety of elective courses had a definite advantage over the students whose schools offered only limited numbers of, or no, AP courses and few electives.

The non-strategic side of this seeming advantage was an overconfidence that made some students feel they didn't need to do some important academic work which had the potential to backfire due to their lack of experience with the expectations of higher education. In most classes, attendance was not mandatory, but it was still vital to achieving top grades.

The writing course addressed a need that was expressed by many students. Some of the students who were relatively novice speakers of English or who had the weakest English backgrounds surprisingly enjoyed and got the most value out of their introductory composition classes. Panyos (a Pleaser) found that even though he had "big trouble" with his English course, his professor worked with him on improving his writing and he spent a lot of time reworking his essays. Panyos stated that writing was power and, therefore, he planned to do more reading to improve his writing. Martine (a Searcher) was highly motivated in this class: "I've learned so much from it. I've learned how to write better. It was, like, my weakest subject in high school....It's made me want to take English next semester again." Laila (a Searcher) indicated that: "I really dislike English cause it was really difficult for me, just to get the noun and subject in the right place. But, right now, I'm like more into my English class than I'm into my bio-chem."

These students indicated the value to them of developing proficiency with the dominant language because it was "power" and central to their academic success. Despite the controversies raging for years over the power and value of language and the appropriate types of instruction in higher education, these students were strong advocates of quality instruction in English. They had a thirst for learning authentic and appropriate applications of the dominant language. How rare it is on campuses to hear students wishing they could take more composition classes than those required! Ira Shor (2000) and others (see, for example, Gee, 1998; Shor & Pari, 1999; Valdes, 1998) tackle the English composition classes as sites that performed the "**cooling out**" function that "was a bureaucratic process of gatekeeping, diverting non-elite students from upwardly-mobile liberal arts to downward choices" (p. 108). In the process, the students were stigmatized as "cultural deficits" guilty of "illegal literacy" if they jumped through the hoops of academic language barriers in non-traditional ways. Shor invokes Bourdieu's (1991) concept of "**symbolic violence**" when examining how writing instruction is a politicized process of maintaining the status quo through assimilating students into a narrowly accepted range of academic discourse. Shor, other writing instructors, and these HEOP students understand that language is a political tool that can be used to challenge the inequities in education and society, not reproduce them.

The students were attentive to developing other academic strategies. A number of them found the summer experience helpful in learning how to succeed with large lecture courses, a staple in the academic diet of first-year students. HEOP students often worked collaboratively on coursework. Other students observed that they were learning how to study and how to avoid cramming for test. James (a Skeptic) best summed up what the students sought to acquire in strategies: " I guess I'm learning how to learn. Because they're giving it to us by ourselves. You have to learn how to learn! ...How to basically look at things more in depth. Research things on your own. And teaching you how to retain as much as you can fit in your head at once!"

Most of the students were making modifications as the semester went along. Marie (a Searcher) shared her challenges: "I know what I need to do next semester. I'm not so disappointed. I know I'm not probably the only one that thinks it's real hard. It was kind of hard in catching up the work. I do what I can for now. I know what I have to do for next semester: a little more....I'm learning how to be more responsible for myself." In addition to strategically keeping up with the work, some students found that they needed to alter their strategies in dealing with teachers. Laila (a Searcher) stated that in her dealings with professors: "I would have to conduct myself in a formal manner in classrooms. I feel, for me, to conduct myself in a formal manner is so that the professors will take me seriously. It's all a professional manner." The students were constantly experimenting with formulas for success, and were willing to experiment with different strategies, most of which they had never needed in high school.

Building academic capital, as swiftly and effectively as possible, was a daunting task. Some students came into Ivy University lacking confidence in their abilities. Roberto (a Pleaser), who had been out of high school for two years before his citizenship process allowed him to enroll, was concerned. "When I came here, I was kind of scared. 'God, is my brain rusting? Oh, my God, my mom expects me to do good and I don't remember everything.' It's not like math is second nature to me...It was just kind of like diving into a pool, not knowing whether it's hot or cold. I just didn't know what to expect." High school didn't necessarily provide the best preparation. Laila (a Searcher) explained some of the new challenges:

> I know that if I go to any college, I'm going to have a bumpy transition, because high schools do not prepare you to come here. I knew I would have some difficulties in some areas....It's not so much that it's too much work, but I'm just not managing the time right....I have too much down time. That's the problem with college. Things are so spread out, time is given to you and you do whatever you want with that time.

Many students echoed this dramatic difference between high school, which presented little challenge, and college, which was remarkably less structured in terms of time and tasks like homework. Tiana (a Searcher) was an exceptional case. She realized early on that she was having difficulty acquiring the academic mindset and skills that she needed:

> And there's nothing to keep me in check in here. And I don't like that. But I'm learning how to deal with that. I'm trying to make my own

> homework. But I can't blame myself totally. I'm a freshman. I just got here. No one can blame me too much. If I don't do great in my classes this year, yeh it screws up my GPA, but it was my first semester....I think I'm learning nothing academic at this point. I'm learning just life lessons, that's what I'm learning....You can't always trust everybody and you can't always have your guard up....How to take drugs, drugs. It's so true. That's what you learn here. You don't learn anything academic....I would never ever in New York [City], ever do anything like this or anything remotely close to this.

Tiana was floundering, especially with drugs, at the end of the semester, near the time of our second interview, and she was the only student out of this research cohort who did not return to Ivy University for her second year. She was one of the few HEOP students who disclosed a history of alcohol or drug abuse.

Despite the challenges that faced the HEOP students, they were strategically acquiring academic capital and succeeding in many aspects of their courses. Their first semester (the previous year), Jason (a Searcher) achieved a 4.0 and Yasmin (a Searcher) was on Dean's List. Most of the students who complained that they were struggling were still making mostly "A"s and "B"s. At the end of the first semester, 50% of the incoming freshman HEOP class was on the Dean's List and 17 of the 23 total participants had achieved a semester GPA of 2.5 or better (out of 4.0).

Collaboration with Others

Central to the formation of identity is interaction with others. The students were actively engaged in developing strategies that assisted them in their interactions with professors. Collaboration with professors and students would be critical to their success, although some did not realize this at the onset. This was new turf and old strategies may not be as effective as they were in the past. For the Pleasers, just being quiet and cooperative in class did not result in an automatic "A" or in the attention one needed to stand out from a crowd of skilled students. How to extend oneself to effectively relate with academicians was being actively questioned and negotiated. Some students elected to work hard enough to ensure good grades and, therefore, avoid being forced to deal with the professors on a one-to-one basis, or they just chose to avoid them as much as possible. Others sought assistance and received minimal or unsatisfactory response to their efforts. And some managed to create a viable working relationship with all of their professors. The "soft sciences" and humanities seemed to be more natural places for positive rapport, although a lot seemed to depend on the ability of the students to extend themselves and to work at carving out relationships.

A number of the students handled their relationships with faculty by choosing *not* to initiate a relationship. Students often responded to my questions about meeting with faculty by indicating that they thought they were "too busy" to be bothered by students. In examining the purpose of a university and the significance of the early transitional weeks and months for newcomers to the university, finding time for students would seem a vital and high priority item, especially if there is a desire to retain students. Some students were probably uncomfortable with this new teacher-student paradigm. They had been used to a more oppositional dynamic with high school teachers, and understanding that professors might best be used as resources would take some getting used to. Paolo (a Pleaser) stated that he rarely had academic problems, and if he did, he kept them to himself rather than seeking assistance from a professor. Other students indicated that they felt more comfortable speaking with friends about any academic problems and found it intimidating to approach a professor.

Although a number of students acknowledged that there were some social opportunities set up by various departments to speak informally with professors, they each offered various reasons for choosing not to attend, ranging from class conflicts, to lack of time, to lack of interest. The students often described courses as impersonal and rather inflexible, which provided little incentive for them to extend themselves to socialize or even try to meet during office hours with faculty. Damon (a Skeptic) admitted that he had not made time to connect with his professors outside of class. "It's because I'm always so preoccupied with so many other things....I should do what I did in high school. Even if you don't have a question, you go talk to him."

There was a general acknowledgment that professors were resources for academic capital, but students were easily rebuffed, and one bad experience may prevent them from taking the risk again. Jason (a Searcher) claimed that he never got close to any of his professors because of this, even those who he enjoyed in class:

> If anything, I had bad experiences. Like with my economics professor.... He just like totally disregarded everything I said cause he's very, very unapproachable. He's almost a genius, so I've heard. So, he really doesn't care about the students too much.

Students were easily put off by teaching styles and assumed that an impersonal style in the classroom naturally extended into one-on-one relationships outside of class. When professors were perceived as boring, uninterested in engaging students in class, or unskilled in teaching, the students did not seek them out for assistance.

The Pleasers had acquired an automatic respect for teachers, earned or not, and this could be an asset when dealing with academic situations. However, this automatic respect potentially impeded communication with an esteemed "elder." Any indication of disapproval or disinterest made Pleasers likely to shy away from contact outside of class. Panyos seemingly made excuses for his engineering professor who was also his advisor:

> He is somewhat different. He [doesn't] really give me a lot of input. He [doesn't] really say much. He says, "Okay, okay. Do this." I would like to hear more from him, what he thinks. It's like stereotype for engineer students. They stay to themselves.... I think he probably has his own stuff and is too busy. He has a lot of responsibility. I can see that. He's a counselor, he's a faculty advisor, he's a professor, a lot of things.... I do not expect much from the engineering department.

The Searchers did not enter Ivy University with the automatic high regard that the Pleasers generally held for teachers and they found negotiating that fine line between personal and professional relationships challenging. Tiana assumed that certain behaviors and attitudes would be acceptable at college and quickly found that her Spanish professor did not respond as positively as her English professor. Tiana explained that: "If anything, she [her Spanish teacher] seems to have a attitude. I'm kissing butt just so I can pass this class. So, she blew up at me about my attitude. She says I treat her like she's beneath me." Tiana seemed somewhat confused by her interactions with her professors, but she was making and trying to keep appointments with them in an effort to improve these relationships.

When professors seemed approachable, the students generally responded by extending themselves in class and they were able to develop working relationships outside of class. A psychology professor was described by several students as reassuring and accessible: "I go up to him most of the time, actually, after class, and I go up to him and say, 'I don't understand this.' And he's really ready to answer me. He's really nice and approachable. He's not like he has a intimidating way." The students enjoyed his class lectures and he spent time outside of class advising the students and helping them understand how to study for psychology tests. Tiana (a Searcher) who had so much trouble with her Spanish professor, was effusive in her praise for her English professor: "I love that course! I love my teacher. It's all on the teacher. They don't understand how dependent on how good your teacher is." Teresa (a Skeptic) also found her American Literature teacher to be "...the best English teacher compared to my high school teacher....The way she talks and explains things is like we have the best conversations and it's so profound and deep, and most of what we talk about is race, class and gender." In each of these cases it seemed to be the one-on-one attention and feedback received from the professor that made a difference.

Not all professors were as naturally available to students as those just described, but many of the students strategically resisted being rebuffed and sought to understand how to survive different teaching styles. James (a Skeptic) made a cogent observation about the difference between high school and college: "[I]n high school, you had teachers and they taught you. And in college you have professors and they lecture you. They regurgitate material from the book, and they basically just tell you to what you are expected to learn. Now go and learn it....We're expected to get outside sources to figure out how to do the homework." Several students explained that they made a point of getting to know each of their professors and felt positive toward them all. Tran (a Pleaser) habitually remained after class and talked with his professors about things he didn't understand, as well as e-mailing them. Roberto (a Pleaser) was actively engaged in class, making his presence known by answering and posing questions. He said that his professors were hard on him, but that was the way he liked it. Roberto's rapport with all of his professors was remarkable:

> I meet with them during office hours. I've met after office hours. I've seen them walking, and if I had something that was concerning me I'd like stop and talk with them, so it's not just office hours. Whenever I see them. Through e-mail....My teachers are always available, even if it's after class I can talk to them....they make time.

Roberto was disappointed that he might get an "A-" in English and describes how he strategically collaborated with the professor:

> I can honestly say I deserve the "A-." Like in the beginning, I wasn't too enthusiastic about the class. It was really boring, and we were reading boring stuff. I went up to her [the professor] one day and I was like, "You know I'm not questioning your teaching abilities, but maybe you could have class discussions so the class could get into it." And she was like, "OK." And the next day she said, "Does anybody have any suggestions?" And everybody gave her suggestions, so the class is much better now....She criticizes some of the things that I write, but I tell her, although I'm taking English and I need to get a grade, I don't feel that I should be writing for her. I should be writing for myself.

Students who experienced success in establishing a working rapport with their professors were flexible in their expectations and sought to maintain close contact with them. Martine (a Searcher) had been able to develop a working relationship with all of her professors, perhaps because her attitude was to get as much out of this opportunity as possible. She made appointments with faculty and found them helpful and considerate, especially her English professor. Martine had this to say about all of her professors: "I've enjoyed my professors this semester. I've learned a lot from them. And they make me work harder." She also stated that she didn't expect anyone to hold her hand.

The students seemed more connected to professors who taught courses in the "soft sciences"—humanities and social sciences. Mai's (a Pleaser) English professor was the only professor who was mentioned who spent time explaining the cultural differences in learning styles. She and Mai discussed how Americans approach the writing task in a way different from Vietnamese. She worked with Mai to adapt her writing style to conform more to the expectations of American English classes. Mai still disliked writing essays, but she understood why she was having difficulty and had, in the professor, a resource to help her improve. It may have been significant that many of the introductory English sections to which the students responded so positively were taught by graduate students who were also students themselves, and that these were smaller classes. Many of the students observed increased difficulty in large lecture classes especially in the sciences and math. Several Searchers indicated that in math, "I'm just there in the class, taking up space," and "If I'm on top of the auditorium, I can't really see him [the professor] and it's hard to listen to him. Too many people, I don't feel comfortable." Physics, engineering, and chemistry classes also received negative notice due to size of classes and lack of contact with the professors.

Manipulation of the System

Most of the students had yet to deal with course registrations, curriculum requirements, rules and regulations that governed many activities on the campus, and the host of experiences with a system of higher education that can intrude on the life of a student seriously engaged in the learning process. At this early stage, the college "honeymoon" was not yet over. However, when problems cropped up in their first semester, HEOP students were creative in trying to use the system to their advantage.

A survival strategy that a number of students used early in the quarter was to drop a class, bringing them down to three rather than four classes. This often helped head off damage to their GPAs, but it slowed accrual of academic credit and the withdrawals would show on their academic records. Several of the students also mentioned that their attendance was spotty in several of their classes. They might not get up on time, or might be lacking motivation to attend. The large lectures were easy to miss; no one noticed and the content was usually at an introductory level that they believed they could get from the text just as well as from the lecture. However, smaller and more difficult classes motivated the students to attend. Laila (a Searcher) explained that in biomed, "If you miss it there, you miss eternity." With no one monitoring their behavior, some students seemed prone to strategically pushing the limits on optional aspects of courses like attendance, which could backfire painfully.

Not surprisingly, the most problematic bureaucratic red tape in the academic system was financial aid. Roberto's (a Pleaser) problem was representative of a number of the students: "Financial aid is always like losing something. Like my aid is taking so long to disburse because they lost something I had given them during the summer." The students spent extraordinary amounts of time and calls home trying to straighten out the financial arrangements and locate the right person to talk with and the duplicate forms to complete. Students complained of filling out the same forms a number of times, and sending copies of financial statements over and over. Sybill (a Skeptic), with two years under her belt, went so far as to call financial aid and the bursar's office "...crooked. I can tell you that now and I'm not joking. Like, you pay money to the bursar's and they take it. I swear they do not apply it to your account." The older students talked about learning the hard way to circumvent the financial aid system by working through the HEOP office, but only after spending several semesters wasting a lot of time. Vanessa (a Skeptic) became so frustrated by unresolved problems with financial aid that she finally sought assistance from the ombudsman. The HEOP office made copies of forms for the students and intervened when possible with financial aid. In addition, they made arrangements for students who were out of funds or whose financial aid was delayed, so they needed temporary support just to survive on the campus. The students exerted themselves to use the resources of the institution to enable them to successfully navigate the maze of the institution. However, it took time to become savvy in the ways to best manipulate the available resources and HEOP helped circumvent some of this.

Strategic Self-Awareness

A HEOP advisor employed a beautifully constructed food metaphor for the critical process that engaged the students in developing self discipline and trust in one's own judgment:

> I think it's [adjustment to college] also the exploration. I kind of look
> at it, when you're in high school, and I use this example, when you're
> in high school, they let you eat at McDonald's. There's a set menu and
> this is what you have to eat. Do you want it for here or to go? And if
> you are going to sit here, the chairs do not have cushions on them, so
> don't plan on staying here too long. They just want you in and out, a
> lot of numbers. That's probably why it says, "numbers served." So, it's
> more on quantity. And so when you get to college, it's different,
> because it becomes more quality. But, in the same sense, you can get
> overwhelmed with the amount of quality that there is. So, when you
> get to college, instead of going to McDonald's, you end up going to a
> all-you-can-eat buffet, where they serve all kinds of foods, from the sal-
> ads, the light stuff that you can just get by, that your stomach can
> digest very easy, to the heavy mashed potatoes and fried chicken type
> of thing that is a heavier course. And then, it's up to you to decide how
> are you going to attack this buffet? Do you get your well-balanced
> meal first, or do you just go straight to the dessert bar because you
> have that freedom to do that? It's not dictated to you that this is what
> you will do. So along with that freedom comes a lot of responsibility
> and learning to discipline yourself, in terms of time management and
> in terms of your thought processes. How much can you possibly take
> without over-eating and becoming sick to your stomach?

This fast food/buffet analogy aptly represents the students' dilemma in transitioning to a new environment and meeting new expectations. The students had a lot of choices placed in front of them, but not nec-essarily comparable amounts of guidance in dealing with decisions.

<u>Personal learning styles and values.</u> Many of the HEOP students were coming to terms with their own personal learning styles and were searching for how best to accommodate them within the course struc-tures. The rigor of courses and teacher expectations quickly woke them up to the realities of college and their reflective comments indi-cated the seriousness with which they pursued their college educations. There was a level of resistance to the academic "code" as their self-awareness increased. Several of the students found large lecture class-es frustrating because they had to sit and listen for a long period of time and the classes allowed so little interaction with the professor, the material, and other students . They felt much like Tiana (a Searcher):

> Oh, goodness. I didn't like that class at all. That's not my kind of class.
> I hated it. I don't know. Maybe because the professor sounded like the
> dry eyes, red eyes commercial....He's a good professor, but I can't....He
> drones on and on and on....I don't like lecture classes.

Professor styles came under close scrutiny and some students were vocally critical of professors, both in personal style and with their unrealistic expectations. Some students took issue with the subtle mishandling of race, like Stacey (a Skeptic). She commented that her English professor never called her name when taking attendance because: "She just knows I'm there, because I'm the only Black person there."

The students' responses to a question about what they were learning at Ivy University were indicative of their expanding self-awareness that went well beyond the classroom. Some immediately went to the academic skills that they were acquiring, especially time management and how to "work hard." However, for these students the college curriculum extended beyond textbooks, classes, professors, and grades. There was a larger curriculum of life that was voiced in these representative excerpts about what they were learning:

"[H]ow to be a person as a whole"

"How to think."

"[B]asically being independent, being able to motivate yourself."

"How to survive in the working work, basically."

"They want you to be well-rounded, able to meet the needs of society."

"How to balance your social life."

"Tolerance, patience...I'm learning how different people are."

"Not just a degree in their hand, but knowledge in their head."

"I see now how the world really kind of works...which is making me stronger, but it's kind of sad."

"I guess just learning more of like a way to mold myself as an individual..."

"If you have that degree, you're an educated person."

"A lot about myself, in terms of my capabilities, my strengths and weaknesses, what I want out of life, what I won't settle for."

"There is no Success 101....These days, you really have to get education outside of the classroom because that's where it really starts.

"I'm proving my theory that your soul makes you who you are, not your body."

Classroom learning was valued for the educational credit that it conferred that would eventually reap a coveted job. This type of learning would create the perception that as graduates the students were "educated" people. Some of them especially enjoyed engaging in the controversial social issues that were debated in some of the smaller "soft science" courses. Others, like Martine (a Searcher), were slowly awakening to their discomfort around these sensitive issues and the realities of racism and sexism that they had never faced before. However, most of the HEOP students agreed that the true education happened outside of the classroom and that the most valued education was the social and self awareness that each of them was acquiring.

<u>Autonomy.</u> When problems cropped up in their first semester, HEOP students often attempted to deal with them in autonomous ways. They were a self-sufficient group of students, used to relying on their instincts to guide their way. Often they sought out advice, but then chose not to follow it, if they were skeptical of the person providing it. Luc (a Pleaser) faced a peculiar challenge with her courses because she was a fourth year student who was a new transfer into Ivy University. She knew few students in her classes, none on a friendly basis, and dreaded having her GPA decline, which she explained is often the case right after a transfer. She had difficulty with courses in her major and attributed much of it to her inability to form or join constructive study groups. The advice her advisor gave her was to enroll in five chemistry courses in her major the next semester "...just for fun....just so I can feel that I'm not a[n] outsider....I hate them almost already.... What kind of a plan do you call that?" Luc decided to ignore this advice and enrolled in her remaining nine credits the next semester, which was also her last semester before graduation. This type of advice made students reluctant to approach others when they really needed assistance. Several students have already shared their misgivings about going to a professor when their grades were suffering. Working through academic rough spots autonomously was empowering and enabled them to strategically protect their self-esteem and bolster their resiliency in an elite atmosphere.

At times, healthy exercising of autonomy as a learner went to the extreme and became non-strategic. Students chose to withdraw at times out of a need for self-protection, when they felt too vulnerable to take risks. This occurred most frequently with professors, like Jason (a Searcher) explained: "And then, most professors I just don't feel comfortable around....I think if I was in academic difficulty, I wouldn't approach them at all. I think I'd feel even more uncomfortable approaching them than if I was like doing well." Teresa (a Skeptic) blamed herself for struggling in a class and was reluctant to approach the professor: "No, I haven't talked to him because I still feel that it's me. Until I get to the point where I'm satisfied with the way that I'm studying and then I do bad, then I'll go talk to him. But until then, no." Withdrawal was safer than placing oneself in a position to be criticized or rebuffed.

Luc's (a Pleaser) situation was the most extreme as she struggled with the new learning environment in her engineering major:

> There's one professor and he asks too much of me. Also, he expects too much. Last time I had his exam, it was the first time I ever failed. I was below average. I studied a lot and I thought I understood the materials, but I didn't.... A lot of students did well, so that's my problem.... I've never met any [of her other professors]. I think I'm scared of them.... I'm just totally isolated from that department. That's my fear and I don't know.... I'm scared of the chem. department.... I failed in a class miserably and I never even say, "I need help. Could you help me with this?"

Luc truly found herself an outsider in her classes at Ivy and was too intimidated by the situation to approach her professors or fellow students for help. Luc stated that this was not a manifestation of her cultural location, but her own problem with shyness. However, this had not been an insurmountable problem at the two other colleges she had attended. Her responses resonate with the self-devaluation that frequently occurs for women when they feel silenced within an academic space (AAUW, 1992; Felder et al, 1994; Hall & Sandler, 1982; Sadker & Sadker, 1994; Smithson, 1990). Luc had proved herself capable before, yet could not find her voice in this environment.

While withdrawal was a protective strategy, it was also a "default" strategy, when other options did not seem open. It prevented students from accessing resources in a proactive way. Some students began to miss classes when they felt the academics were sliding. In addition to not working with professors, some found reasons to avoid working with fellow students, as well. Yasmin (a Searcher) felt that classes for her major just attracted unusual people: "It seems like all the math majors and physics majors are people that look like aliens. They don't socialize. They sit there and punch in numbers." Also, when students felt they were not taken seriously in their classes, they elected to not invest energy or interest in making social and strategic connections.

There was also evidence of being overwhelmed by too many decisions and issues to resolve, and not yet having the resources and strategies in place to assist them. Paolo (a Pleaser) majored in psychology, but his career plans sounded non-existent: "I don't know. I haven't really checked out the stuff. I personally don't care. It's stuff to think about and worry about....I'll just find something to do." While many students had direction and even passion for their chosen fields, Paolo sounded like he was avoiding serious career exploration and that this choice of major was the path of least resistance. Paolo was expending great energy in confronting other things, namely his sexual identity. For him, just having a major and not worrying for a while about the future might have been strategic self-preservation.

<u>Intrinsic and extrinsic goals.</u> Beyond dealing with the novelty of higher education's curriculum and bureaucracy, the first semester was a time for exploring the reasons behind attending college and the directions the students wanted their lives to take. The initial and primary thrust was deciding the "correct" major. This was an intense search that commenced before they began college, but continued as they were bombarded by information through classes, acquaintances, and family. As the students tried on personas and identities, they were becoming more aware, with each choice, of the competing options and the tremendous range of opportunities before them. Many factors interplayed to influence their decision about their goals. They vacillated between seeking goals that satisfied intrinsic, personal desires and needs, and extrinsic goals which would literally pay-off in terms of career and financial security, and in the eyes of the family. Many, like Tran (a Pleaser), felt the urgency to earn the credentials for a good job: "I don't believe in fortunes and things. I have to finish college and have a definite job."

Sorting through the constantly growing mass of information about the rapidly changing disciplines of knowledge could become an overwhelming challenge for anyone, let alone a college freshman on the brink of major life decisions. The students demonstrated the importance of flexibility and the push and pull of intrinsic versus extrinsic goals when they tried to explain their deliberations about their majors. The Pleasers seemed to undergo more changes in their majors than either the Searchers or the Skeptics, as the following students illustrate:

> *Ileana*: I was thinking of economics and psychology, double major. And then my father wanted me to be a chemist. But when I came here in September, I was like, I don't want anything to do with the sciences. But I was thinking. I don't want to do anything and regret it later in my life. So, I wanted to take biology second semester....I want to do something with economics and psychology because I want to have my own business. And I want to know why people do stuff...because I really love to deal with people and the way they think and the way they

act....I love psychology, economics and choreography....Because I want to be a choreographer... but that's just on the side. I don't want to do that as a career, because they don't do well.... [Five years from now] I see myself in an office just directing people, being the boss.

*   *   *   *   *

Roberto: OK, I was taking my optics courses [his original major]....I tried to stick through it and I was like, "God, I'm not going to do this." And I got discouraged from chemistry; I was just not into it anymore. So, I dropped out of chemistry, dropped out of electrical engineering, and I added Spanish because I always liked Spanish. So, I still had one gap to fill. So, one day I was with my friend and she was like, "Why don't you come into my [psychology class]?" ...I went to the class and I just loved the class.... My friends are crazy. They're killing themselves with biology and chemistry and calculus. I don't know. I remember when learning was fun. Although it was strict in Jamaica, it was fun. Right now, it's fun for me; I enjoy it.

The Pleasers also seemed to labor under heavy parental influence, especially the Asian students. They often justified their choices of major and career by delaying their personal gratification in order to please their parents:

Panyos (Thailand): [R]ight now, I would say I would like to finish college and get a degree, so that my mom and dad will be happy about it. They have done so much for me and I believe that this is what they want to see. So, I want to give them what they want first and I'll think about what I want next.

It appeared that they worked academically for their parents as much as for themselves:

Mai (Vietnam): Yeh, I really worry about school. I think because of the culture. I really afraid to get a low grade, that would make my parents really unhappy. Sometimes I remember when I got really low grade, I tried to hide it....They didn't want me to go here. They wanted me to go to [a local school] instead. Because in Vietnam, we just try to stay close together and then when we come here, the children when they grow up, they leave home and go to learn.

There is a temptation to generalize from the Asian students' sense of familial responsibility and attribute it to their cultures, which has been indicated in numerous studies and articles about the Asian model minority (see, for instance: Bankston, 1997; Chan & Wang, 1991; Lee, 1991; Walsh, 1993; and Zhou, 1997). However, it became apparent that Tran (a Pleaser from Vietnam), under similar conditions, evaded family influence and was able to strike out in a more individual way once at college. These students, like other racial and ethnic clusters of students, do not express a singular and uniform process in developing core identities within the contexts of college and family. Instead, similarities overlap, in some respects across cultures and genders, but then turn around and evidence differences across these same tenuous boundaries. Each student forged an identity path sometimes around and sometimes through the family base.

These freshmen fearlessly sampled a wide range of disciplines in their search for the best fit, heeding the advice of the HEOP staff. They were keeping their options open and they were unafraid to make changes that could refine their search. Many students raised questions about the availability of jobs in their preferred career areas, about competition for entrance to professional programs, and about the lucrative aspects of various jobs. Economics and employability, the extrinsic rewards, were top concerns, as Veronika (a Pleaser) expressed:

> I want to be, like as soon as I get out, I am going to grad school and everything, but I would probably want to work for a while after college, before going on to grad school. So, you know, I guess I'm looking for something where I can get a guaranteed job as soon as I get out of school. I mean, that might change next year. That might change next week-end.

But, beyond the practical concerns of income and job availability, students also desired the intrinsic rewards of personal satisfaction and social mobility. Many students lamented the over-emphasis on success being equated with money. They were actively engaged in striking the right balance between intrinsic and extrinsic demands.

The Searchers came into Ivy University with fairly clear career goals, although they were not reluctant to switch majors to help them better achieve these goals. They were exploring options with which they could live, that would provide financial and professional security for themselves (and probably shared with immediate family) and peace of mind for their parents. There was not as much switching as the Pleasers, and not as much questioning of their decisions. These students mounted a search for self-satisfying careers, rarely influenced by family desires. Alicia talked about following her passion, despite her parents possible disapproval:

> I think I am a artist. I've had a couple of shows. I think I'm not established. I think I'm still a art student, but I think I am a artist. I've always been interested in it, since kindergarten, specialized junior high school for art, specialized high school for art.

Interestingly, the Skeptics changed majors and goals about as frequently as the Pleasers. However, the major difference was that parents were not influential with this group, even less so than for the Searchers. Their choices were contingent upon new experiences that had not been available to them until they entered college. The exposure to one class that led their thinking in new and exciting directions could be the groundwork for a new career path. The Skeptics reflected on the narrow career choices that had been impressed upon them from early on. Few options beyond professional medical or law degrees were promoted in their schools, and their parents lacked time and/or resources to provide additional inspiration. Four of the seven Skeptics had considered becoming a doctor during high school. Upon entering college, the "buffet" of choices led to lots of sampling of new fare that altered their original career choices. Those who did not change, held fast to idealistic goals of making the world a better one than they and their families had experienced. One student was going to become the English teacher that she had never had in her urban high school and another was going to clean up politics and become President of the United States. While concerned about making a living in a respected career, the extrinsic factors, they were strongly influenced by intrinsic drives that would lead to personal fulfillment.

As idealistic as some of the students were, there were real pay-offs at the end of college if they strategically made their way through the system. Luc (a Pleaser), a graduating senior, despite problems with her department, demonstrated a level of engineering skill that made her attractive even before graduation. Her sister was employed by a large local company as a chemical technician and they were willing to pay Luc $30,000 for a similar position without finishing her degree. For personal reasons, Luc would only accept a local job, and she questioned the wisdom of not jumping at this opportunity, the bird in hand. However, she decided to complete her program at Ivy University, and early in the spring semester, she had accepted a far better position with this company, commencing *after* graduation. She deferred, but not rejected, plans for graduate school until after she had earned enough to help her family and establish some financial security. Luc's story is representative of the remarkable level of resiliency that these HEOP students showed in the face of academic endeavors that were often marginalizing and oppressive. By holding fast to lofty goals and dreams, these students strategically resisted conformity and surrender to the limitations of elite academia.

Institutional Features That Affected Strategic Instrumentalism

There were certain institutional features that the HEOP students identified as *enhancing* their development of positive strategic resistance techniques:

1) professors who made a point of being approachable;
2) smaller class sizes;
3) one-on-one interaction with professors;
4) opportunities for discussion and interaction in classes;
5) and, courses in the "soft sciences" which often met all of the above criteria, plus pointedly instructed students in the real life application of concepts they were learning.
6) While not a feature of the institution, students were more likely to successfully create and employ resistance strategies if they had solid preparatory classes (such as AP) in high school and brought with them a strong motivation to prevail under any circumstances.

Most of these attributes have been discussed in previous sections. Sybill (a Skeptic) provided a useful summary of the student perceptions of the "soft" and "hard" science course differences:

> Well, my non-science courses, like my history and English, they tend to be smaller and I get a more personal relationship with my professors and I like those classes better. They get to know me and we get to know each other better. Expectations, they expect a lot out of me because they know I can do the work. But my science classes, they are typically weed out classes. Because of [the teaching hospital], everyone wants to be a doctor and they know that. They are very unsympathetic to anyone who is not performing at a "A" or "B" level.

The institutional features that students indicated *impeded* their efforts to become strategically resistant and often forced them into non-strategic behaviors were:

1) inaccessible teaching styles;
2) professors who were intimidating and who held unrealistic expectations for students;
3) large classes;
4) lecture formats, especially those that ran over one hour;

5) courses in the "hard sciences" that often met the above criteria and failed to extend the learning into real-world application;
6) inadequate academic advising;
7) and, lack of institutional support and follow-up to the summer program.

Many students voiced concerns that the professors had unrealistically high expectations for their students and were not overly willing to assist students in learning. Nicole (a Skeptic) had three years of experience to frame these comments:

> Some professors, I believe, they really forget that you're learning this stuff right now and that you don't know it as well as they do, and I think a lot of professors have a problem with that. They expect you to pick things up just like that. After a reading, you're supposed to fully understand that reading and they don't really understand that some people, me being one of them, don't really understand everything just because it's presented to them. Of course they're smart; they're teaching it! Everybody is not at that level yet.

In addition, some professors were inaccessible even during their office hours because they were busy conducting research or working at a company, or out of the country for extended periods of time.

Several of the older, more experienced students faulted the university for not providing more academic advising. They commented that no one was "held accountable for like academic planning." An academic support unit that was designed to assist students with academic planning and to answer questions was not helpful: "Like the people in [the academic support unit] are so ignorant!...They treat you, well, they treated me, like they really insulted me." Most of the students seemed to rely on the HEOP advisors for academic advising, even though they were not thoroughly familiar with some of the majors. Stacey (a Skeptic), a freshman, had already found the academic advice she received from her HEOP counselor less than informative. She made an appointment to set up her courses for the next semester and was disappointed with their brief talk: "Sign the paper. Made a photocopy...didn't even take ten minutes!"

Some students observed that there was no follow-up programmatic support like the summer program. Ivy University does not offer a first-year or freshman seminar type of course which many universities are providing (see, for example, Gardner, 1992). These courses are typically designed to integrate the new students academically and socially to the particular campus culture and to the expectations of higher education. Several of the instructors and counselors also commented on the lack of university support during the first year, as this HEOP counselor noted:

> I think that at [Ivy University] basically you're admitted, you're here, now learn and learn everything. Learn to adjust and adapt socioeconomically. Learn to adjust academically. Learn to understand what the professor is saying. Learn how to go and ask questions of your professor. But, I don't think they do anything. They don't train any student to be a college student here.

In addition to lacking a first year experience type program, the orientation at Ivy University is a short, one day before the beginning of fall semester. HEOP intervened when appropriate, but there seemed to be few available resources to assist students beyond this program. The ombudsman was mentioned only once, and academic advisors seemed to have little time and too little contact with the students to be a useful connection during this transitory phase. They did not expect to be pampered, but the students found the "sink or swim" boot camp mentality worrisome.

CONCLUSION

Academics were the proving ground for the HEOP students. Gaining admission to Ivy University was only the first step. They then had to quickly learn to break the "academic code" and show that they could achieve well in their classes in order to continue to take advantage of this opportunity for education at an elite university. Their success would come on their own terms through what I have called *strategic instrumentalism*. They developed strategies to allow them to resist total conformity to the dominant, Eurocentric cultural ways of learning and living, while coexisting and achieving their goals on this campus. They were trying to make their marginalized positions locations of strength.

The students demonstrated a high level of resiliency, the ability to continue on in the face of challenges to their identity and feelings of self-worth. Many of them felt disadvantaged by their high schools' limited opportunities in some of the courses and it was obvious to them that others brought far better academic capital to the learning experience. The structure of the courses often made professors inaccessible and the system of education more impersonal and inflexible than their high school experiences. However, the students were fairly philosophical and were able to see beyond the individual courses and the curriculum to the larger curriculum of life that was available to them through the college experience. The HEOP students were taking risks just being in college, but they seemed to feel that they had little to lose. They grabbed the opportunity at Ivy University and threw themselves into the work of making a place for themselves. They expected to work hard and they were not disappointed. If things didn't work out, they would often blame themselves and work a little harder, but they did not complain very often. They were able to verbalize the changes they observed within themselves and the lessons they were just beginning about life and the world beyond. There were frustrations, but overall, the HEOP students narrated an enthusiasm about learning, their futures, and who they were becoming.

CHAPTER 5

Searching for a "Home of My Own:"
The Use of Time and Space

> [C]oming to college is a little bit different than when I moved from Ghana
> to America because, I mean, in my neighborhood where I live, it's still the
> same kind of people. It's mostly Blacks and Latinos, and here it's every-
> body. So, that's like a major difference.
>
> *—Veronika, a first generation immigrant from Ghana*

In the first few months on campus, in addition to understanding the
academic "climate" of Ivy University, consisting of physical and curricular
elements of college life, the Higher Education Opportunity Program
(HEOP) students attempted to establish a routine of daily life and to
engage on some level with their peers and the organizations and activities
that were arrayed before them like a sumptuous smorgasbord. Striking
a balance in their daily lives that allowed them to create a space that
could be their home away from home, that attended to their academic and
career goals, while also incorporating pleasurable activities in their daily
routines, was a stiff challenge that all of these students struggled to address.
The culture of college life beckoned them to immerse themselves in a
bewildering plethora of activities, some academic and many social. The
choices they made during these early stages could have a lasting impact
on their college experience.

Many researchers (most notably Vincent Tinto, 1987, but also Bean,
1980; Cabrera, Castenada, Nora, & Hengstler, 1992; Pascarella, Terenzini,
& Wolfle, 1986; and others) have underscored the importance of both **academic and social integration** of incoming college students into the college
environment as predictors of their willingness and ability to persist at that
institution. The body of persistence research indicates that how these two
processes occur varies widely between institutions and among individuals,
but that the amount and quality of academic and social integrations directly

impact the success of the new students in making the transition to college. Bean (1980) calls this quality and quantity of integration "institutional fit." The congeniality of the environment (institutional fit) determines the level of social and academic integration that will occur for each individual, and the stronger the fit, the stronger the student intentions and commitments to achieving their academic goals at this institution. The academics required strategic negotiation on the part of the HEOP students, but they were even more out of their element in understanding how to manage the social, daily aspects of living in this foreign environment.

Other persistence research also pertains to this study of HEOP students by highlighting the positive effect of adequate financial aid in providing a more equal opportunity for academic and social integration to occur for low income students (Cabrera, Nora and Castenada, 1992) and the critical necessity of institutional commitment to enhancing strong academic and social integration, especially for academically underprepared students (Walleri & Peglow-Hoch, 1988). In terms of adjustment to college, the academic integration through strategic instrumentalism that was explored in the previous chapter and the social integration which is the topic of this and the following chapter, are critical factors in the successful transition of students to college, and even more so for students from low income and/or disadvantaged educational backgrounds. The HEOP students employed strategic instrumentalism in their navigation of the social environment at Ivy University, but not as consciously as with the academics. There was also more departure between the social adaptation behaviors of the three groups than seen in their academic endeavors.

The choices that the HEOP students made which fostered institutional integration reflected their stages of identity development, especially the level of need for affiliation of various types. This chapter explores the part of the process of social integration that the HEOP students experienced, especially in terms of their use of time and space. Because they were clearly not planning to make a clean break from their pasts and leave their home identities behind while forging brand new identities at Ivy University, the process of separation from their social support systems at home will be briefly discussed through the first stage separation effects of the prefreshman summer program. This period of transition and growth created, sometimes in a sad or painful way, space for new people and experiences to fill the partial void that the separation from home brought. The remainder of the chapter focuses on the outside identity that these HEOP students constructed on campus when they returned in the fall, those manifestations of changing identity that were most visible. One level of identity development can be viewed through the way the students' physical living space within the dorms and their "free spaces" were organized, sometimes through choice, but often through the university's arrangement. Another level of discovery and development relates to the students' daily routines and activities, the extracurricular organizations and clubs that they chose to join, and their purely social activities. These levels of social engagement impacted the identity construction and the social integration of the HEOP students in complex ways, raising questions and doubts, or clarifying long-held beliefs about who they wanted to become and how they were going to go about doing that within this select environment. As much as with their academic integration efforts, strong resiliency was called for in adjusting to the cloistered lifestyle that many found oppressive and oppositional.

PREFRESHMAN SUMMER PROGRAM: LEAVING THE HOME PLACE AND LOOSENING TIES

Ivy University was an academically focused academy that had originally educated White male students who dominated the cultural, political, and social spheres of this country, and the university still showed remnants of those days through symbolic and social practices. Becoming bicultural in this environment became a necessary survival strategy for the HEOP students. **Biculturalism** is described by Antonia Darder (1998) in relation to immigration, but it is equally applicable to the college transition stage:

> There can be no question that biculturalism in the United States has evolved from a set of conscious and unconscious adaptational strategies to preserve significant dimensions of cultural knowledge and collective identity, adapt to changing material conditions, and resist institutional forms of psychological and physical violence (p.133).

The students were without their families to mediate the cultural transition. They would have to create their own strategies for maintaining the essence of their cultural and collective identities, while coping with new expectations, experiences, and pressures on the college campus that would have certain impact on their identities. Veronika (a Pleaser) expressed the anxiety-provoked conflict many of the students experienced when faced with this unknown world: "Oh, it was really exciting." And then, in the next breath, "I wanted to go home. Coming over here by myself on the bus, I was thinking there's going to be so many people. I know nobody. I was wondering if I'm going to be able to get along with them, because I don't really talk a lot."

Socializing During the Prefreshman Summer Program

Initial feelings of uncertainty gave way to pleasant surprise at how socially engaging the summer program was. A strong social component was constructed around a core curriculum of courses by six older HEOP students who were hired as program assistants (PA) for the summer and a graduate student who served as a program director. All of these employees lived in the dorms with the students, and the PAs were assigned to attend classes with them and to plan social programs. A careful web of support was constructed from the beginning to cushion the entry of these students into the college environment. A welcoming barbeque, trips to the local malls, an excursion to an entertainment theme park, and an outing to a local crafts festival were some of the planned activities in which all of the students participated. A further social acclimation was the assignment of roommates for the summer program.

Most of the students found the transition far less painful than they feared. Veronika's experience represents what many of the other students related, the awkwardness at the beginning, followed by welcome *bonding*, one of the programmatic goals that was introduced in Chapter 4:

> Even at the barbecue, my chips were pouring, my soda was going in. Oh, God, it was awful! My roommate was really nice. The next day another girl came in and we just clicked, so now she's my best friend on this campus. It was so amazing because we built like a family, during [the summer program]. We all went out together, we'd all have time to study and then after studying, someone would say, we're having a party in my room....It was so much fun.... I didn't really expect to form those close relationships. I mean, everybody is different. So what if you're all in [the summer program]? We still have different backgrounds. We really didn't know each other. We're only here for a month. But, it seems like we've known each other for years. That was pretty strange. I think that was a good thing. I wasn't expecting that, so it was a good thing to happen. I remember, like in the evenings, you would have people playing with shaving cream, running up and down the hall, throwing water on people. And I'm like, oh my God. I mean, we all just came from high school, but I was imagining that we were going to a college and everybody would try to be conservative, you know, put aside all those childish things. But, it was really amazing, because you had like juniors and graduates who were playing along with us....Like me, I'd think, like I'm in college and I can't be looking like a child. But everybody just let go and we became children again. Running around, having the time of our lives.

The tremendous pressure of the new and unknown college experience may have led to an overly exuberant playfulness during free times. There were some "emergency" meetings held by the staff to handle some behavior problems that developed during the course of the program. However, through these experiences, this group made some strong bonds and friendships that lasted into the school year. Perhaps some of the "childish" behavior was the escape from what the students perceived to be rather heavy academic demands.

On the whole, the HEOP students were pleased with the social engagement engendered by the summer program and to find that the focus was not strictly academic. Several of the students talked about the benefits:

> *Tiana* (a Searcher): I loved it [the summer program]! I had a really good time. I'm going to apply to be a PA [program assistant] during the summer. Uhm, I met a guy during [the summer program] which, we got really close, so that made it all worthwhile. We're really close. We're still best friends....I think it's a good experience for kids.

*   *   *   *   *

> *Teresa* (a Skeptic): My roommate in [the summer program] I couldn't stand her.... She had low self esteem, and now I wish so much that she was my roommate because I know her and I can trust her....I can talk to her about anything. It's kind of weird how [the summer program] kids share their strange distant bond...

Many of the students commented on the immediate bond that developed between students in the summer program and most of the students concurred that it was a relief to have made friends in the summer who would be there for them in the fall.

It must be noted that there were intragroup exceptions to the strong social integration that took place over the summer. Paolo (a Pleaser) hated his roommate and, at the time of the interviews, didn't speak to the students who went through the summer program with him. He explained that "...I'm a very reserved person most of the time." Paolo's inability to form bonds and friendships during this time was explained away as part of his nature. Tran's (a Pleaser) voice is noticeably absent in the discussion of the program. In order to graduate and enter college in the fall, Tran attended a local high school summer school to finish up his credits. Unfortunately, he was unable to attend the HEOP summer session. He did comment that he felt somewhat left out, but he was not really aware of what he had missed. Alicia (a Searcher), for the most part, was not impressed by the students in the summer program and had a lot to say about this:

> The students, they were all very fake. I always act the way that I am,
> my whole life. I never put up a front, a barrier. I never hid that. But in
> [the summer program], people did that a lot....This was supposed to be
> a learning experience and you were all putting up a front. So, what are
> you doing?...I think on the most part, they were kind of dumb. It's real-
> ly bad. I'm not saying that I'm smart, but I didn't have much in com-
> mon with them....They were up for parties. I like parties, but like, come
> on, there's only so much you can do. We all came from different back-
> grounds. I was more like passive—diplomatic, not passive....I thought
> [the summer program] was going to be more well-rounded. I saw a lot
> of people kind of the same, either really urban and into science. There
> wasn't much variety. I guess everybody was from New York State for
> HEOP...The thing is, I wasn't from where they were from. They were
> more like from Washington Heights, Brooklyn, Bronx, and I'm from
> upper west side, which is pretty.

HEOP is composed strictly of New York State students. However, the
summer program at Ivy University also included about twenty students
from all over the country who appeared by their entrance portfolios to
be similar to the HEOP students and could, therefore, benefit from the
summer program. Yasmin (a Searcher) was one of these students who
had attended the prefreshman program the summer before, and was
now a program assistant (PA) for this year's group. She was from Florida
but informed me that she was just like the HEOP students and received
the same amount of financial aid, just not from the state. Yasmin's perspective on this class was also somewhat negative:

> I think, what we [the PAs] all thought, was they had more book smarts,
> but they have less street smarts. Less common sense....I mean, they're
> not even here long enough to establish tight bonds with anybody that
> you can hold sacred, like bonds that you know you can trust a per-
> son....They were very immature. I'm not even sure if I acted like that.
> I mean I acted like that to a certain extent, but I knew where to draw
> the line.

From Alicia and Yasmin's comments, plus the emergency meetings to
discuss behavior, it seems safe to infer that there was a lot of socializing
that included some risky behavior. Some of the students talked about the
good times they had together just running wild, but there were dissent-
ing comments about the negative aspects of the socializing among this
student group.

Alicia's statement that she had little in common with the HEOP students, further emphasized by the comment that she "wasn't from where
they were from," needs some examination. Alicia, by virtue of being

admitted to the HEOP group, had a lot in common with these students, beyond the fact that she was from New York City like the vast majority of the HEOP students. They just didn't all happen to live in her borough of the City. This tendency to distance oneself from potential membership groups further highlights the tension that exists within groups of people who are monolithically classified and defined by others using such descriptors as minority, Hispanic, or Latino/a. In Alicia's case, it also demonstrates the class issues that exist within groups that are seemingly culturally similar. In order to qualify for HEOP, Alicia's family would be defined by the state as poor and/or working class. However, factors beyond economics enter into a self-definition of class. For Alicia, her parents' high level of education (both have doctoral degrees from Peru) and their area of residence, even within close proximity to some of the "other" students, indicates to her that she is not one of them. Several researchers have discussed immigrants trying to break from any association that might be made between them and groups who have been historically marginalized and oppressed within the American system (see, for example, Hirschman, 1996, p.54; Matute-Bianchi, 1991, p. 207-209; Portes, 1995, p. 248-262; and Waters, 1996, p. 172). They avoid identification with those they consider, as Portes (1995) calls them, "downtrodden." This intergroup tension rarely surfaced in the HEOP group and Alicia is a notable exception. The important point for now is that there were minor tensions that began to appear during the summer for a few students, but the majority found the prefreshman program helpful in terms of connecting with a group of individuals with whom they could continue friendships and support networks when the fall semester began. To set foot on the campus in the fall with familiar faces around them provided a measure of comfort and achieved a major goal of HEOP.

The introduction to the seriousness of college expectations helped prepare most of the students for the reality of college work and they appreciated the opportunity to establish fledgling friendships with others in HEOP. However, they certainly had other concerns, one of which Jason (a Searcher) voiced:

> [M]e and a couple of other Asian HEOP students were talking in the library during the summer. We were talking and we were like, it's going to be weird when everyone comes, because it was just basically us, you know. There were a couple other people walking around campus, but it was just basically us, you know, so it's nothing like, no big deal. But we had our worries, you know. Like, would you be embarrassed to say "I get like full tuition and everything," compared to other students, and things like that.

Jason anticipated the culture shock that might occur as the full student body returned in the fall and the HEOP students no longer had the campus virtually to themselves. Several other students worried about the artificial nature of the summer program and the instant bonding that took place.

Loosening the Family Ties That Bind

For most of the Pleasers, the summer program was the first major separation from their families since they arrived in the United States. They had traveled a long way to reach this point, from their countries of origin where they lived the dominant culture, to American neighborhoods that served as intermediary stops between two distinct cultures, and finally to an elite campus. During this time of transition, beginning with the summer program, but continuing into the fall, relationships with family and friends from "back home" were challenging to handle. There was an internal dialectics constantly moving between preservation and change. The separation from earlier alliances was under way, but for most of the Pleasers it was only partial. Friendships and positive family relationships remained a part of their lives. Their **"segmented assimilation"** (Portes & Rumbaut, 1990; Rumbaut, 1996) into the US led to different patterns and degrees of becoming bicultural which impacted their affiliations with family, friends, and the university.

Students were exploring their ties with the family and how to become independent students and young adults. Much of their identities were still wrapped around home and, lacking the constant support of their families, they found the college separation a painful struggle with which to cope. Many of the Pleasers spoke with their families frequently, some daily, by phone and some returned home every other week. At mid-semester, Mai had already been home four times (her home was only a little over an hour away) and was planning another visit at Thanksgiving. She said, "...it just feels good to go home....I just let it out. I took a test and I didn't get a good grade, so I go home. Even though they yell at me, I feel better." However, the frequent absence from campus made it difficult to develop much of a social base from which to draw support.

The pressure to achieve at the same level as high school was weighty for these entering students whose family cultures fostered compliance, obedience, and achievement. Veronika felt that her family had little conception of the difficulty of the coursework and the reality of her college life:

> She [her mother] thinks because I was doing well in high school, I
> would do the same here. I told her I got a 84 out of 140 on my chem-
> istry exam and I mean that was a good score; that was like a "B+"
> because the curve was so messed up. And she's like, "What? An 84?
> Damn, you should really stop going to all those parties." I'm like, you
> don't even know what you're talking about....I did better than most of
> the people.

The family who set so much store in the college diploma could not begin
to comprehend why the student may have found it impossible to compete at the same level as before. The immediate response was to blame
the student for not trying hard enough. With this reaction, the nature of
communication home would certainly change to less revealing and less
specific information.

Other Pleasers relied less on the connections to home to bolster their
college experiences. They carefully selected what they shared with their
families. Paolo and Roberto confided little in their families and returned
home infrequently, perhaps more at ease with this because both of them
had experienced lengthy separations from one or both parents before
immigration. However, Paolo appeared to be adrift, without the support
of old friends and with minimum engagement with his family.

For Tran and Luc, because Ivy University was in their hometown,
their family and friendship relationships changed but they played a
prominent part in their daily life at college because they were so accessible. Their identities continued to be tied closely to the past. Proximity
to home made the transition more of a challenge for Tran because it was
not as easy for him to leave his former life behind. Luc's situation was
somewhat different because she transferred to Ivy University in order to
be able to live at home. She had a short commute to school each day and
enjoyed being with her family. Luc appreciated the proximity and
explained that, "...whenever I have trouble with school, I'm always
looking forward to going home." She shared many of her experiences
with her family but avoided talking about some things because she
didn't want to upset them. Her ties to her family resembled Mai's, and
this was her final year of college.

The three and a half week summer program was the first time most
of the Searchers had been away from their families for any length of
time. Tiana was the exception in this group because she had attended
boarding school during her high school years: "I've already been away
from home. What's the difference? I didn't mind." However, several of
the other students expressed separation anxiety. Martine indicated that
she found it difficult to say good-bye to her parents, even though she
wanted to begin the separation: "...my parents brought me up here and

my mother was crying when they left and she knew I would be back in a month, but then I would be leaving. I started crying when I saw her. I wanted to be on my own. I'm not going to change my mind. I really want to go away and be on my own." Despite the separation from family and finding themselves on a campus quietly removed from the urban pace that had been the rhythm of their lives, these students did not express the same level of anxiety and bewilderment as the Pleasers. They wasted few words in describing the transition between home and college.

The students also worked at establishing their independence from home. Most of the Searchers expressed the importance of making the separation. At our first interview, in her second month at college, Tiana talked about this:

> I know people who've been home twice already. My goodness, just leave it alone. Let the transition happen. You know what I mean? If you run home every time you feel like you want to be with family, you're never going to get used to this place. Just stick it out.

She indicated that she was fairly honest with her family about her academic struggles her first semester, but that she didn't feel that they could begin to understand what she faced at Ivy University. Tiana knew that her family was proud that she was the "only real college student," but she wished that they would show their pride in being more supportive financially: "But if they're so proud, why don't they try to help me out? I need things. I need deodorant. I need cigarettes. I have a very bad habit. The least they could do is buy me soap and send it to me, and write a little note saying it was all I could buy you, you know?"

Separations seemed harder on the parents than the Searchers. Martine relished being on her own, but had been back to New York City four times by the end of Thanksgiving week-end. In addition, her parents had visited her twice. She commented that her father seemed to have the hardest time with this separation: "He always says, am I lonely, am I this? I think he wants me to say I'm lonely so that I can say that I miss them. But I'm not really that lonely. I'm okay." Martine spoke with them about school, but only in the most general terms. She knew that they wanted her to transfer to a school closer to home. Several other students spoke of identical situations.

Each student's separation experience was unique and challenging. However, the Searchers seemed more eager to draw the lines of separation between their lives as college students and their lives as family members than the Pleasers. They understood their parents' struggle to allow them independence, but the students were seeking respect for handling their lives responsibly. They wanted to prove that their parents' fears were unfounded.

Many of the Skeptics made notably fewer trips home in their first semester, although they maintained contact, some very open and honest, with their families. Nicole shared little with her family about her academics because she didn't want her mother to worry and she visited home only on breaks, if then, in her first few years at college. However, now in her fourth year, she found she went home more frequently and she maintained fairly regular phone contact with her mother. She speculated on the reason for the change: "I guess maybe because I'm just so fed up with being here and going home is so much better." In contrast, Stacey made only one trip home to New York City, but she phoned her mom everyday and her father several times a week mostly to check on their well-being and not to discuss school. This group of students spoke with less intensity about their families and about the urgency of regular visitations in maintaining their relationships. Many of them experienced financial restrictions on the amount of travel they were able to schedule, but they indicated little disappointment in this situation. Nothing was mentioned about homesickness or negotiating independence from the family, contrary to both the Pleasers and the Searchers.

Damon and Sybill were remarkable in their strong family affiliations that resulted in weekly visits home. Close proximity to their homes made it easy for them to run back and forth on a regular basis. Sybill spoke with her mother a great deal and went home every week-end. Damon talked to his mother everyday and shared most things with his father and brother. He went home mid-week to work with his father and stopped by every week-end. These two students made distinct separations between home and school, but sacrificed neither one for the other. They both expressed satisfaction that they were able to have the best of both the academic and familial worlds. They seemed the most able of all of the students to strike a balance between their intrinsic and extrinsic needs.

Hometown Friends

Of the friends "back home," many of them were involved in transitions and identity shifts of their own. With the majority of friends being academically minded, they spread out to colleges throughout the region and surrounding states. However, the closeness of these high school relationships was hard to maintain long distance, and some of the HEOP students found that their friends had truly gone their own ways. One student vented his frustration: "I tried e-mail, phone, letters. They don't respond. I say, screw you. I'm not begging you to be my friends....Well, that's not my loss; that's their loss....But, personally, I say, with how close we were, they should have given me at least a phone call. Once in a while, say 'Hi, how are you?'"

Most of the students were experimenting with the frequency and types of contact that could be maintained. After the first phone bills arrived, many of the students decided to depend on e-mail and requested phone cards as gifts from their parents. Some friends lacked access to computers, so the phone bills ran high. Surprisingly, several students frequently wrote to their friends, an art that's reportedly dying out. Other students were able to visit home, even when it was New York City, with enough frequency that they could stay in contact with their friends who attended college there. For students whose families and friends were "well-connected," the ease of e-mail communication had radically altered the probability that relationships could be maintained from a distance.

Filling the Gap: The Role of HEOP

The dynamics of identity construction continued as these students left one family and social support system behind in order to find another. HEOP positioned itself to provide the support that would enable this transformation to take place within the college environment. Despite the fact that this was the first time many had been away from "home" and family for this long, that the HEOP students were in residence at an elite university whose milieu was totally foreign to them, and that their peers were total strangers, the prefreshman summer program was not an "othering" experience. The reverse was true. By the time they headed home (and most of them were eager to go home), these students had formed bonds and connections with peers, faculty, and HEOP staff that would be sustained well into their first semester. They had grown to feel comfortable with making their way around campus and accessing some critical resources. The "taste" of academics was challenging, but not beyond their capabilities. HEOP had carefully, thoughtfully, and purposefully constructed an experience to make the students' transition to Ivy University less disruptive, jolting, and traumatic than it might have been without the summer program. After observing much of the summer program, my sense was that this program succeeded in creating some critical continuities for these students that would carry them through the inevitable discontinuities that awaited in their college careers. There were few head-on assaults to the identities that these students brought with them, that of being someone's son or daughter, and that of a successful student, a number of whom had negotiated numerous cultural adjustments to school systems that marked them as outsiders based on their immigrant or ethnic identity. They left the summer program with their identities intact, although changed through continuous construction in the academic environment, and buoyed by the bonding experience. In leaving one family, they had found another, and HEOP banked on this shared experience to ease the culture shock of the fall semester.

LIVING SPACE: FALL SEMESTER...AND THE REAL WORK BEGINS

The initial phase of college in the fall for the HEOP students was described as a culture shock by several of the instructors and HEOP advisors who were interviewed. Despite all of the careful groundwork that was laid in the summer, there was no way to detour around the collision of two very different cultures—that of the HEOP student coming from an urban experience of economic and educational disadvantage colliding head-on with an elite academic culture of higher education, steeped in over one hundred years of tradition and high expectations. A writing instructor who taught the HEOP students in the summer and continued to see some of them in her fall classes and a study skills group commented:

> I think culturally there's a huge challenge. I think that the first year is just trying to negotiate how to act in college and, granted, all students have to learn how to do that. But, I think with HEOP students, there's a bit more of a challenge in that. This really doesn't resemble any sort of educational setting that they are familiar with and, of course, this is very obviously an upper class, very white, homogeneous campus. So, finding your position and even feeling that there is space for you is something that's very difficult....They say that a lot.... They can prove something which is very similar to a culture shock. And, I think that the [summer program] is the first stage of the culture shock, where you are ecstatic, everything is wonderful, new, you're meeting people and all works out well. But by the time they come back, they're in the second part of the culture shock, which is that downer, that feeling alien, feeling very different from the rest of the population and very lonely.

This instructor attributed the shock to students who were used to being around *diverse* populations in their schools and neighborhoods now encountering a homogeneously White and contained environment. However, one of the HEOP advisors took the opposite perspective of homogeneity, that of the HEOP students coming from culturally *monotype* environments and being surprised by the increased diversity to which they must adjust:

> A lot of students are coming from, particularly our HEOP students, maybe coming from schools where it's a homogeneous type of environment, either all White and rural, or largely Black and Hispanic. And when they come here, it's different. It's very different and they will encounter people who have never met someone of color and so their perception is based on whatever was said to them by the media. We know we can't count on the media to be sensitive or accurate when it comes to those kinds of issues.

Coming from either of these backgrounds, the HEOP students faced a major cultural challenge.

In a focus group, Clarissa and Veronika compared the transition to college to their immigration to the United States:

> *Clarissa*: It's been pretty similar in that you have to really adjust to...I guess this could be compared to my first year in America and going to school, public school that was different.

> *Veronika*: Yeh, I think the same thing too. They're both like, well, like leaving home for college is like traveling to a whole different place. Because, you know, once again you experience a whole different kind of people and it's not like you're in your country where you see most of your own people. And America is so diverse...everybody here.

These young women and instructors spoke of cultural ruptures in the school setting and in the social fabric to which the students had become accustomed in their home settings. In the fall, the students became aware immediately that this space was unlike any they'd experienced. Here the population appeared homogeneously White, while also containing diverse elements, however small, that had been absent "back home." The summer program could only allude to what this felt like. Home started to sound like a welcome refuge for some of the students, as they began to feel marginalized within the institution.

The Dorm: "Home, Sweet Home?"

Trying to make a "home away from home" became one of the first issues for most of the incoming freshmen. All freshmen and sophomores were required to live on campus, and the incoming students had little say in room assignments.

Because Luc was a senior, she chose to live at home with her family. All of the other Pleasers were in dorms; three of them had their own rooms and five had roommates. The students with roommates established a civil, if not friendly relationship with their roommates. Of these students, Clarissa seemed to have formed the closest relationship with her roommate, including her and several hall mates in the outer circle of her friendship group: "...they come over, but we're not all in the same grade and not always together." Tran had a comfortable relationship with his roommate who was also Vietnamese, but described him as very studious and not often in the room. Interestingly, the most consistent friendship with dorm mates came from Paolo, the self described anti-socialite. His friendship group was mainly composed of students from his floor, although he qualified the depth of their relationship: "Sometimes the word 'friends,' that's a bit too close. I like 'acquaintances.'" Mai also developed a rapport with some of her hall mates. They spent a lot of time together, studying and eating. However, Mai had no roommate, complained of being lonely sometimes, and went home frequently. None of these students seemed overly enthusiastic about their living arrangements, and they certainly never referred to this space as "home." However, they didn't complain about the living space other than to mention that they might prefer to be in a different dorm, and their words indicated that they were carefully negotiating alliances or truces with their roommates and hall mates.

Five of the seven Searchers had roommates and the remaining two had suitemates, but their own rooms. These two, Martine and Tiana, enjoyed the advantage of having others around for socializing yet being able to close their doors for solitude. Martine was adamant that she wanted to continue this arrangement in future years. Tiana was one of the few HEOP students who referred to the dorm as her "house" and entertained her friends frequently in her suite.

Jason had a bad experience with his freshman roommate who was "into bad stuff" that he was trying to get away from. He was somewhat lonely without his girlfriend, and when conflict flared over his smoking, he elected to move to a single. However, in his second year, he again had a roommate who was "strange and weird" and was living in a dorm that didn't appeal to him. Despite this, he indicated that Ivy University was like his home, "...but it still kind of gets to me." The remaining Searchers were fairly content with their roommates. Yasmin, a second year student, was allowed to choose her roommate and chose to room with her best friend, even though they were total opposites. Laila was coming to terms with cultural differences: "It's good in a way that I have a Caucasian roommate, because it exposes me to a different side." And Marie was not unhappy with her roommate, but she was disappointed that the floor didn't do much together, and she rarely saw her resident assistant. Her comment was the only one of the Searchers that betrayed a tinge of homesickness: "Yeh, it's good dorming, but it's so far away from home. I miss the family."

If there's any truth in the old adage "home is where the heart is," the Skeptics clearly did not see Ivy University as home. Nicole, in her third year, chose to live off campus and wished she had done it earlier: "And like, moving off campus has been the best thing, the best decision I've ever made!" However, Nicole was quick to comment that freshmen would not be ready to handle it. The remaining six Skeptics lived on campus, but Sybill lived in a dorm complex at the edge of campus that made it feel off campus. Despite this, she indicated: "I have my space, but I'm always home on the week-ends....My home is still my home!....This is just a place I sleep." Damon and Teresa, whose families were local residents, were also home with great frequency, usually more than once a week. They both had roommates with whom they had civil, if not friendly, relations, but the lure of home was strong. Teresa found the noise in the dorm too distracting and had no success in urging others on her floor to keep the noise level down, especially at night. Damon was somewhat disgusted by the mess that his floormates made, but he was so involved in community projects and working with his father that his home base was truly his family home.

Vanessa stated that she and her roommate were quite different but they got along well. They had established workable arrangements for sharing the physical and audio space. She looked forward to winter when she could eat in the cafeteria downstairs and then hole up in her room. She commented that, "I'm going to be a ghost. Like, no one is going to see me." Stacey started out her first semester with a roommate and was actively negotiating a tenuous relationship. She spoke about several situations where her roommate had been insensitive, climbing on Stacey's bed with her boots on, opening the window at night while Stacey froze, and mysteriously and permanently removing her VCR from the room when Stacey was absent, which she perceived as an unfriendly action. By the second semester, she was in a single room, but still confused about home:

> I don't even know where my home is right now. Like my dad just moved two weeks ago. I mean, like I know physically, like I have the address, but I've never been there. Home is still where I was living before. That's why I say home, that's still what I think of. And I'm like, oh, that's not home anymore. My room is gone....I don't know what home looks like or anything. I feel every time I say home, I still think of where I used to live.

Stacey had only been living with her father for a little over a year before she entered college. So, she did not have a stable conception of home to begin with, but her father's move so soon after she left made the transition to the dorm more complex. Stacey indicated that she had called the dorm "home" at the beginning, but was no longer doing so.

James, in his fourth year, was living in a single room in an all male dorm. He had always had singles and liked the arrangement: "I had a room to myself that you can close and stuff. So, I mean, I still see my friends. I usually only go home to sleep. I usually have so much work." He didn't hesitate to use home synonymously with his dorm space.

However, living in the all male dorm was a chance circumstance not of his own choosing:

> I was actually going to be roomed with some guy in crowded housing. And they were basically going to turn the lounge into another room for us. The guy really didn't feel comfortable doing that with me. Basically, we didn't know each other. There was only one closet. So, he had a best friend in [this dorm], and he convinced his best friend to move in with him, so that they could make arrangements together, and I took his best friend's single. So, that's another one of those lucky things.

James viewed the situation optimistically, but there are undertones that raise other interpretations. It would take a great deal of convincing for most students to sacrifice a single dorm room. While James never commented on the racial aspects of this situation, he was a Black student being thrown together with a student who was, in all probability at this institution, not Black. In the experiences of many of the Skeptics, while they may not have consciously viewed their dorm situations as unusual, there were clashes of culture, evidenced by the use and abuse of social living space. None of these students had close relationships with their roommates and many of them elected to be as far from campus as possible. None of them mentioned programs within their dorms that enhanced the ability of students to live together harmoniously.

In a conversation with the director and assistant director of residence life at Ivy University, they both held reservations about allocating specific dorm space to ethnic or religious groups. While they saw the pros and cons of self-segregation among racial/ethnic/religious groups within the dining and living areas of campus, they indicated that these spaces provided excellent opportunities to break down stereotypes and cultural fears. However, they were contemplating creating a minority club building that would provide some "free space" for group activities that currently had to search for space in the common areas of the campus. In the meantime, there seemed to be an absence of programming that might encourage more awareness of and sensitivity toward student diversity within the dorms and other campus spaces.

Greek Organizations

For some students, fraternities or sororities are optional living environments. However, for the HEOP students, these were not residential choices for which they were eligible. The fact that all of the Greek residential buildings were dedicated to White fraternities—no sororities or racial/ ethnic fraternities—was a bone of contention for a number of students. They quickly ascertained that the fraternities in the Greek buildings had only White members and mostly White students attending their functions. The ethnic fraternities and sororities were, for the most part, social organizations that met in common rooms on campus. There were some shared events between these groups, but much of their activity revolved around week-end parties on campus or group trips to other campuses to attend ethnic functions. One of the English instructors who was a graduate student at Ivy University commented on the state of the minority Greek organizations:

> I am in a sorority and I can honestly say this, that Black organizations here are not representative of what we're about....Our numbers have traditionally been a lot smaller, for understandable reasons, and so sometimes people will randomly say, "Okay, we're going to live together," but it's nothing as organized that it's really sanctioned by the university.

None of the Pleasers seemed interested in joining fraternities or sororities at this early juncture in their college careers. They observed that the drinking parties seemed to be confined to the fraternities (frats), for the most part, and could be avoided by not attending the frat parties or joining these organizations. Typical comments were: "There are also parties at the frats, but they're not my kind of parties," and, "I heard that fraternities always drink, so I avoid drinking and smoking." Ileana decided not to join after some consideration: "My friend wants me to do one with her. I think that's a big commitment, and I don't know much about them. It kind of scares me." Clarissa and Roberto also rejected the idea for different reasons:

> *Clarissa*: I don't know what it's all about, and I was asking around. Most of the upperclassmen aren't in sororities. I wanted to know what they go through, if they have to humiliate themselves and stuff like that, cause I can't do that. I can't take people talking down to me and stuff like that....One of my hall mates also told me that it's like you have to pay $600.00 to join. I don't know if I need to pay $600.00 to make friends.

*   *   *   *   *

> *Roberto*: I don't know, cause they're just so silly. All fraternities fight. That's why I wouldn't join. It's supposed to promote brotherhood, and they, they're like fighting each other. It doesn't make sense to me.

The Pleasers clearly valued an academic atmosphere that promoted seriousness about learning. They were attending Ivy University for an education and were keenly aware that this was an opportunity they didn't want to fritter away through drinking or committing their time to frivolous activities, which, in their eyes, were epitomized by Greek organizations. They were willing to commit most of their waking hours to academic pursuits, although there was a wistfulness underlying their narrations that seemed to imply that if money were not a constraining issue for them, they might be having more fun, or at least more choice about pursuing entertainment, just not within the Greek organizations.

The Searchers voiced more interest than the Pleasers in the Greek organizations, but none of them had joined within the first year. Laila shared Clarissa's concern: "I heard that sororities, just the simple fact of pledging....I don't see myself being subjected to something like that." Martine was thinking about joining a sorority: "If anything, probably a Hispanic one, though. But there's not any on campus, so....And this school only allows fraternities, right, to have houses?"

Jason was very interested in forming an Asian fraternity on campus, which would be the only one in the immediate region. After the summer program, he had started hanging out more with Asian people and found common interests, "Something I could relate to." The group had trouble getting recognition at Ivy University, even though the woman who accepted their application for fraternity status told them, "We love diversity so much." Jason was frustrated with the delay and reiterated the inequity of the Greek system on campus: "All the basically Caucasian fraternities dominate all the campus with like the big fraternity quad out there....Like a lot of the minority fraternities don't really have any of that." He was further frustrated because he viewed his fraternity's goals as being a positive influence for the campus:

> I don't want to sound like we're just a party fraternity, because it's not like that.....Like, set up more like cultural workshops and have things about like the Asian culture. Something that everyone could really attend....Partly the reason that we can have like an impact [is that] more like a city, New York type culture that could be imprinted on the campus....Not only that, but like share like hope for everybody we work with. Like do some community—like we did some community service already.

The Skeptics were adamantly opposed to joining Greek organizations. When asked if he would consider joining a fraternity, Damon unequivocally stated: "Absolutely not! Don't get me started on fraternities, especially African-American fraternities. I have a problem...well, I don't want to get into it." James was also negative in this exchange:

James: I wouldn't be doing it for the right reason if I did. I would probably be doing it for the reason most people do it...to wear a jacket, stroll around and look cool...and have a lot of parties. And that, and the fact that I don't think it's worth getting beat over. I've known some people, like, I'm like, "Okay, he's 200 pounds. That's a pretty big guy with a fractured tail bone." I mean, that's a lot of hitting. Not me!

LG: What do you mean? They fight all the time?

James: No. They haze! Although they, they, they don't haze, you know...quote, unquote.

LG: They still have lively activities?

James: But they do, they do [haze]. And I don't think I'd go through that for any fraternity.

The females were equally skeptical toward the value of sororities. Stacey had investigated their activities and loved the volunteer work they promoted, but was dismayed by seemingly insignificant rituals and the lack of housing for the organization. She observed: "This is a men's college." Nicole flatly rejected sororities for herself:

> It's not so much they have a bad rep[utation]. I guess it's just like all in your preference, you know. Some people feel that they need a sorority or fraternity to boost them up socially or whatever, but I really don't. I can't see the immediate benefits to it. I know it's a good network, socially, but I think a lot of kids do it to boost themselves up socially and I don't agree with the standards, what you have to do to be there. They're good organizations, but I guess it's all a preference.

Sybill concurred with her peers and also denounced the emphasis on alcohol and drugs: "I mean, because you have the whole fraternity quad. It's just...I mean, kegs and kegs. I can imagine someone as a freshman....Like freshman year, I really didn't see it, because I really didn't go over to the frat quad. I just didn't see like alcohol and drugs as being as much a problem until [that day]." Sybill referred to a special day late in the spring semester when the fraternities pull couches and chairs into the open quad and party all day. Numerous kegs are visible and the administration quietly avoids any interference into the activities of the day. This event has a notorious, historic reputation on campus and becomes a drunken day of abandon, a true spring bacchanal.

Fraternities and sororities have come under fire for many of the issues that these students raise. Laura Meyers (1996) noted in her study of college women that there were calls to abolish the Greek systems on campuses all together. Her study also pointed out the high consumption of alcohol at Greek functions and the exclusive nature of these groups. She called for examination of the marginalizing effects of the Greek system on students from underrepresented groups.

Free Spaces for Hanging Out

The notion of "space" has been explored in a number of contexts, including physical and psychological space. Beverly Tatum (1997) expressed the need for space in the development of the Black identity:

> Though the cultural symbols for this generation [of college students] are not the same as for mine, the process of racial identity development is the same. Black students practice their "language" in Black student unions and cultural centers and at college dining halls on predominantly White campuses all over the United States. And they should not be discouraged from doing so....they need safe spaces to retreat to and regroup in the process of dealing with the daily stress of campus racism (p. 77).

In their recent ethnography of young, poor and working-class African American, White, and Latino/a men and women, Michelle Fine and Lois Weis (1998) used the concept of space more expansively:

> These spaces offer recuperation, resistance, and "home." They are not just a set of geographical/spatial arrangements, but theoretical, analytical, and spatial displacements—a crack, a fissure, a place to come together and restore sanity, and to imagine possibilities....Not rigidly bounded by walls/fences, the spaces often are corralled by a series of (imaginary) borders where community intrusion and state surveillance are not permitted....Young women and men, in constant confrontation with harsh public representations of their race, ethnicity, class, gender, and sexuality use these spaces to break down public images for scrutiny, and invent new ones(pp. 252–253).

In another perspective of space, Antonia Darder (1998) works off of Gloria Anzaldua's notion of a "third space" which she created as a "shock culture, a border culture, a third culture, a closed country" (as quoted in Darder, p. 138). This space is a critical location for "border crossers:"

> In the safety of the "third space," notions of bicultural identity are constructed, deconstructed, and reconstructed anew, all while negotiating the tension of ongoing interactions with social and material conditions of subordination (p. 138).

Employing aspects of each of these survival spaces, the HEOP students found a way to work within the physical constraints of the university to establish a comfortable space, both physically and psychologically, for themselves, away from the constant surveillance and "othering" that was part of their daily lives on this small campus space.

Because the Pleasers were continually making adjustments to a new environment and culture, I was interested in how they created space for themselves to escape the stresses and where they didn't have to be "imposters," what others expected them to be. As Mai stated it: "My life has really changed since I've been here. Totally....Sometime it's better and sometimes for the worse. I'm so tired sometimes." Mai felt like her world became the campus and that there were few "escapes" from this environment. Therefore, she focused most of her energy on studying and found her "space" in the library, "...first floor, in the reference room. It's real quiet....I just go straight to my, I declared it as my own place....I think nobody want to go there. It's really quiet." Panyos also used the quiet of the library when he needed to study for a test, but usually he preferred another section of the library where the students had access to computers, as well as open study space. "I mean, people say [the computer area] is noisy and too much socializing. I don't have any problem. Sit down, do what you have to do, cut yourself off." Ileana agreed: "And a lot of socializing in [the computer area]. People just go to [the computer area] to make friends." Mai had visited the computer area, but decided it was too noisy, that people were always "jetting all around." Tran also spent a lot of time in this part of the library, "...but mostly I spend it in my room. Some people like to go somewhere else."

By far, the dorm rooms became the haven for these students when they wanted to just be themselves. Clarissa explained that she made space, "In my room pretty much, because my roommate and I are friends and we have another friend down the hall. So, we just hang out, get silly and loud. People might walk in and wonder what is going on, but we're having fun." Veronika ended up with a single room after the first semester and enjoyed the privacy: "Like, I'm a lot freer now. I can play music whenever I want. Because, like you know, when you have a roommate, maybe she might be studying, and you know, you want to do something. You have to leave the room and go somewhere else. But, now, it's just do whatever you want when you want." Veronika indicated that she usually had friends in her room, but she appreciated the freedom to choose solitude. Roberto found "space" in the dorms, but not in his own suite. He explained that he was rarely in his own room and always in other freshmen's rooms. Luc appreciated that she had more options and stated in a focus group: "I have residence here with my family....It's too much stress at school. Just go home." It was interesting that neither Veronika nor Clarissa, who were in Luc's focus group, wished that they were living off campus and could "go home."

The computer library space that was favored by Panyos and Ileana was the overwhelmingly popular hang-out for the Searchers. This space was particularly attractive because it was open all night and had banks of computers that the students could freely use for e-mail as well as academic work. Many of the HEOP students and six of the seven Searchers did not own a computer so, for them, this area was an important communication hub on campus. Martine and Marie made ample use of the space, but tired of the endless trips between their dorm and the library. However, a side benefit was a relationship with a young man that Martine struck up while studying there. Jason indicated that he spent a lot of time socializing in the dorm with his friends, but he and his friends were at this library area most of the night during the week. This was an invaluable location for studying, socializing, and communicating, and the Searchers expressed a distinct preference for the companionship they found here. Their needs for space revolved more around the social and communal aspects than for the Pleasers who frequently chose solitude.

The Skeptics were not as dependent on the library space as the other two groups, although three of them relied on the computer access for e-mail and academic assignments. Vanessa identified this space as a social area, but she used cassettes and headphones to block out the noise when she needed to study. She usually hung out in this area until 2 AM, and often met up with a male friend there. Stacey also lacked a computer and spent long hours in this area of the library working on the computer. Most evenings from 8:30 until 2:00, James combined study and socialization in this space he identified not as much a library as an entertainment center because even TVs were visible from most parts of this area.

Damon found that his dorm space provided most of the accouterments that he sought each day, but he was often away from campus working on family and community activities and, therefore, accessed other campus spaces minimally. Nicole often left campus and returned to her apartment even between classes. It was a rare occurrence for her to hang out on campus, although I did meet up with her in the library area one evening as she chatted noisily with a sizable group of friends, all Black females. Sybill went home most week-ends and, during the week, she found that her dorm space provided enough separation from campus and enough solitude that she rarely spent time elsewhere when she had free time. These Skeptics clearly did not need and chose to not avail themselves of this library space on a constant basis.

However, this library area was truly a social and communication hub for many of the HEOP students. Most evenings groups of them could be observed studying and socializing. This late night population had a different visual presence than in the remainder of the library. Here, one could clearly see that the racial and ethnic minority groups found the space more suited to their needs and desires. They displayed a measure of comfort and freedom that was not noticeable in other spaces on the campus. The environment took on a different tenor, with the level of noise and activity remarkably more lively than in the remainder of the library and even in the open spaces in the student union. One of the HEOP staff members indicated that when the office needed to locate HEOP students, that was the first place they looked, followed by a visit to the largest cafeteria. A summer HEOP instructor observed that this area of the library was: "...sort of the minority student social center....It's not a very user friendly space though. It's really kind of gross." But the students weren't concerned with the aesthetics of the place. Besides the open hours, the access to computers, and the prospect of companionship, this area was located right next to the major bus stop on campus, which served both the campus and community bus lines. This, together with the mini canteen that provided light snacks, meals, and beverages in the hallway outside of the computer library space from late morning until early evening, made the space even more attractive.

DAILY ROUTINES AND ACTIVITIES

Living Each Day

The Pleasers seemed, for the most part, surprisingly organized and efficient in their daily routines. Most of them rose in the morning with enough time to shower and have breakfast before their first class. Several of them skipped breakfast, but not class. Classes were concentrated between 9:00 and 4:00, with some study groups and elective classes meeting in the evening. In between classes, most of the students made effective use of the time to study or use the computer lab to catch up on correspondence. Lunches and dinners were eaten, but usually at odd hours and more unplanned than planned in terms of who ate with whom. Evenings, nights, and early morning hours were spent studying by *all* of the Pleasers. Even Luc stayed on campus until early evening to study in the "torture chamber," her name for the library. As the semester progressed, students found that schedules became more "tangled," as Tran described it, and not as easy to maintain. Tran indicated that his planned time to go to bed had slipped from 10:00 to 12:00 to 2:00 as the semester wore on, and Clarissa slept through her morning class the day of our second interview late in the semester. She had stayed up late for a few nights to prepare for a biology exam, and it finally caught up with her. Missing a class was not the normal routine for any of these students.

Most of the Searchers had a difficult time describing a routine day due to the erratic lifestyle they chose. Marie described the most disciplined regime of rising early enough to iron her clothes ("Father is the type of person that's so neat and he's always like, 'Why don't you iron these clothes?'"), and always eating three meals a day at planned times, often with friends, although she complained that she couldn't adapt to the food and often felt rushed. She called her parents most evenings and observed a reasonable bedtime that gave her eight hours of sleep each night. After Marie, there was a swift descent into erratic schedules and behaviors. Laila got up in time to make her 9:00 class, but she ate irregularly and was not always hungry. She did practice a lunchtime ritual with a group of seven friends who always sat in the same place in one cafeteria. She did most of her studying and a lot of snacking late at night. Martine and Tiana went to bed in the early morning hours and often missed their morning classes. Martine expressed some concern over her inability to sleep and to eat. Tiana also expressed disgust with the food and complained of stomachaches and lost weight. She recognized that her chaotic late night schedule wasn't productive for her, but she valued the socializing during these times and seemed only slightly concerned about changing this behavior.

Yasmin described her days as "crazy" because she crammed so much into them. She attended most of her classes, spent considerable time in labs and at meetings, and worked part-time. She managed to eat with a group of four friends at scheduled times. Her sleep schedule usually included at least six hours. Yasmin was accomplishing a lot each day academically and socially, but she expressed some frustration that she was behind in several classes and hadn't been assigned a tutor she'd requested. Jason's days were also somewhat crazy, but he got a late start in the morning and included some relaxation, exercise, and study time in each day. Meals were unscheduled, and he often preferred to eat by himself and read.

None of the Pleasers mentioned watching TV and indicated through their rigorous schedules that they had no time for it. However, the Searchers often included some viewing time as a form of relaxation. Their study time was more flexible and did not consume every free minute.

The Skeptics narrated more consistent daily patterns than most of the Searchers. Teresa indicated that a typical day found her either at work or doing work. She was a college intern for the company that had employed her during high school. When on campus she was either reading, writing, thinking, or processing, but always engaged in some type of academic activity. Teresa did admit to watching cartoons when she just didn't want to think anymore. Stacey also described a structured day where she rose early enough for breakfast, attended all of her classes, ate three meals a day, and spent most of her free time in her dorm room studying, watching TV, or listening to the radio. She indicated that she was pretty much of a loner on campus:

> I feel kind of weird sometimes sitting at a table all by myself eating. It does get kind of lonely down there [in the cafeteria]. At least if I'm in my room I can watch TV. Most of the time I'll take the food and go to my room....People would say, "I haven't seen you for days." I've been here in my room; that's pretty much it.

James and Damon described tightly packed and structured days that included attending all classes and eating healthy meals with friends. Interestingly, these two both discussed their use of power naps during the day to boost their productivity. James got little sleep at night, but wedged a few hours in between study sessions, and caught up on sleep during the week-ends. Damon took three power naps a day, worked part-time off campus, did volunteer work with his father and another program off campus, had a student government position that required weekly office hours, frequently read the local paper, yet still stated that he had some time to "let down a little bit" and watch TV or play occasional video games. Besides the power naps, his key was multi-tasking: "I can socialize and do my homework at the same time. I can type up something on the computer and listen to music at the same time, and talk while I'm typing it up."

Sybill and Nicole also attended all classes and ate regular meals with friends. Nicole preferred to stay on campus to eat ("I'm lazy.") and took pride in her improved eating habits. Both of these young women worked on campus and carefully planned their study schedules so work would not interfere with academics. Neither one discovered enough time for television during the week. Of the Skeptics, Vanessa's routine was the loosest. She frequently missed her morning classes: "These are the classes I don't really have to go to. I can just read the book and do well." However, she described days that included a considerable amount of study time, as well as regular meals with friends, some work hours on campus, some volunteer hours off campus, and late nights. The Skeptics did not seem as intensely focused as the Pleasers, but their days sounded more structured and efficient than the Searchers.

Jobs on the Side

HEOP discouraged students from working for pay especially during their first year on campus. While the intent was to allow students ample time to focus on academics and get started off on the right foot, the policy was unrealistic for these students. HEOP attempted to provide enough financial assistance that students would not have to work, but the reality was that over the years the funding for the program had become tighter and tighter, so while the state and institutions provided most of the tuition and first year book fees, many of the HEOP students did not have family resources or personal savings to help defray the cost of personal necessities that all students have beyond the academic costs. Many in this group of HEOP students found it necessary to take jobs on the side, and sometimes not share that information with their HEOP counselors. The comments of one of the HEOP counselors indicated that they were aware of this:

> Even though we don't like our HEOP first year students to work, a number of them will end up finding a job because they just can't do it. Their families can't support them, can't send any little bit of money and, of course, we have had some older students who work and send money home. It's expensive coming to a school like this.

The majority of these students worked from the beginning of their first semester. Usually the weekly work hours were contained to a reasonable eight to ten hours, just enough to earn some spending money. But, in some cases, students were working 20 or more hours. Damon (a Skeptic) worked 20 hours at a job off campus that he'd held for a few years. James (a Skeptic) had worked up to hours a week after his grandfather passed away, and he became self supporting. Yasmin (a Searcher) was working three jobs which varied in the number of weekly hours, but quickly added up to over 20 per week. Most of the students were eligible for on-campus work study jobs which were more convenient and tailored around a student's schedule. However, the competition for these jobs was stiff, and several of the students indicated that they would have to wait until the next semester for jobs to open up. Those students who did not work their first semester were looking for work the second semester. Sybill, who was working 16 hours a week, provided her rationale for these hours:

> That's why I work so much. I don't want to ask my mother for money. My sister, she's not working her first semester, and I want my mom to help her get the same chances she gave me. I work a lot to support myself.

It was difficult getting off campus to apply for jobs, but all of the HEOP students who worked and who were looking for work understood the necessity of a job and did not complain about working. Several students were willing to work at more than one job.

PARTICIPATION IN EXTRACURRICULAR ACTIVITIES

Organizations and Clubs

Organizations that the HEOP students found attractive, at the beginning, centered around ethnic or racial affiliations. The HEOP office published a list of multicultural organizations at Ivy University that included fourteen clubs. The numbers of students belonging to one or more of these organizations included: seven of the nine Pleasers, four of the seven Searchers, and all seven of the Skeptics. Five of the students participated in the African Caribbean Culture Club, six students in the Spanish and Latino Students' Association, three in the Vietnamese Students' Association, and ten in the Black Students' Union (BSU). Three students had been asked to assume leadership positions in the BSU within the first semester. Jason was involved in trying to organize the first Asian fraternity on campus. The levels of involvement in organizations varied tremendously, with a number of students expressing their support but indicating that they didn't have time to be actively involved, or that they were somewhat frustrated by the lack of coordination between the groups and they felt fractured in their time and allegiance.

In addition to the multicultural groups, some students were attracted to other organized activities such as sports, mostly informal dorm floor pick-up games. Teresa (a Skeptic) had tried out for the women's volleyball team, but was told that she was too short for the team. She shared her disappointment:

> I went out for the volleyball team and I was basically told I was too short. Yeh, right. There are people on the team shorter than me, which stumped me...But I understood the reason was because at my high school we didn't play upper level volleyball. If we got the ball over the net, that was a good thing....Yeh, but there are some girls on the team that did not come from a structured volleyball background either. That's why, oh my goodness, why didn't I get on the team? But then again, after he told me, "You might have difficulties," he didn't say he wasn't going to let me on. He just said, "You might have difficulties because a lot of the girls are taller than you." But after he said that, I was totally discouraged.

Vanessa (a Skeptic) was a cheerleader for the football and basketball teams. She found the spirit lacking for the sports teams and was considering dropping cheerleading in order to crew. Students involved themselves in other groups ranging from martial arts to dancing, bowling, and debate.

Some of the HEOP students joined professional and service groups like the National Association for Black Engineers, the Society of Hispanic Professional Engineers, and the Optics Society of America. In addition to professional organizations, some were active in volunteer groups that tutored high school students or did other types of community service.

There was a lot of tentative interest in many campus activities, but a reluctance to overcommit too quickly. When clubs didn't seem to be immediately productive, the tendency was to stop attending and refocus one's energy. Religious organizations offered other types of opportunities for connection and participation, although only four students faithfully attended, two Pleasers and two Skeptics. Among this group of HEOP students, Tiana (a Searcher) was the only one who was not actively invested in some extracurricular group.

Hobbies

Besides formal activities, the students continued with other pursuits and interests that they had developed before college. Eight students were avid readers, and one was an active book collector. Several enjoyed writing and keeping journals. And five (four of them male) expressed interest in cooking their ethnic specialties. Clarissa was fortunate to be in a suite with a kitchen and had managed to assemble the equipment to create some aromatic curries. Art was also an outlet, and three students engaged in various formats including photography, drawing, and painting.

One of the most commonly shared interests among all of these students was music, whether through listening, dancing, or creating. Veronika (a Pleaser) talked about impromptu dancing in her room and, like Ileana (a Pleaser), danced in a credit course. Ileana also participated in an extracurricular dance group, and sang and played the guitar. Tran (a Pleaser) continued to sing and play in a local Vietnamese band that he had formed in high school. James (a Skeptic) mentioned that he had produced three music videos. Martine's (a Searcher) passion was collecting compact discs, as well as listening to them. Tiana (a Searcher) voiced an interest in playing around with the clarinet again, but she lacked access to the instrument. Almost all of the students indicated that music of some kind was an outlet for them when they felt stressed or bored.

Social Activities

Friday Night

The weekday structure seemed to relax minimally over the week-end. When asked how they spent Friday night, many of the students included studying as one of their activities. While studying didn't have the same urgency on Friday night as it did on other week nights, most of these students did not view Friday night as a night to let loose and party, contrary to what is often popularized as the case on most campuses, especially with freshmen tasting the freedom of no parents and no curfew for the first time. Ileana and Veronika were the only Pleasers who talked about attending parties, and both of them indicated that they had attended parties at the beginning of the semester, but after the mid-point, Friday nights became study nights. They observed that everyone seemed to be studying or catching up on their sleep. However, Roberto and Clarissa tried to take a break on Friday nights, but usually found themselves at loose ends:

> *Roberto*: That's my problem with this school. There's nothing to do. Most of the time I just visit all my friends' rooms or something and we just act silly. Or we go to the [campus food court] and we order something and we stay there for two hours acting silly, and then we go our separate ways. Sometimes we'll call each other and sometimes we'll play [video games] or something. I'm thinking of transferring.

*   *   *   *   *

> *Clarissa*: Friday night is the one night we don't know what to do. We sit around trying to figure out where to go. We call each other complaining we don't have something to do, or we walk around. We might go to [a friend's room] and watch a movie if they get one. We wait until [a friend] gets off work. We all walk to pick her up and we go somewhere, someone's room to go and talk or just to watch TV.

These students were constrained by their lack of resources to go off campus and purchase entertainment, but there was also a distinct atmosphere built into this campus that valued a serious focus on work and not play. Over and over students commented about the intensity of the studying that went on all of the time. I observed this wherever I went on campus. Students might be talking over lunch, but they usually had books or notes out and were discussing a class or project. Even walking behind students, I noticed that they usually were chatting about a course or a professor. The library was always well used, especially during the evening hours and on week-ends. Students were burrowed away for intense studying in the farthest reaches of the isolated book stacks, or were congregated in small groups around the larger wooden tables found in the more open areas of the many floors. The groups were always observed to be working on problems together or on some type of research project. All of the computer stations were well used. Wherever I observed students lounging, inside or out, a book or notes were evident. Occasionally a student would be catching a quick nap, but these were short in duration.

On Friday nights, the Searchers did not share the academic fervor voiced by the Pleasers. Only Yasmin studied on Friday night, and then only because she had a physics lab that was due every Saturday morning at 8:00. Jason was usually on road trips to other schools with his pseudo fraternity. He, like other Searchers, emphatically stated that he didn't want to pick up a book on Friday. Even when students couldn't get off campus, they made a point of not touching schoolwork. Relaxing with a video perhaps shared with friends, sleeping, or watching TV were preferred activities.

The Skeptics did not describe wildly exciting Friday nights, either. James and Damon worked at paying jobs on Friday nights. Damon had worked the same job for several years, knew some of his fellow employees well, and they would go out to a local restaurant/hang-out after work for a few hours. James worked on campus setting up sound equipment for functions, which had its own advantages. In between set-ups he could study:

> Like my second semester of freshman year to probably like the beginning of my junior year, during those little time periods I would study, and I would do a lot of core studying at late night. I would do a lot of work in between those times and study during late night. And, the way my job was, I would sometimes actually do some of the parties. Like I set up the equipment and stuff for the parties so that allowed me to earn money and I was still able to go out on the dance floor and dance.

Sybill usually drove the hour and a half home on Friday, where she spent the week-end with her family.

Nicole, Teresa, and Stacey (all Skeptics) were the only HEOP students who indicated that they spent time with romantic partners on Friday night. Nicole explained that their time together was usually with a group of friends who might go out to dinner and a movie. Teresa went to dinner with her boyfriend of several years and then the few minutes to home where she'd study or sleep. She complained that her boyfriend would frequently call during the evening: "He's inside me. He needs to be with others." At the time of our first interview, a month after beginning college, Stacey wasn't seeing anyone. However, a month later she'd met someone at a campus party and spent most of each week-end with him. It wasn't unusual for them to see four or more movies each week-end.

For most of the HEOP students, Friday nights assumed a more casual pace than the week nights. However, none of them sounded like they were having the great time that one of their writing instructors envisioned as part of the college life:

> I think you have to have a good time. This is the time to do it. When else are you going to be where you don't have to worry about being responsible, paying bills, dangers? It's a pretty protective environment. This is a time to do all those kind of wild and crazy things cause you're not saving that.

These students were already burdened by expectations and constraints that forced them to actively resist some "opportunities" in order to focus on their intense academic work. They strategically prioritized and evaluated activities that were instrumental to the achievement of their goals.

Alcohol and Drugs

The impression that Ivy University was a serious school and not a party school was reinforced by the students' behaviors, the professors' expectations and comments, and the image created by university publications and public relations personnel. While touring the campus with a small group of potential students and their parents and led by a trained student guide, the guide made a point of stressing how the public lectures and cultural events were always standing room only, while the sports events could hardly muster a cheering section. In scanning the student and the university newspapers, there were only occasional references to any type of talk or workshop aimed at educating students about drug and alcohol abuse, which is a rampant problem that's being aggressively attacked by colleges all over the country. I was surprised at the absence of advertised programs to raise awareness about drug and alcohol issues. The understanding that students conveyed was that students were free to do anything they wanted as long as they did it behind closed doors and didn't disturb others. However, I kept noticing short police briefs in the student newspaper about students who were found passed out or seriously drunk and taken to local hospital emergency rooms. Exploring this issue a bit further with the HEOP students revealed that they had some real problems with the amount of drinking on campus.

A number of the comments about drinking were prompted by my question about whether the Pleasers would consider joining a fraternity or sorority. Other observations were volunteered when they spoke about their dorms. The students told me stories of witnessing drunken episodes on their floors and hearing second-hand about incidents in the fraternities. Some bouts resulted in dorm mates being taken to the hospital. The Pleasers voiced displeasure over the amount of drinking and drunk behavior they observed. Most of them indicated that they didn't find drinking appealing:

> *Clarissa*: People drink from Thursday to Sunday. I don't know. I guess parents and the restrictions they have on them when they're away. I mean my mom was strict, but I didn't try it, even away here, I don't drink. It's just not something I do. My roommate, she doesn't drink either, which is lucky. We don't drink or smoke.

*   *   *   *   *

> *Ileana*: I'm not going crazy because people used to tell me that because of my father, that he used to have me be so sheltered that I was going to go crazy, that I was going to go drinking, smoking, and having like 20 boyfriends. And like I'm not doing anything at all. I'm straight-edge, so I don't drink. I don't even go to parties.

Panyos observed that there was drinking out of boredom on campus, but he didn't seem bothered by parties. "It's not a lot of parties. It's quiet. This is my kind of school."

The Pleasers observed a great deal of drinking around them, but the Searchers brought this up more frequently in describing the general college body, and it was often in relation to fraternities. In fact, Jason found the social life "depressing" because the frat parties were the popular events and he found them boring because he'd already had parties in high school that were "a lot crazier" than these. As he put it: "My first impression on campus, which is probably why I have all these stereotypes, all they did was like listen to Metallica, drink beer, smoke pot, and I was like, 'I'm in college now. I have to get as far away from this stuff as possible.'" Laila saw a definite division among students based on drinking:

> I feel that there's a diverse differentiation between students. There's a high tendency of drinking alcohol on this campus and some feel like that compared to those who drink heavily and to those students that don't drink. They feel that the student that is in the fraternity or sorority and drinking heavily still ends up getting "A"s on their exams....Children have had alcohol poisoning. This is a heavy drinking school.

Laila commented on seeing beer bottles around the garbage and students strolling around with beer bottles in their hands, not making much of an effort to conceal it.

Despite the emphasis on drinking and partying that the students perceived, they were amazed at how well most students did academically. Laila's comments above marveled at the ability of the partiers to get "A"s while most of the students she knew were struggling to get "B"s and "C"s and did not have time to party. Yasmin also commented on how the freshman class seemed able to do this: "The students, I think they're smarter than us, because they'll sit there and stay partying every single day until late and then turn in their work and not even put effort into their work and still get good grades." The Searchers seemed to characterize their fellow students as partiers who did well academically despite their heavy partying.

Tiana was the only HEOP student who shared her penchant for drinking. She complained that it was "...hard for an underage person to get liquor here." So, she would go to NYC and bring it back with her. "Like I spend a large quantity of money on stuff I'm not going to drink for a long time. But this way I don't have to harass a friend to drive and go get me whatever....The first week we were here, we were lushes." She explained that she was no longer drinking as often because, "Yeh, I'm trying to do school right, now....Up here, because you have a lot of problems and financial problems and this-and-that, you're more prone to drink and smoke, cigarettes, weed, and other drugs...Honestly, this is such a bad influence. I think I'd rather be in the City; I'd be doing less." Tiana also shared her experiences with buying Ritalin from other students and snorting it to get high, something she'd never done before she came to campus where she had easy access to this medication. Students were selling their prescription medicines and, in some cases, their siblings' controlled substances. Tiana indicated that some students were willing to ingest about anything, including horse tranquilizers, that might alter their physical states. The irony in Tiana's story was her dire financial straits, which made it difficult for her to keep herself supplied with toiletry products, yet, somehow she found money for liquor, cigarettes, and illegal drugs.

The Skeptics shared the disgust that most of the HEOP students voiced about the preponderance of drinking on the campus, and concurred that most of it centered around the White fraternities and their week-end parties. When I asked Sybill if she thought drinking and taking drugs were used as outlets for stress, she summed up many of the HEOP students' feelings toward intoxicating substances: "As being an outlet? Not to offend anybody, but I don't think so much for the Black population as the White population."

Many of the HEOP students called themselves "**straight-edge**," indicating that they didn't indulge in alcohol, drugs, or cigarettes. The rowdy, inappropriate behaviors and garbage generated by these activities were an annoyance that the HEOP students accepted as part of being on a college campus, but they viewed the blame as lying elsewhere. A number of them indicated that it seemed to be a White student problem, but that it was a problem that certainly affected the entire campus, even though the university officials seemed to turn a blind eye.

CONCLUSION

Life at Ivy University for the HEOP students was distinguished by a daily and weekly routine that was quickly established, anchored by the organizations and activities with which they aligned themselves, and by the creation of a "home" space which could accommodate comfortable relationships with peers, enhance academic and career goals, and provide opportunities for some pleasure. This chapter examined the transition between home and college, detailing the ongoing negotiations that the HEOP students enacted on a daily basis when creating a home away from home, when finding and/or creating their space on campus in which to "become somebody." Going away to college was truly a milestone for the students. They would never be the same after this experience, and going home again would never be the same.

The HEOP students made a valiant effort to quickly adapt to the culture of college at Ivy University. It was not as easy a task as the summer program led them to believe, and these students needed and were seeking some type of connection or "fit" within the institution, a form of social integration on their own terms. However, they were certainly not living the wild and crazy high life that characterizes the stereotypical college student. They strategically eschewed many of the lifestyle choices that other college students were making, and they astutely avoided spending time or energy on breaking the social codes of campus, especially when they were deemed inessential to accomplishing their instrumental goals. They found few extrinsic rewards in the social milieu, so they sought more intrinsic satisfactions that could be gained through strategic use of time and space, while still achieving an acceptable level of biculturalism within the college culture. Without sacrificing their identities and familial values, the HEOP students were negotiating the dialectics between home and college that would enable them to forge identities enhanced, not diminished, through their academic and social accomplishments. They became more resilient in the face of these challenges.

CHAPTER 6

Peer Relationships:
Building Bonds and Trust

It's really like hard. Let's say, if you're somewhere, let's say in a public finance class and there's only one other Black guy in my class. It's just me and him. It's really hard because like you're treated two ways. One way is they always want you to represent the Black voice. Either that or they're afraid of you and they really don't want to associate with you. They don't want to talk to you. So, you have two extremes and there's nothing like down the middle. Either you have to be the Black voice and anything you say you're speaking for every Black person on this campus. Or they just don't talk to you at all.

–Nicole, third year student from New York City

The quality and quantity of social and academic integration of incoming students into the college environment are crucial determinants of the likelihood for successful achievement of the students' goals and objectives at a particular institution. Chapter 4 explored the academic integration of the HEOP students at Ivy University and Chapter 5 opened the discussion of the students' social integration experiences. As we have seen, in order to survive in the elite atmosphere of Ivy University, the HEOP students engaged in strategic instrumentalism, devising and experimenting with coping techniques within the academic and social settings that were strategically productive and furthered their achievement of goals, or that proved non-strategic and self-defeating. Throughout this process of breaking academic and social codes within the institution, and deciding how best to negotiate these systems while sustaining one's identity, the students managed stigmatizing situations on a daily basis. This chapter continues the examination of the social integration process by turning away from the external, physical aspects of daily life on the campus that were explored in Chapter 5 in order to focus on these internal, less visible aspects of social integration experienced by the HEOP students. William Cross and Linda

Strauss's (1998) theory of identity functions, which was constructed to demonstrate how Black people manage stigma, will help illuminate the college adaptations of this even more diverse HEOP population.

Using the identity functions as a frame, this chapter focuses on the students' narrations of interactions with their peers that reveal layers of peer clusters and associations. Peer relationships were finessed within the contexts of ethnicity and race, gender, and romance, but not without problems and challenges. These peer relationships and interactions were central to the students' identity development and expression. Humans are fundamentally social animals and the opportunity to flex our identities through our engagement with others is a pivotal stepping stone in our identity development. Josselson (1987) describes identity as developing through this social process:

> Identity becomes a means by which people organize and understand their experience and deeply share their meaning systems with others....Our identity is fundamentally interwoven with others' to gain meaning; contrasting ourselves with others heightens our sense of what is uniquely individual.... Often we learn who we are by discovering our differences from others (pp. 10–11).

The HEOP students had ample opportunity at Ivy University to experience a range of student/peer identities that stretched their comfort zones in many directions. Often the discovered differences became problematic at this elite institution and necessitated stigma management strategies.

IDENTITY FUNCTIONS: THE MANAGEMENT OF STIGMA

Noticeably absent in the students' narrations was the constant undertow of discriminatory tension that pulled at them in many different contexts. They described many situations where they felt marginalized within this institution, but they did not consciously identify those institutionalized experiences as primary stressors. Many identity theories have evolved that describe how individuals cycle through stages of awareness and engagement with aspects of racism and discrimination in their lives (Cross, 1995; Helms, 1990; Marcia, 1966; Phinney, 1993; and, Tatum, 1997; among others). Some of the students had not yet become developmentally aware of the persistent presence of racism and other forms of discrimination. However, they were coping with these forces on a daily basis and devising strategies to counter their effects, just not in a conscious way.

In order to explain the psychological steps that Blacks negotiate in order to develop a social and group identity, William Cross and Linda

Strauss (1998) refined a theory of **identity functions** that included five strategies in which individuals engage. These are not *stages* in that there is "recycling" through these functions on a regular, even daily basis as needed. Cross and Strauss defined functions as "...action choices that logically follow from the fusion of ideas and emotions, as stimulated by various context variables" (p. 270). They called this theory the "stigma management perspective" and defined **stigma** as "...associated with a situation or predicament that has the potential for delimiting the response options of the person toward whom the stigmatization is directed" (p. 268). I find Antonia Darder's (1998) description of stigma more explicit: "...subordinate communities continue to be stigmatized by both external and internalized perceptions of inferiority and deficit, whereby their members are, for the most part, viewed as inadequately prepared or socially unfit to enter mainstream American life" (p.134). Among the HEOP students, these feelings of stigmatization on the campus bubble to the surface with some regularity, as this chapter will continue to point out. Cross and Strauss's concept of functions are useful in explaining the strategies that students employ when they are actively engaged in identity producing and altering situations within a hegemonic environment, like that of an elite college. Therefore, I am appropriating this concept of functions and applying it more broadly than exclusively to the Black population. From my observations, it is relevant when explaining the identity processes that *all* of these HEOP students experienced because they were allocated marginalized positions within the college culture where they needed to manage stigma on a daily basis. The following sections describe each of the five functions that Cross and Strauss (1998) identify with some applications for each of them in the actions and narrations of the HEOP students.

Buffering

Buffering is a strategy that provides a buffer or shield to reduce the impact of stigmatizing events when they can't be avoided. It is "psychological protection against racist situations" (p. 270). The person must differentiate between racist and race-neutral situations and employ buffering to "filter" out the racist elements while still benefitting from those aspects of the situation that are race-neutral. For many HEOP students, buffering seemed to occur every time they set foot out of their own living space. As they traversed the campus, they were subject to stares and comments that they constantly filtered to determine a racial or ethnic motivation. In their classes, the students perceived racial isolation and difference in treatment that could have derailed their academic involvement if they weren't able to create a personal buffer zone which protected them from covert racial assaults, while allowing them to get what they needed from the class. Luc (a Pleaser) didn't let the fact that students in the class excluded her or perceived her as Chinese, not Vietnamese, deter her from completing her courses with high marks which led to a coveted job offer. Ileana (a Pleaser) and Nicole (a Skeptic) tired of being the Hispanic and Black spokespeople in their classes, but they continued to attend and did well.

Another buffering strategy is **"reactive bonding,"** recognized as the self-segregation that so puzzles White students and educators. Beverly Tatum's (1997) informative book called *Why Are All the Black Kids Sitting Together in the Cafeteria?* offers an in-depth exploration of this phenomenon. She even employs William Cross's model of Nigrescence (1991) from which elements of the five functions of stigma management are derived. Both Tatum and Cross agree that self-segregation is a necessary strategy and a protective function that minority students employ in a predominantly White environment that feels threatening. In observing the students on campus, there was trans-ethnic evidence of reactive bonding among the HEOP students. They continued to group and cluster together, which annoyed some HEOP students, but which provided strength and support for many of them. It was easier to face each day together than by oneself. Some students maintained singular ethnic attachments, while others connected more eclectically. However, the groupings were of minority students bonding (self-segregating) as a response to the environment. Their level of penetration of the social structuring of the university system usually allowed these students to perceive the stigma as a problem that could be blamed on the system, not themselves. This insight allowed them to maintain their amply expressed pride and feelings of self-worth. They found their greatest support came from students who were going through experiences and challenges that mirrored their own. HEOP facilitated the reactive bonding, especially during the summer program. The director of HEOP previously shared his understanding that reactive bonding was a necessary response to what the students often found to be a hostile environment.

Intrinsic Bonding

Intrinsic bonding, as distinguished from the reactive bonding from the previous section, differs from buffering in that it is not a reaction to an external threat. It is a chosen affiliation that expresses the pride one feels for one's cultural position. It celebrates the culture, heritage, and experience of being Black, West Indian, Latino/a, Dominican, Vietnamese, Thai, or whatever culture best expresses one's core identity. Through affiliation with groups and individuals who share this identity, one is nurtured and sustained. It has little or nothing to do with the White world outside, although it is not an outright rejection of elements of the White culture that are useful. It does not depend on establishing the binary opposition that frequently pits one culture against another as good or bad, right or wrong, all or nothing. Seeking a space on campus in which to be oneself is often a bonding experience because it usually results in finding companions who share values and belief systems. Clarissa (a Pleaser) got loud and silly with her West Indian friends and cooked curries for them. Mai (a Pleaser) studied with her Asian friends because they were serious students who thought as she did. Tran (a Pleaser) maintained connections with his Vietnamese high school friends who had a band and who played Vietnamese music and wrote poetry. Damon (a Skeptic) was actively involved with the Black Student Union where Black students shared concerns and engaged in social activities of their creation. Several of the young women liked shopping with their friends who appreciated the same type of stores and styles. In their narrations, the HEOP students were seeking these types of bonding affiliations. Their efforts were hit-and-miss at first, and they resisted involvement in activities which did not feel authentic, which may indicate that their cultural values were a top priority and they were feeling their way toward connections that made them feel at "home," the ultimate bonding experience. However, they were clearly open to engagement with White peers and activities, so this was not about rejecting the dominant culture of Ivy University.

Bridging

Bridging engages the social skills that allow one to bridge over difference and establish intimacy with someone with a different world view. These relationships are achieved *through* difference, not because of it. Difference is understood as engaging and unique, not strange and in need of change. The HEOP students frequently expressed a desire to bridge to different students and groups on campus as part of their learning experience. Several students wished that others were more open to experiencing diverse groups, so the student clubs and organizations would not be segmented entirely along racial and ethnic lines. A number of the faculty wondered why there were no required courses that focused on learning about cultures and social justice. In their personal relationships, the students seemed willing to extend their friendship groups to different cultures and, as we see later in this chapter, some succeeded. Developing bridges requires social skills and strategies that students from all backgrounds may not have acquired. Bridging has to be a two-way proposition. Students within dominant groups need opportunities to develop these skills, as do students from underrepresented groups. There is also evidence of need among faculty, staff, and administrators at Ivy and other universities.

Code Switching

Code switching is a form of impression management where one puts on a front in order to meet the expectations of certain situations contrived by other individuals or by institutions. One's preferred and innate identity is suspended when there is a need to obtain something or to fit into a situation that requires certain modes of dress or behavior. This is a temporary, one-way transaction where "one plays the game" because it is politically advantageous. It requires that the individual possess the social capital that will allow bicultural switching. When students indicated that they put on different behaviors designed expressly for the academic setting, this is an example of code switching that they perceived would either advance their academic purposes or protect them from stigmatizing assault. Laila (a Searcher) was not yet exactly clear on how to successfully carry this off, but she recognized the need for it when she commented that: "They [professors] are pretty much like what I expected, but I act different though cause, like in high school, I felt different. I felt more confident. But in college, I'm kind of intimidated to go up and talk to the professor." The need for these students to seek private spaces to be themselves is indicative of the strain of code switching in most of their daily encounters, presenting a certain face to a university bureaucrat or professor in order to accomplish their objectives. It is exhausting work to have to continually change identities in order to extract required services and outcomes.

The Black students with whom Cross and Strauss worked when refining these functions, insisted that they include the term **"fronting"** when describing code switching. Putting up an artificial front was something some HEOP students chose not to indulge in on a regular basis. A number of them sought single dorm rooms in order to evade the need to constantly be someone who they were not. Tiana (a Searcher) definitely resisted the notion of code switching with her professors, even though this ended up a non-strategic tactic that made her more academically vulnerable. The exertion required to code switch on a daily basis, or the consequences of choosing *not* to "front," undoubtedly led to some of the stress the students experienced, even though they did not directly identify this as a contributor.

Individualism

Individualism as a function recognizes that some actions are pure expressions of an individual's personality that may have nothing to do with their racial or ethnic locations. When individuals engage in this function, they are not thinking about race or racism. However, their personal expression may indeed have been shaped by their racial or ethnic background and may be a part of that identity. The HEOP students, especially Martine (a Searcher), wanted a break from the focus on racial issues in the summer courses, a time to just be themselves without a racial connotation. They sought spaces where they would not be observed or judged as representatives of a certain race or ethnic group, where they could be individuals. We have seen that many of them found this in the library computer center, where students from dominant and minority groups met, but which became a known hang-out where students felt they could group, cluster, or behave as they wanted without the constraints of a classroom, institutional bureaucracy, or the rules and regulations of communal life in their dorms. A prime example of the function of individualism may be found in the common thread of music that just about every HEOP student expressed that had little to do with race, but everything to do with the effect music has on the human soul and spirit. The students' tastes in music may have been driven by their cultural backgrounds, but they had individual modes of expression and appreciation beyond that. Another situation that highlights this function was Veronika's (a Pleaser) confession that she confused her friends because she was moody; sometimes she enjoyed their company and other times she craved solitude. In either of these cases, she was not making a racial comment about her friends or herself. This was her individual personality that she had to honor. A White friend may have felt rebuffed for racial reasons in this case, unless there was an ability to understand that the individual response can be race-neutral. Teresa wondered if her exclusion from the volleyball team was racially motivated, but had to accept that she, as an individual, may in fact have been too short and too inexperienced to contribute to the team. This is a function that opens up a tremendous amount of confusion and conflict between races when it is assumed that one always represents and operates through the socially constructed attributes of one's race, and the individual is easily overlooked. The difference between a collective and individual identity can be difficult to sort out.

THE IVY UNIVERSITY STUDENT BODY AT LARGE

In order to understand just how the student culture on campus created the potential for stigmatizing situations for the HEOP students, it's important to look more closely at the students, the peers, with whom the HEOP students interacted at Ivy University. The director of admissions shared some statistics about the incoming freshman class of which most of these students were a part. Fifty percent of their SAT scores were in the 1220 to 1400 range, with significant numbers at the high end of the range. High school grade point averages were not recorded but were used in the admissions review process. However, 56% were in the top 10% of their high school graduating class, and 80% were in the top 20%. There were no "feeder" schools for Ivy University; students came from all over, representing private and public schools equally. New York State contributed 54% of the population; 13% were from New England; 12% from the Middle Atlantic states; 4% from the South; 7% from the Midwest; 2% from the Southwest; 5% from the West; and, 4% were international students. Males made up 56% of the population and females, 44%. From these figures, a slight majority of Ivy students were from New York State and all of the students had achieved well in their respective high schools. The male/female ratio was approaching parity. The HEOP students may have matched the high school ranking of this group, as many of them were top scholars in their schools. However, their SAT scores were not as high. All of the HEOP students were from New York State, and this group of freshman HEOP students was predominantly female (14 of the 22 students). A statistical data base had not been assembled to record the numbers and demographic characteristics of first and second generation immigrant students, so it was difficult to speculate about how much company the immigrant students had within the general student body.

In addition to admissions scores and geographic origin, the admissions director discussed the racial/ethnic composition of this class. According to the admissions office categories, the incoming freshmen identified themselves as 81.1% White, 12.7% Asian American, 5.4% African American, 3.7% Hispanic American, 0.3% Native American, and 0.7% multiracial, a new category that year. None of the HEOP students in this research cohort identified themselves as White, so they all were part of a racial and/or ethnic minority on this campus. The Asian first generation immigrant Pleasers—Panyos, Tran, Mai, and Luc—were part of the largest non-White group making up almost 13% of the incoming class. However, most of the Searchers, the second generation students, were Latino/a and thus a part of the very small Hispanic American group, 3.7% of the incoming student population. All of the Skeptics, whose families were well beyond the early immigration generations, fell under the African American category, which was clearly a minority on campus at only 5.4%. According to the U.S. Census Bureau, population estimates for the United States for various groups during July 1998 (when these students were entering freshmen) were predicted at: 11.2 % for Hispanic Origin (of any race); 72.3% for White, Not Hispanic; 12.1 % for Black, Not Hispanic; and 3.6 % for Asian and Pacific Islander, Not Hispanic (Population Estimates Program, 2000). Except for White and Asian students, the student numbers at Ivy University were well below the national percentages for sub-groups within the population, and certainly different from the composition of the urban neighborhoods that many of the HEOP students left to come to college.

Beyond the admissions office "objective" statistics, the faculty and staff who were interviewed shared their subjective impressions of the Ivy University student population at large. They used a range of descriptors which summarized their perceptions of this group. Among the quotable, notable descriptors were: "from good backgrounds," "had very good opportunities," "homogeneous," "dress alike," "same kind of activities," "Caucasian" (or "White"), "studious," "serious", "energetic," "complacent," "more diverse than 20 years ago," "less diverse than four years ago," "motivated," "inquisitive," "career oriented," "ambitious," "smart," "critical thinkers," "hard to get them to question," "Ivy League material but less snooty," "conservative," and "elitist." Some of these responses were diametrically opposed, such as the comments about the amount of diversity on campus and about their critical thinking abilities, and these responses were dependent on one's position in the academic world of Ivy University. The discipline in which one worked, the context within which one interacted with these students, and the number of years at the institution all shaped the professional's perspective. From the interviews with these faculty and staff, those who had been at the institution in a teaching capacity for longer periods of time tended to view the current population with higher regard for their abilities and for their expectations for learning. The instructors who were themselves graduate students working on doctorates, seemed to be the most critical of the student body, taking them to task for being conservative, unquestioning, and elitist.

Several English instructors and a history professor who had been on this campus more than 20 years posited the students as from a "culture of entitlement," bearing the conviction that they deserved to attend a university in the Ivy League. They were described as Ivy League "wannabes" who were somewhat surprised and frustrated to find themselves at Ivy University instead, which had also been described by these professionals as an Ivy League "wannabe." But they were even more surprised to discover that they weren't catered to and that more academic demands were placed on them than they felt they deserved. However, despite the supposed elitism of Ivy University, several staff and instructors remarked that the Ivy University students were not predominantly from upper class backgrounds, even though they appeared to be homogeneous and "advantaged." There were students from all socio-economic classes in attendance. The financial aid office indicated that almost 65% of the students received need-based financial grants, based on family income, size, and assets, and the number of college students in the family. Given the fact that tuition was over $20,000 per year plus another almost $8000 for room and board, this percentage of students needing some type of financial assistance is not surprising.

Another history instructor described the students as products of popular culture, a culture of consumption. They were pleasure seeking, and not really sure why they were in college, other than to get a "ticket" to a career with upward mobility. Howard Greene (1998) conducted a qualitative study that explored life and learning in America's elite colleges and referred to students and parents as: "...'consumers of education.' More and more, the higher-education agenda of parents and their children has more to do with chances for admission to and preparation for graduate schools than with the inherent value of the collegiate experience. I share the apprehension of educators who see students using their liberal arts training more as a vocational stepping stone..." (p.11). Several English instructors decried the tendency for the more popular majors in the sciences and technologies to devalue the humanities and critical inquiry. They perceived that the university was becoming "more technically, scientifically molded," and in the process it was centering the more prestigious and high ticket career areas. As a result, the students frequently resisted the humanities and social sciences, leading an English instructor to observe that by choosing prestigious majors, "...they're doing the right things, but it's not very interesting." The university did little to promote foreign languages or cultural exploration in classes. A psychology professor summed up these students at Ivy University as "...people who have come to the university who knew the university is where hard work is a good part of the picture. They play hard, too, but I think the ambitious, serious student comes here. We aren't any kind of a party school." There was no question that students were expected to give their all in the pursuit of certain degrees, as the HEOP students were discovering. Few of these students could be described as "pleasure seeking," although they saw students around them whom they would describe that way, that they worked and they played hard, hoping that college would "pay off" in the end.

HEOP FRIENDSHIPS

Complications with the Student Body at Large

HEOP friendships seemed to arise as much from a reaction to a social climate that they either couldn't understand or of which they didn't want to be a part as from the intrinsic bonding that was enhanced by the summer program. Their true friendships did not develop from the dominant, White population with whom they interacted in class and in the dorms. When describing the student body at Ivy University, the HEOP students used different words but voiced some of the perceptions of the faculty, especially the psychology professor who didn't see Ivy University as a party school. The HEOP students spoke with energy and enthusiasm, with no apparent guarded hesitation about their perceptions of their Ivy peers.

Most of the Pleasers concurred on the studious nature of the students. Veronika commented that:

> Everybody is just as smart. They all seem to know what they're doing....Friday night you go to parties, but Saturday morning you go to [the library] and before 10:00 there are people waiting to go inside to study or write papers. It's really surprising cause I never thought that people would be that studious in college. I know the work is hard, but come on! It's a Saturday morning. It just really surprises me. Everywhere you pass, you see someone studying. Buried in his or her books, studying.

Other Pleasers were not surprised by the level of academic focus. However, Roberto saw smart students all around, but "...they just don't maybe apply themselves as much as they should....I have friends who their parents can afford to send them here, and because of that, they don't try as hard as my friends whose parents can't afford to send them here." Very rarely did the HEOP students describe students in terms of economic class, although Roberto's comments made it evident that they observed some of the implications of economic advantage. Several of the professors felt that economic class was not very apparent because the majority of students conformed to clothing styles and all of them lived in the same dorms. However, Roberto observed an attitudinal difference within his circle of acquaintances that he attributed to economic privilege.

Beyond the studious nature that they observed, many of the Pleasers seemed confused by the general student population, and they were reluctant or unable to interact effectively with it. They were finding it difficult to develop the skills needed to bridge between different cultures. However, there was a strong need for affiliation and "fit" as Tran indicated when I asked him whether his social relationships were as meaningful on this campus as in high school:

> I think so, because I don't want to be alone. Yeh, it's very important. If I go anywhere, I have to know someone. I want to do that. I want to be a home person....I mean, basic reality, I don't know anybody here,

but I just have myself say, "Oh, I know everybody here, so approach them and talk to them." With that attitude, I find that they are pretty friendly.

Despite this optimistic outlook, comments that the Pleasers made to students were not received as they intended, and they often felt rebuffed by their efforts to engage other students. A number of the Pleasers called the students "weird," like Panyos in this exchange:

Some of them are weird. Some of them like to get to know you. In general, they are nice. I don't have any problems with anyone....I felt a bit of tension because most of my friends are Asian. I don't know like standard[s] in order to be accepted into Caucasian or some other stuff....In class, I don't really know much. When I see them having conversation, I try to jump in. Not really working. I don't know why, and when I see it's not really working, I think I should try harder....I try once or twice and then I stop. I don't want to make a fool of myself.

Panyos felt uncomfortable because he couldn't understand how to relate to "Caucasians," which he attributed to always having Asian friends and never having to learn these skills. Barbara Okun, Jane Fried, and Marcia Okun (1999) expand on the cross-cultural confusion that takes place when people attempt communication but are unaware of or inexperienced with the complexity of others' worldviews:

The creative process [of effective communication] requires dual awareness of self and other, as well as attention to the interactive processes of communication and to the strange attractors of strongly held values, beliefs, and norms. Although a person can learn a lot about a different culture before actually meeting people from that culture, no cross-cultural interaction is completely predictable (p. 30).

The risk inherent in these unpredictable interactions may partially account for the limited engagement between student groups that other students observed: "...the campus, everyone doesn't mix as much as you'd expect. It's more that everyone is in their little clique.... Everyone was so closed off and I guess, their own. You don't see a lot of people mixing anywhere, except those who were in the [summer program] together....So, you don't see a lot of interclass." The reactive bonds among like groups, which were buffering strategies, made opportunities for interaction across groups seem very superficial, limited to registering a "hi" or a smile in passing. The Pleasers seemed to be trying to find how to break this student code and bridge with others from diverse backgrounds. However, they were novices at this and were experiencing limited success.

The Searchers had their own perceptions of the Ivy University students. They did not seem as bewildered by their interactions with students as the Pleasers, but that may have been because they had spent their lives in bi- or multicultural environments and, having "been there and done that," they were not as willing to experiment with trying to engage many of the students around them. Of this group, Marie was the only one who made positive comments about the student body when I asked her to what extent she interacted with students who were from different backgrounds:

> I interact with them. To me, I don't really care if you're from different backgrounds. Sometimes it makes it odd because we don't have similar interests. Like we don't have too many things in common to speak about. But there's so many other things like schoolwise....It's different, the environment, especially from where I come from. At first it was kind of hard. They act differently. They're more mature. They don't show like they're talking behind your back. They're very nice and they say, "Hi."

However, Jason's response was more typical. He felt a distinct difference between the high school student environment that he had left and the college student ethos. He just went through the motions of being a normal college student but: "Basically, I was just like, 'I don't want to be here....You know, these people I can't relate to. I can't understand them. I really don't want to go and attempt to understand them.'" Race and ethnicity were not the only elements that complicated the ability to bridge between groups. Jason observed class differences in lifestyles around him that felt foreign, especially the attention that parents showered on their students during frequent visits that involved a considerable amount of time and money. Like Roberto (a Pleaser, above), he was very aware of the economic gap between himself and other students. In searching for relational comfort with the peer group at large and finding effective means to bridge between groups, most of the Searchers opted to avoid these relationships altogether. They opted not to become the "bridge over troubled water."

The Skeptics had a lot to say about the Ivy students and little of it was positive. Several of them commented on fractures across racial and cultural lines:

Stacey: I guess to me most of them (students at Ivy) are different to me because I can't imagine my roommate is scared of cities, of big cities....I can't imagine having that feeling of being scared of the city just because it's big....This one girl asked me if they had houses in the city (NYC). I looked at her like she was nuts. I was thinking she probably was thinking about Manhattan. Even in Manhattan there are houses. She was like, "with trees?" Yes, there are trees and lawns and people have swimming pools....I was for a moment like outraged, and then I just had to laugh.

*   *   *   *   *

Teresa: My roommate's from Connecticut. And she's like really, really White. Like, she has no street smarts whatsoever....I like the classes but I just don't like the people. Everybody seems so fake to me. Maybe it's just me. I don't find any comfort in being here. I feel a little more comfortable at home.

*   *   *   *   *

Damon: I don't think there's much interaction between African Americans and Whites. I don't know if there should be, but there's not much interaction. There's some, but the vast majority...you go to a fraternity, a African American fraternity party and you won't see any Whites there....You can go to [a dining hall], you'll see some, but mostly you'll see African Americans and Hispanic sitting together and the vast majority are Whites sitting together. This may be a social evolutionary type thing. People gravitate toward people they look like, or who they can relate to on music. That's not a bad thing. It's just important to know that other things exist and you're not alone out there. And you need to be aware of other peoples' cultures.

Damon observed the reactive bonding between groups, which functioned as protective buffers. However, what is notable with the Skeptics is that all of these students critique the difficulties of relating with students who have observable differences from them, yet they all eventually highlight the necessity and desire to transcend some of the differences long enough to reach a higher level of cultural understanding, the bridging function. They were the most skilled at seeing through the structures of race and culture, and expressing the desire to move on to the point of enhancing understanding. Perhaps their historical location with generations of bicultural experience made the Skeptics more aware of how and when to bridge between cultures, even though they were out of their element in this elite environment. Nicole comments at some length and with considerable insight on her experiences in class, gleaned from three years at Ivy University:

> The ones, like in some of my classes, whether it be a White person who wants to study with us—you know who doesn't mind. I'm telling you, some kids, they really don't want to be around. Maybe they get intimidated. I don't know. I can't describe it. Those who don't mind and that aren't intimidated, I feel free to like. I don't look at a person's color and discriminate against them. But, if I feel like kind of on edge if I'm talking to you and it makes me feel kind of weird because maybe I make you feel uncomfortable or something like that, that's when you get kind of turned off....I just really had to realize that some kids are like that because they've never been around minorities before and you have to understand that. Just like some minorities have never been around White people like this before. You have to understand where people come from and just be accepting.

Nicole's statements highlight the confusion that exists among all students in attempting to develop the skills necessary to interact successfully and bridge across racial, ethnic, and class locations. White students cannot be assumed to be more skilled (and may be less skilled because they have not had opportunities or felt the need to develop these skills) at intergroup communication than any of the other student groups. And clearly, successful communication is a two-way process. Most of the HEOP students perceived little reciprocal effort from the student body at large.

Friendship Groups

The HEOP students described the Ivy students as not particularly friendly or easy to get to know, a dramatic difference in how they described HEOP students, for the most part. The faculty and staff who worked with the HEOP students during the summer program and beyond, observed the challenges that this group of students had in establishing meaningful social interaction beyond their own group of HEOP peers. The HEOP staff talked about encouraging the students to join a number of groups and branch out, but how difficult this was, especially in the first year when they were working hard to establish themselves academically. The staff worried about the students' polarization and lack of community, which was also evident in the larger student body. The reorganization of the university had magnified the relationship problems for the HEOP students because the student body was smaller and more homogeneous, which made the HEOP students stand out in terms of their races, cultures, and economic class. The faculty and staff described them as being "cliquish," "birds of a feather," who traveled in "little packs" of fellow HEOP students. It was notable that all of the faculty and staff spoke of the need for the university to build better bridges between students and provide more opportunities for networking and creating a community on the campus that might break down barriers and the stigma with which many of the HEOP students lived. And most of the HEOP students would agree with them. However, this group of students had the added pressure to perform at high academic levels from the beginning or to lose their college funding. This often got in the way of social outreach.

The strong group affiliation of the HEOP students could be directly attributed to the intrinsic bonding that took place in the HEOP summer program that connected these students with each other, and the fact that these students quickly recognized their areas of commonality. Among themselves, there was little need to engage in the work of code switching. This was even more obvious when they talked about the friendship groups they created in the fall.

The Pleasers

The Pleasers described the HEOP students as "normal." The majority of them maintained the friendships that had budded in the summer HEOP program, and built on them in the fall when their intrinsic bonds helped buffer the culture shock. Most of them described friendship groups that contained students strictly from their cultures, although several made a point of emphasizing that some of their friends were HEOP students from other racial/ethnic groups. However, the Pleasers engaged in bridging cultures even within their HEOP "family." Clarissa describes her friendships centered around commonalities, but reflecting an awareness of intragroup differences:

> My friends from [the summer program] and even my roommate, we're pretty close. We spend all of our time together....We'd all have lunch together and then we'd all meet up at 6:15 for dinner....It's kind of like a little family....We're all friends, but we're always together, always getting on each others' nerves. We talk to everyone else from [the summer program], we talk to them, but you don't always hang out with them....Personality wise, we're all a little different. We're all from the West Indies, but we're not like all from the same country. So there's that difference. We like music.

To some of the Pleasers, these friendships were substitutes for family and friends that they had left behind. Veronika narrated the optimism that these relationships would eventually become as significant as her previous friendships: "I figure I'm going to be here four years of my life.

It's good to make meaningful relationships. You're going to go through a whole lot of problems and it's good to know you have someone you can count on." Trust was a big element in all of the HEOP students' relationships. They surrounded themselves with students who shared and understood the work of managing and surviving in this elite institution.

Even within groups sharing cultural commonalities, intrinsic bonding was not automatic. Tran found it difficult to relate within his *own* ethnic group due to his difficulty with English. He explained it this way:

> I think I can socialize and be friends, but I still can't find the connection sometime within a group, with my own Vietnamese group, too. They speak in English. As soon as they speak in Vietnamese, okay. But as soon as they switch to English, they have their conversation and I feel like I'm invisible or something. I can't find something to talk about....I guess I have to like hang out more and more with the Americans or something like that. I need to get the feeling of how the culture of the language goes.

Luc, who had just transferred to Ivy University in her fourth year and who had missed the summer program, was an important exception that underscores how critical the early summer bonding experience was for the students. In previous chapters, we heard her difficulties in making the transition to this school and to her engineering department. When I asked about her friends on this campus, she stated:

> Not really friends, maybe partners, group members....But then I'm not going to tell them my personal life....I think it's the reason why I feel so isolated. This is probably because of myself. Also, I'm very shy. The Vietnamese guy [in her classes], I only talked to him yesterday and I've been in the class two or three months already. So, it's not because I think of him as Vietnamese or anything; I'm just too shy to talk to anybody....I really hope I can get better. It's not good. I wouldn't recommend this to anybody. Reach out, talk to other people, join clubs.

Luc's experience was dramatically different from that of the incoming freshmen. She spoke of her isolation as self-imposed and her fault, a function of individualism; however, she was caught in an unfortunate web of poor timing coupled with few resources from which to draw. Transferring as a senior made her an anomaly in a department that was not renowned for creating a welcoming environment for any student. While trying to get up to speed with a new program and the rigorous academic requirements, Luc had little time left to become involved in new, extracurricular activities. As a Vietnamese and as a female, Luc was physically different from the majority of the students in her major and was set apart instantly as the "other," the isolated self that she keenly felt. Luc had no transition program like the summer program to help her gain a foothold on Ivy University's campus culture. HEOP could provide her with welcome opportunities to connect with HEOP advisors and other HEOP students (mostly younger) through individual counseling sessions and group workshops, but it was beyond the program's scope to affect her experiences with her department and peers. Living off campus also prevented Luc from having the casual, everyday opportunities to develop comfortable relationships and to bond with fellow students. So, while Luc blamed herself for her inability to establish friendships, there were obvious external structures that made her transition difficult.

It was evident that even with the summer program, some HEOP students felt an intragroup tension that resisted the intrinsic bonding that others found so easy. A reluctance on their part prevented an automatic association with other HEOP students, perhaps because they saw little need to bridge over their differences, or they felt the threat of being tainted by association. Panyos stated that:

> The HEOP students, they are, I don't know, pretty much in my situation. I get along well with them. I don't have any problems. I don't really spend time with any of them. I mean, they would say, "come and visit with me." I was going to say, "why don't you come and visit me?" I hold back. I say, "I'm sorry, I don't have time." I say "hi" to them. But I saw a lot of them bunch up together....The thing is I don't think I need to. But sometime I should for old time's sake. We've been through the summer together.... But, the thing is, I understand why they want to be together. They want to have a sense that they belong. It's pretty tough being alone on this campus. So they feel, "These are my friends, I know them; I know they're nice people, so I belong to some group that welcomes me."

The Pleasers seemed actively engaged in trying out relationships and quickly disengaging from groups and individuals who didn't measure up to their initial appearances. Much of it came down to trust and learning who could be trusted without suffering in the process. As Ileana described it: "I think I talk to everyone. I just don't trust everyone. I talk to a lot of people and a lot of people think they're my friend, but I just don't trust anyone who is not my sister." Close friendships were not created overnight nor within the first few months of college.

The Searchers

The Searchers were more cautious than the Pleasers in establishing peer relationships. Several of them acknowledged their self-imposed isolation from most Ivy students. Their friends came from narrow segments of the international and HEOP groups who were most like them in cultural backgrounds. They recognized their need for affiliation with fellow HEOP students and how that led to clusters of friendships within the group, but which excluded most other Ivy students. In fact, Martine commented that she did not interact very much with students from other cultural backgrounds on campus and chided herself:

> I really should. I mean, I find myself going to Hispanic parties. Like, since there's such a small amount, it's like, when you hear there's a Hispanic party, whether it's here or on another campus, everybody comes together. Everybody gets ready and goes to show support....I really don't associate with, like the White community unless I go to a frat party or something.

Martine also observed that she felt excluded by Whites, not just because they were White per se, but because they had "different interests." She confided that what she really liked about her friends: "The truth? The fact that if I want to start talking in Spanish, they're both going to understand me." Martine also appreciated that they were going through the same academic and social experiences that began with the summer program. The students did not overtly reject the White culture, but they clearly found the intrinsic bonds easier and more natural.

Laila indicated that some of the difficulty in developing bridging skills that would foster intercultural friendships came from segregated high schools like hers which was all Black:

> ...up here it's like kind of difficult for me because now it's people that like different music than I do, dress differently than I do, and different thinking than I do, and different colors. So, I do have Caucasian friends and Asian friends. I have Indian friends and African American friends. I'm glad. That's one thing I didn't want to go to, another all Black college....But sometimes too, when you reach here, you kind of like stay with certain similar people.

Two females described themselves as "social butterflies" who thrived on their friendships that seemed to cut more across groups of students, although they both agreed that the HEOP students did tend to segregate themselves and they, at times, followed suit.

The Searchers viewed the HEOP population as distinct from the general Ivy University student body. Several of them identified their shared economic class location as a feature of their bonds. Tiana began describing HEOP students as not like her, but continued on and listed many similarities: "I think they're all real poor, of course, because that's what HEOP does, takes the poor people. We're all poor and, for the most part, intelligent....I mean they're smart, happen to be underprivileged. They're trying to make it through their college life with their own trials and tribulations." Martine focused on how the students' financial dependence accounted for how hard working and "book smart" the HEOP students were: "They know that they have to do work because no one's going to be paid for it. It's kind of like you know that the school is looking for mistakes to take it away from you. So, you work hard. But, yet, I don't see them really working hard. A lot of them." Martine was conscious of making a slight distinction to derail a class generalization about all HEOP students.

More than for the Pleasers, trust was an important theme in the Searcher friendships, and they didn't waste much time in deciding where to place that trust. Their bonds seemed to be reactive, serving to buffer perceived assaults from others who proved themselves unfriendly and untrustworthy. Tiana discovered this: "...You can't trust just anybody on this campus. I figured that out the hard way." Trust was found most frequently among students most like them. Jason's Asian fraternity "brothers" were his closest friends because of the trust that this group engendered: "...Especially after like what happened in high school; it was really hard for me to like trust people and have friends again. I was really hesitant to do that....It's like I rebuilt that trust with these guys." The friends shared the same hobbies, interests, music, senses of humor, and academic seriousness. He indicated that some Asians seem to fit the "model minority" stereotype (Chan & Wang, 1991; Suzuki, 1994), although he resisted accepting this classification for his group: "I would say with some Asians. But, some Asians who just instilled it in them, and it's just you should work hard...It's like most of the Asians I hang out with, we do our studying, we get good grades, but, at the same time, we know how to have fun."

The Skeptics

The Skeptics also valued their summer bonds, but indicated a desire to not be tied down by only the intrinsic bonds of race, ethnicity, or class. Most of them made strong friendships within the HEOP group and showed a level of respect similar to Damon's:

> I think a lot of them are determined. They're hard workers, the ones I see. They have other jobs in addition to working. A lot of students here don't have to get another job, but a lot of HEOP students, they struggle to do the work, and they try to stay on top of things. I think that's really good. That's something they should be proud of. Yeh, they're hard workers. They're really into it, in tune to each other.

They frequently discussed the importance of their friends being genuinely interested in their lives, and sharing some kind of common interest, from music, to humor, to classes. They found these elements most frequently in the students they met in the summer program. As Teresa explained, her friends "...all have the same issues, the same stresses. We think about the same things, but not the same. Thoughts and goals create a bond." Sybill provided proof that the quick summer bonds could in fact become lasting friendships. Her best friends in her third year were students she had meet during her summer program. She viewed these friendships as more lasting than high school, based on shared humor and intelligence: "We're all intelligent and we want to succeed and do well. We don't let other people slow us down."

The Skeptics voiced an impatience with other students who often asked strange questions and made naive assumptions about their cultures. This group was most concerned with how time- consuming social relationships were, and they just couldn't or wouldn't afford the time to work on relationships. Therefore, a number of them felt that HEOP students gravitated toward those who were most like them and comfortable—the relationships formed through intrinsic bonding that took the least amount of time and work. The Skeptics seemed convinced that the pay-off in college would come from the academic and not the social aspects.

However, many of the Skeptics voiced the need to bridge out of the confines of the HEOP population, and to go beyond the comfort zone of intrinsic bonding. Nicole in her third year, reflected on this, and voiced a criticism of the younger freshmen:

> It takes a lot of moving around, it does. I switched my social groups, my group of friends, I guess, like three times. I've kept my best friends, but I've changed my social groups. I think my friends when I was a freshman, they were accepting to me and I was here alone, and we all hung out. But then you get comfortable here and then you say, okay, you see differences and you see similarities with other people and you are attracted to other groups.... A lot of us [upper class HEOP students] feel that these freshmen aren't as accepting to us like I remember my freshman year. I would always go to the upper classmen for advice or whatever it might be. But these freshmen are very to themselves.

Many of the first year students migrated naturally toward students who were more like them in terms of backgrounds and challenges, but some searched for meaningful relationships that expanded their worldviews. They sought authentic relationships, where they could bridge without having to code switch. Damon indicated that he valued his lifelong friends, but:

> Connections on the college campus are very important because these are people you'll be working with in the real world in the next 10 or 15 years. It's important to get along with them because it makes your four years that much better. But it shouldn't be your driving factor. You shouldn't go out of your way to impress people. It's important to live on campus in college because you want to get that well-roundedness and meet new people.

After indicating that she had little time to hang out with any of the Ivy students, including her HEOP peers, and how everyone seemed so "fake," Teresa launched into a classification system that offered a stinging critique of most of the student body, while underscoring the need for authenticity and acceptance of difference:

> If you're from NYC, they are so pro-NYC, they are never going to change. They are always going to talk like they're from NYC, act like they're from NYC. They will never conform to the ways of this university, no matter how much they try to break them down; it's not going to happen. But the other kids, then you get the really, really White kids...who are totally excited and upbeat, on valium or something...Then the one White girl from rural New York and she is so down to earth, like stupid. It's so easy to communicate with her; she understands everything I'm talking about...Then you have the foreign students; some of them are still fully engaged in their culture and I think that's excellent cause you never want to lose yourself. But there are others who are totally and completely so far away from what they used to be. I'm pretty sure that their parents have aspirations for them to become great surgeons, but you do not have to change...Show people that you appreciate the richness of your culture. Everybody that has slanted eyes are not Chinese; there's Chinese, Japanese, Cambodian, Thai, and Laos.

Friendships Between Genders

Among the HEOP students, friendships seemed to form easily between the genders. Many of the students included students of the opposite gender in their inner circle of friends, and not in a romantic connotation. This was true for males as well as females. I observed this phenomenon early on during the summer program, when students began to form mixed gender groups that would comfortably hang together both in and outside of classes.

Several of the male students indicated that their female friends were, "...more understanding than guys are." They found it remarkable that they could find as close friendships among females as males. These relationships were characterized as comfortable, honest, and open. In contrast, Roberto (a Pleaser) described his relationships with older male students as being tense due to perceived code switching and inauthenticity:

> There's only a certain few I speak to. Most of them—how can I put this?—most of them aren't productive. They act like it's all about them. It's just not cool to be friends with most of these guys. Most of them aren't even friends with each other. I mean, they'll smile. Like, I'll be sitting at a table with a bunch of upperclassmen, and one of them will be like, "Oh, God, I can't stand this guy coming over here." But as soon as the guy comes over, he'll shake his hand, and he'll be like, "Oh, what's up?" So, I do not want to be around stuff like that so I just stay to myself....Like, I'm very, very close to all the guys in my class, but not with upperclassmen."

The male HEOP students found it difficult to be themselves around some of the other males. They resisted "playing the game," wearing one face around some students and switching to another identity around their friends. They often decided to avoid socializing with the students who required more "fronting" than they were willing to give.

Several of the young women indicated that their friendships with males resulted from their distrust of females. Martine (a Searcher) stated that she'd had bad experiences with females: "With girls I would be like jealous, or they would be mean. With guys, it was more like they would tell me the truth. They wouldn't say things for a motive." Tiana (a Searcher) worded it differently: "Other women, women are trifle. I don't know if that's a word in the English language, but that' s word in my ghetto language. Women, you don't trust women." These male friends were usually HEOP students they had met during the summer program.

On the other hand, Sybill (a Skeptic) did not find meaningful friendships with the males on campus because she found them immature. And Yasmin (a Searcher) was not as interested in striking up friendships with males as with openly flirting with them. She admitted she was playing with guys and made a game of it when she was out with a group of friends. But, as a whole, the HEOP students voiced a desire to be involved in *authentic* relationships and were open to these coming from either gender. The intrinsic bonds that formed around race and ethnicity superseded concern over the gender of friends, as long as the person was deemed trustworthy.

ROMANTIC RELATIONSHIPS

Interestingly, it was one of the English instructors who taught HEOP students in the summer program and during the academic year who raised a raced gender issue that affected her as a graduate student on this campus. Because there were so few Black males on campus, especially compared to the number of Black females, she personally found limited opportunities to develop meaningful relationships with males on this campus. Her work as an instructor and a doctoral student kept her tied to the campus, so she had no time to explore the social possibilities in the broader community. Her observations about the campus situation foreshadowed problematic gender issues for Black female students:

> ...then to get a guy who is serious, who doesn't think I'm going to have three or four girls, that I'll get one on campus, one that lives in [one dorm], one that lives in [another dorm]. You don't get to establish those kinds of romantic relationships.

This lack of opportunity may have been partially responsible for romantic liaisons among HEOP students assuming a lower priority than friendships. Laura Meyers (1996) also described this dilemma of a lack of Black males when doing her doctoral research at an elite university. The HEOP students in my study were adamant in not wanting romance to side-track them from achieving their academic goals, which was the strongest reason they gave for the lack of focus on romance in their lives.

Of the nine Pleasers, Veronika was the only student who was seriously involved romantically and trying to maintain the long distance relationship. She had been dating a man who was a year older than her for about two years. In the first semester she described their relationship as very compatible, and claimed that they were in love and had a great time together. However, she also related the challenges of long distance relationships:

> Every time he calls, he tells me I'm changing, and I'm like, "What are you talking about? I'm not changing, just because I want to leave for college." He says, "You don't notice it, but I do." I don't exactly know what he means by that. I mean we go through so many arguments, but really it's unnecessary. I guess that's what a long distance relationship does.

While Veronika could not see it, her boyfriend described what Howard London (1992) identified as the costs of upward mobility achieved by attending college: "Moving up, in other words, requires a 'leaving off' and a 'taking on,' the shedding of one social identity and the acquisition of another" (p. 8). By the time the focus group met in the second semester, this situation had played itself out and Veronika had broken up with this boyfriend. However, she expressed an interest in being in a relationship and indicated conflicting emotions about this:

> It is always in the back of my mind, that you know, like I'm in college. This will be like the most appropriate time to find somebody that you can hopefully spend the rest of your life with. But, then again, I'm like, well, it is college and it's not really all about trying to find someone. I'm here to get an education and not really to focus on how my relationships are going to be....it's really confusing.

Veronika's initial statements sounded like many of the young women whom Dorothy Holland and Margaret Eisenhart (1990), and Angela McRobbie (1978) researched, who placed top priority on securing a romantic partner in their lives. However, Veronika quickly checked herself and gave voice to the conflicted situation in which many young women find themselves today and which the women in Laura Meyers' (1996) study felt. She observed that it was at the critical juncture of anticipated motherhood that women's career plans were thwarted by the realities of childcare and being the "good mother." There was a scaling downward of career expectations for the women in her study, but as freshmen, few of the HEOP women had yet reached the perilous moment of contemplating motherhood that Meyers noted. Even for those who did not speak of romantic partnerships and issues, there are questions that they all will face as they work on developing their career and gender identities. Does one focus on education and career to the detriment of developing meaningful personal relationships, or is it possible and appropriate to achieve a balance between all of these aspects? What is worth noting, however, is the *lack* of attention and focus that these young women had on romance in their narratives.

Several other Pleasers were gingerly venturing into romantic liaisons. Ileana had a blossoming relationship with a guy who she had met at the minority student week-end in the spring. However, being away from home for the first time and out from under parental surveillance raised issues surrounding romantic relationships. Ileana felt that she missed being a teenager altogether due to her father's strictness, but now that she had the opportunity to structure her own social world, it was not a smooth transition. She indicated that:

> I don't have like any social life what-so-ever, since this week. But I feel good saying that I don't have any social life, because I'm studying, so....Like I don't have, I'm not seeing like 20 people. I'm seeing one person, right? But, it's not because I'm free now and I wasn't before. Because, like 20 million girls go out with people when their parents don't allow them. So, I don't think that's—I had the opportunity back then and I didn't want to.

Ileana had real qualms about informing her parents of the relationship she'd struck up with the male student. She feared that her father would give her the old speech about: "I told you, in the future. Now you have to concentrate on school. If you mess up, don't come back to me because the doors are going to be closed." She was eager to share with me that after our interview that night, she and her boyfriend and another couple were going to spend the night together, but she was quick to add "...but we're not doing anything bad. We're just watching a movie and, uhm, eating." It was clear that Ileana found this a very meaningful social group and longed to talk about these new experiences and feelings. It seemed that she realized, with some sadness, that her family would not understand, and she could no longer confide in them about all aspects of her life.

Tran spoke about enjoying time he spent talking with a female friend. When I asked if he was just talking with her or dating her, he replied: "I don't know, but personally I think Asians don't date. They just go out, we go as a group. We're pretty shy about it. She didn't want me to tell people, so I [said] fine. She's very shy." Gendered relationships were new to many of the Pleasers who, as first generation immigrant students, came from sheltered backgrounds. Adding the cultural influences of their ethnic locations, such as Ileana's traditional Latino "guard the daughters" experience and Tran's Vietnamese "guard your emotions" response, made romantic undertakings fraught with dilemmas.

Establishing a heterosexual gender identity on a campus was difficult enough, but Paolo's homosexuality posed continual problems for him. He found that his lack of discretionary funds made it difficult for him to date. He described the homosexual community on campus as "closeted" and that many people had not "come out," which limited his opportunity and choice to connect with a potential partner. In addition, Paolo couldn't confide in many people about these difficulties, especially with his family with whom he felt little closeness. Greene's (1998) study of elite college students discussed aspects of this dilemma:

> Today, men and women must make up the rules as they go along. Gay men and lesbians face similar issues, along with concerns about defin-

ing their own sexuality in a closed and oftentimes perilous environment. Combine the inevitable vagaries of youthful sex and love with
the pressures of elite academia, and you have an inevitably volatile
environment (p. 103).

The HEOP counselors became a major source of support in helping
Paolo struggle with his sexual identity and the issues surrounding it. He
did share his situation with several counselors, and they extended themselves to keep the lines of communication open.

The Searchers voiced more romantic activity and interest than the
Pleasers, but the course of love did not run smoothly for many of them.
For those with romantic relationships, problems were as prevalent as
pleasures. Yasmin honestly expressed that she had lots of "guy troubles"
and wasn't sure if the student she had dated on-and-off for a year felt as
strongly toward her as she did toward him. Tiana was the only student
who mentioned that she had a boyfriend back home as well as on campus. The man she was seeing back home was five years older, married
with two children, "...and a wife he's about to divorce." Nonetheless,
Tiana felt that she was cheating on him when she went out with
a student on campus. And Martine was working hard to sort out her
relationship which was based equally on romance and friendship. Her
problem was complicated by taboos that resisted dating across some
culturally constructed barriers:

> I started seeing somebody, as in just hanging around with a person
> more, almost like a boyfriend. He's Black. All-of-a-sudden, my
> Hispanic friends are like, "Why are you with a Black guy?" Or like
> comments as in, "They don't cook their food well," or certain things,
> or whatever. It's like, yeah. Like their friends, his friends will be like,
> "It's a shame that you can't find a beautiful Black woman or whatev-
> er, that you have to cross all the time." ...I get it worse. As in, they tell
> me, "Why can't you stick to your own?" as in your friends. My fami-
> ly also has wanted me to marry a White male, because they assume that
> a White male always brought money with him. You know what I
> mean? As in the safest thing....They see one of yours leaving to some-
> one else, all the Hispanic males will jump on you, as in to try to bring
> you back...I hate saying it, but my White friends, they don't have a
> problem with it....[S]ince I'm a light-skinned Hispanic [pause], because
> even within the Hispanic community there's a lot of racism. As in, if
> you're darker, that means you have African slave or whatever. And if
> you're whiter, you're better, supposedly....All-of-a-sudden it's like,
> "Well, that's not your character [to date a Black guy]." Why? Because
> I didn't find him cute, a Black guy, back in high school, and I found one
> here or something?...I'm still the same person. I still love my culture.
> It's not like that's changing.

While Martine was trying to bridge across cultures, she was stymied by issues raised by her peers, such as **colorism** (Tatum, 1992; Ward, 1999), where the amount of color in one's complexion made a difference within ethnically similar groups. The complexity of sorting through racial and ethnic prejudices became further clouded by her family accepting a relationship with a White male, not necessarily Latino, but not with a Black male. This was an overt distancing from a subjugated group (Blacks who might have slave ancestry) that was perceived to have less status to bring to a relationship than a White person, an issue that has been noted in other research (see, for example, Hirschman, 1996; Matute-Bianchi, 1991; and Portes, 1995).

Martine was not the only Searcher who voiced concern about developing meaningful relationships in this climate of racism. While not the same as colorism, Jason shared his frustrations concerning the stigmatization of physical markers: "I think once they [females on campus] get to know me, it'd be okay, but then based on my outside features and certain things, they'd be like hesitant to approach me." His mixed heritage showed somewhat through a combination of Asian and White physical characteristics, which he feared might be difficult for females to bridge over. Maria Root (1997) comments on concerns like Jason's which evolve from stigmatizing incidents that make multiracial people more sensitive to their environments and appearances:

> In order for many multiracial people to make peace with themselves, they must individually construct a reality that allows for duality and multiplicity, with an awareness that one may be perceived and categorized very differently than one perceives one's self (p. 33).

However, Jason was confident that his individual traits, not cluttered by the racial/ethnic trappings, would be positively received.

The Skeptics were the most romantically involved of the three groups, with six of the seven students having relationships with the opposite sex that they described as more than friendships. Teresa's romance of two years with a local young man was also conflicted by racial difference:

> When I first started going with my boyfriend, I was really having a problem dating a White guy, cause people was really giving me the stare down, blah, blah, blah. He's like, if you're uncomfortable with this, I'm going to let you know that I'm White and, unfortunately, I'm not going to change color any time soon....But, he's like a different kind of White. He's not like New Hampshire White. There's a difference between being [this city] White and New Hampshire White. I mean, New Hampshire is really, really White. I mean, there are no outside influences.

Teresa felt that over time they had bridged over the race issue because he was not as "White" as other Whites, another variation of colorism, although based more on individual attitude than collective physical characteristics. She recognized what Ruth Frankenberg (1993) identifies as the absence of a unitary collective white identity or culture. Teresa found the relationship solid and supportive, and indicated that her family was comfortable with her interracial dating.

The rest of the Skeptics were involved in a variety of romantic relationships, ranging from those formed only recently at Ivy University or at neighboring colleges to long term relationships being maintained in hometowns, as far away as New York City. None of these romances were complicated by intergroup differences, although they all presented the various challenges of maintaining any romantic relationship.

Even though most of the Skeptics had romantic attachments, they were not overly focused on them. In fact, little came out about these relationships until I asked them if they had a "partner," intentionally phrased this way to minimize any gender bias attached to asking if they had boyfriends or girlfriends. However, I learned that even this was too broadly framed when Damon's response was, "For what? Lab?" On the second pass, he understood that I meant a romantic partner and stated that he had none; he was still trying to find the "perfect first lady," a reference to his desire to become president and to his high standards. Obviously, romance was not the first thing on his mind!

In a focus group later in the second semester, Nicole and Sybill were very vocal about their expectations for their romantic relationships and marriage. They hoped to eventually marry and have families, but their thoughts about timing differed greatly:

> *Sybill*: Whenever I say this, I swear I feel guilty. Women look at me like I'm in the '50s or something, but, like I've been in a relationship the last five years. Like, I plan to get married when I get away from college, but I still plan to go to medical school and get my master's. I mean, I'm applying for my master's right now, so, like, I plan to do it all!...It's like anything...relationships, nothing is guaranteed. And I need to always know, whatever happens, I can still pay the bills at the end of the day.

> *Nicole*: And I just don't have time for a relationship. I don't have time for one. But, I also want to get married and I want a family and everything. But, I also want to get my master's degree and I want to get a career before I get anything else....I guess just seeing my older sister and my mother and father. I want to have everything for myself and then, if someone comes into my life and wants to share my stuff, that's fine. But I want to have things for myself. I don't want to depend on anyone to provide anything for me.

                                                                          Resilient Spirits

I compared what I heard from young Black college women in this study with several of the conclusions of Dorothy Holland and Margaret Eisenhart's (1990) study of college women. The times (1970s versus late 1990s), populations (Black and White versus no Whites and a mix of Latinas, Asians, and Blacks), and colleges (both non-elite public versus elite private) of their study were different from this study, but these young women were all academically strong and initially motivated to pursue challenging careers. Like one of the groups that Holland and Eisenhart's study addressed, all of the Skeptics were Black and, yet, contrary to their findings, none of the Skeptics seemed less focused on finding a man than the other women in this study (if anything, they were more engaged in this), nor were they less expectant of future economic support from men (pp. 199–201, 223), because *none* of the women in this research cohort voiced a desire to depend on a man to support them. Perhaps this contrast would have surfaced with a White referent group on the campus, which my study lacked, but which was a part of Holland and Eisenhart's research. This determination to not depend on a male for economic survival seemed to generate more from the Skeptics' need for independence and self-reliance than because they directly doubted men's ability or desire to contribute financially to a relationship, although all of households of these young women had been headed up by single mothers, and the resultant economic disadvantage with which these students had lived could certainly be claimed as a primary influence. All of the Skeptic females were proving themselves capable of achieving a college degree ("doing well", p. 172) and were serious students ("learning from the experts", p. 174), and several of them were on the cusp of graduation. One of Holland and Eisenhart's findings, read backward, is useful in explaining the lack of over attention to romance within this group of women. They state that: "...the decreasing investment in schoolwork coincided with increasing investment in romantic relationships" (p. 220). Applied to this group of HEOP students, the increased and focused investment in schoolwork seemed to coincide with a *decreased* investment in romance, and not just for the Skeptics, but for all of the HEOP females. The instrumental rewards of education were valued over the emotional rewards of romantic preoccupations.

Holland and Eisenhart discovered that a "sexual auction block" (p. 96–107), where male peers informally rated young women's sexual attractiveness, was one means of reproducing and perpetuating an oppressive patriarchal gender hierarchy on campus. Laura Meyers (1996) found a similar system operating at an elite university through the fraternities and enhanced by the liberal use of alcohol within the fraternity lifestyle. Notably, Tiana (a Searcher) was the only student in this study who commented on anything resembling this system:

> I think the idea that freshmen girls are fresh meat, that's rough.
> Everyone knows that. You come in and they tell you that. The guys
> consider you "fresh meat." That's the word they use. So, they tell you,
> watch out for the guys...all upper class males consider freshmen girls
> fresh meat because they're naive, they're new, and they can get in their
> pants, supposedly. But not me. They can do whatever they want with
> everyone else, but they're not getting too far with me. The senior guys
> that I have met are really good guys. They went through their hunting
> for fresh meat. See, they've already passed that stage. They did that.

When Sybill indicated that she had no male friends on campus because
she found them immature, she may have been alluding to what Tiana
describes. However, the most striking conclusion from the lack of discussion of this issue by all the other females in this study, is that they
have strategically avoided placing themselves in this situation. The
majority of them abhor the fraternity system and its attendant substance
abuse, and have nothing to do with it. They choose their friends carefully and demand that they are trustworthy. The intrinsic bonding develops a safer net of relationships, but, undoubtedly, their relationships are
also a result of reactive bonding, where this system that objectifies
women is acknowledged as a threat, and their friendships help buffer
and remove them from these types of peer relationships. While they may
all desire romantic relationships at some point in their lives, the HEOP
students narrated high levels of self-respect, resiliency, and strategic
instrumentalism, even in their relationships. Academic and career goals
took precedence over social distractions and stigmatizing situations that
pressed all around them in this elite environment.

CONCLUSION

Peer relationships for the HEOP students were a central experience, and
for many, they were as important to their education as the academics.
However, as for all students entering a new educational environment,
the paths to friendships were fraught with challenges. The HEOP
students were trying to break the academic and social codes as quickly
and skillfully as possible, but they were truly at a disadvantage because
they had little experience with elite institutions and because they were
faced with stigmatizing experiences on a daily basis. To counter this,
they employed all five of the identity functions which William Cross
and Linda Strauss (1998) described and which provided a useful frame
for examining the behaviors of the students in the establishment of
friendships.

While the students used all five functions, cycling through them on a
daily basis as needed, the intrinsic bonds, based on shared cultural,

racial, and ethnic features, that were formed with their HEOP peers during the summer program served best to carry them through the culture shock of fall semester. They made efforts to connect with the student body at-large, but appreciated most the comforts of being with clusters of students who were most like them. The HEOP students were able to successfully skirt around most problematic relationships by strategically selecting their friends and activities. At the backs of their minds were concerns about survival on this campus and in the future, and they didn't choose to depend on many people other than themselves. They were self-reliant and self-sufficient, seeking only those relationships that were earned through trust. These relationships helped to offset stigmatizing experiences that occurred on a daily basis and bolstered their resiliency.

CHAPTER 7

Good Enough:
Becoming Agents for Success

Students from nonprivileged backgrounds who did not want to forget [their pasts] often had nervous breakdowns. They could not bear the weight of all the contradictions they had to confront. They were crushed. More often than not, they dropped out with no trace of their inner anguish recorded, no institutional record of the myriad ways their take on the world was assaulted by an elite vision of class and privilege. The records merely indicated that, even after receiving financial aid and other support, these students simply could not make it, simply were not good enough.

—bell hooks, "Learning in the Shadow of Race and Class" (2000)

The previous chapters have woven together the strands of influence on the HEOP students as they labored to reap the rewards of their work at Ivy University. They were goal oriented and persistently strove to find ways to accommodate the academic and social demands on campus while maintaining their dignity and self-identity. Some were more skilled at this than others, but all of the students experienced this elite institute as a challenge that would hopefully be worth the emotional price they were paying.

The first part of this chapter highlights the emotional costs of attending this university. The "imposter syndrome" was identified by instructors and students as a response to being in an environment that often positioned these students as marginal participants or outsiders. In addition, the students experienced high levels of stress that made them question the value of being at Ivy University. Their ability to cope within this highly charged context once again demonstrated the resiliency of these students. They employed strategies to reduce the academic and cultural vulnerability and marginalization that they felt in this environment.

One of the most surprising incidents during my research became a flash point for the HEOP students' political mobilization and unity. It became a political strategy that allowed them to resist their positions of marginality and take a courageous step toward asserting their rightful place in this learning community. While it was a controversial move, it grabbed attention and focused the institute's energies on issues that mattered to these students. It is doubtful that they would have achieved this level of consideration otherwise.

Braided through the students' experiences was the HEOP staff and resources. The students' reliance on the support of this program will be underscored in the final section. While HEOP contributed to some extent to the stigmatization that the students felt, it was also identified by the students as one of the few resources on campus that sincerely cared about their well-being

THE EMOTIONAL COST OF COLLEGE

The Imposter Syndrome

Several of the English instructors from the summer program, who continued to work with the HEOP students within regular English courses during the fall semester, observed some of the internal questioning that these students experienced and best captured it by the phrase "imposter syndrome." Both of these instructors were doctoral students attending Ivy University and had sat, therefore, on both sides of the desk:

> *Ms. Smith*: I'm willing to bet you that a lot of them are really feeling like they don't belong. Even with the other minority students here. There's a real urban hip-hop culture here and...these people are clones of each other.... A lot of them [from the summer HEOP] will change the way they dress....A lot of them were feeling that they were alone, like everybody else is doing it, not that they really buy into it.

*   *   *

> *Ms. Jones*: I personally don't come from this culture of entitlement. I'm the first one in my family to reach this point of education and I've always suffered from what I think that a lot of the HEOP students suffer from, which is the imposter syndrome—feeling that somehow I got through the cracks and I really shouldn't be here. I felt that....I think that a lot of the HEOP students feel the same, too.

The instructors who spoke of the imposter syndrome observed a change in dress and behavior by HEOP students as a way to fit in with the culture of the campus, examples of code switching that could reduce the stigma of being perceived as too different.

The only Pleaser who voiced anything similar to the "imposter syndrome" was Veronika in this excerpt: "...like at home I joke more, but like in school I'm a little bit more conservative. I don't just let myself go like what I do at home....when I go outside, I know I can't 'cause of what people would say. I don't like people saying bad things about me." The other Pleasers may, in fact, have felt like imposters at times and employed various façades to mask this, but more often what they expressed were high levels of self-esteem, independence, and pride, well illustrated by Roberto who resisted his mother's wishes in order to follow his own dream:

> My mom is not exactly a rich person. We live okay, but that's not the way I want my life. I look at my mom and how we live....I just wanted more than selling drugs and stuff like that, so, it's not only her [his mom]. Today she thinks I do well in school because of her, but it's because of me.

Clarissa rejected joining a sorority because she was offended by the initiation rites: "I can't take people talking down to me and stuff like that." Similarly, Ileana realized that, "I don't like people giving me orders. I like doing my own things. I like doing things the way I like them being done." Panyos added a philosophical insight that also reflected a confidence in himself: "Yeh, I definitely like to take risks....If you win, you win. If you lose, you lose. You start out with nothing and you lose everything, you don't really lose anything." These students were willing to strike out on their own and bounce back when things didn't go as they planned, a measure of self-sufficiency and resiliency.

Of the Searchers, Tiana and Marie were both questioning their abilities to be students at Ivy University. Tiana was on shaky academic ground and was considering dropping out and going home before she blew her cover and everyone found out that she was an imposter:

> I don't think I'm very smart. I think I'm very stupid. After getting here, I realize I'm not as intelligent as I thought I was and that's why I want to get out of here. I want to get out of here ASAP [as soon as possible], before I prove to the rest of the world how dumb I am. Right now, it's my first semester. I'm proving it to myself. I don't want everyone to see how dumb I am. I don't think I'm smart enough to be here. I'll leave and go somewhere where I'll be where I belong.

Marie also felt challenged by the academic rigor, but was working through it, reassuring herself that others were feeling challenged, even though there was a reluctance to admit this among the HEOP students: "I'm not so disappointed. I know I'm not probably the only one that thinks it's real hard. It was kind of hard in catching up the work. I do what I can for now." And while Laila was holding on academically, she talked about her need to change her behavior depending on the situation, whether she was in class speaking with classmates or the professor, or with a group of HEOP friends. Jason, in his second year, reflected on the façade he created his first year:

> So, basically it's like my first semester. It's like I did all my school work and everything, and I applied to like clubs and everything. Just like if you looked basically, just like at me on the surface, like just based on the things that I did, it would seem like a normal college student. But it really wasn't like a normal college experience like first semester. Basically, I was just like, "I don't want to be here"' I mean, it's not something that I would transfer. It was just something that I said....So, first semester, I was pretty much just like, "I'll do my work. I'll get good grades. I'll worry about my future. But it's not something that I will like enjoy."

The Searchers, more than the Pleasers, were experiencing aspects of the imposter syndrome, as evidenced through their narrations of academic and social insecurity. They were actively feeling out how to best fit in.

Among the Skeptics, Teresa voiced her anger over the poor preparation for college she had received from her high school. She knew that Ivy University would stretch her abilities, but she had no idea how much until she had sat in her fall courses for a short time. She was particularly livid about the lack of depth in her English courses that had left her feeling the outsider in her courses, not even understanding common references to mythology or classics of literature to which most students at Ivy had been exposed during their high school years. So, while she did not identify herself as an imposter, Teresa clearly felt marginalized in this academic community and recognized how her weak high school curriculum had made her academically vulnerable. As a whole, the Skeptics seemed able to put their self-doubts and past histories behind them and focus on the present—doing their best at Ivy University. And the HEOP counselors tried to reassure the students during their individual sessions that these adjustments were normal and to just give themselves some time.

Stress

In the chapter introductory quotation, bell hooks (2000) poignantly expressed the emotional pain that students like those in HEOP endure at an elite university (here she refers to Stanford) where they are pressured to assimilate. Despite the strong levels of self-esteem that many of the HEOP students possessed, their dialogues were laced with insecurities and stresses that accompanied their identity negotiations. Change does not occur without a cost, and these students risked a tremendous amount to attend Ivy University. We have already seen how stressful long distance relationships, separation from family and friends, and the culture shock of entering an elite university could be, and their struggles to strategically maneuver through these challenges. As intelligent and innately skilled as they were, they pushed themselves to perform at the level required by the perceived expectations of the institution, their parents, their professors, their peers, and themselves. This often required that they employ *all* of the identity functions—buffering, bonding, bridging, code switching, and individualism—on a regular basis. Their voices below provide glimpses of their perceptions of the underlying currents of stress with which they lived and tried to cope.

Stress came in many different forms and elicited a variety of responses among the Pleasers. Several, like Mai in this excerpt, were questioning their place at Ivy University:

> Last night a lot of us got together and we were like, "Why are we coming here?"...I don't know. It's so stressful. Sometimes I don't want to be here. But I knew that I had to go to college....Sometimes you feel like you're really happy to be here and because of the tests and homework, why am I coming here?

They questioned each of their actions, searching for ways to more successfully bridge the expectations: "I think a lot about what happened, what did I do today, how is it, how could I have done it differently...stuff like that."

Many students attributed the high levels of stress to the competitive nature of many of the students. Luc, who transferred to Ivy in her fourth year, identified this as problematic and was further perplexed about her relationships with peers. When I asked her to describe students at Ivy University, she replied:

> I'm the wrong person to ask because I've been so isolated. They're okay....There's a lot more stress here [compared to her previous college]. So, I don't know. Just my class, they're very competitive. They

> [the students] watch every move you make in class....And students here, especially my class, they been here, most of them since freshman year. They know each other too long. And I'm here, I see that they look at me strangely. Like, "where you coming from? Why haven't we seen her?"....Yeh, I don't get along with them too well. I got along with a couple people, but not a lot....Because I'm new here, they should come instead of me asking them to come to me. If they come to me, that's okay, because I don't come to them.

Paolo reflected the serious state of flux in which he found himself and delivered the most extreme response to stress when answering a question about what he was learning at Ivy University: "Different ways to commit suicide. Different things you can do...On my hall, I know there's quite a few people who seem depressed." I took his comments seriously, but he resisted suggestions about counseling because he had tried it last year and they had wanted to hospitalize him. He was working with the HEOP staff to address his identity issues and the emotional crises that resulted, and this was not the first nor the worst depression that he'd experienced, as these comments indicated: "I wake up to go running....I do it whenever I feel extremely stressed and suicidal....I end up going to the bridge which is where my first preference is going to be [to commit suicide]....Life's a total bitch and then you die. Literal, horrible, ugly death." Paolo's painful responses are a stark depiction of the reality of male students committing suicide on campuses today that must be more openly discussed and acknowledged in order to combat it. There has been an alarming rise in the numbers of young males, ages 15 through 24, committing suicide in the past two decades. It's the second leading cause of death on campuses, behind accidental death. About 16 out of 100,000 males in this age group commit suicide each year, markedly higher, especially on college campuses, than for females and three times higher than in 1960 (American Federation for Suicide Prevention; National Mental Health Association, 1997). As Janie Ward (2000) points out, students must be taught how to become resilient, and this begins with acknowledging the oppressive situations they face.

Howard Greene (1998) found that students at select colleges face an extraordinary amount of stress:

> ... in the demanding social hothouse of the college campus. For some minority students, a feeling of alienation and emotional depression because of their different ethnic, racial, or economic backgrounds presents the potential for serious repercussions. I have found that many troubled minority students will not seek help from professionals on campus out of a sense of shame, failure, or a culturally bound preju-

dice against psychological help. Appropriate role models are crucial to encourage these students to seek personal support (p.210).

Paolo was attempting to cope with ethnic, racial, and economic issues that Greene mentioned, with even more stigmatization generated by sexual identity issues. Fortunately, he confided in the HEOP counselors who were the closest role models he might find on campus, because he found the medical resources and intervention too intimidating to access. In addition, he lacked strong peer bonds with students who shared his concerns.

Among the Searchers, Tiana also raised the issue of student suicides, especially at Ivy League schools:

> They shouldn't have let this whole college thing get so far that students are killing themselves because they don't feel like their lives mean anything. That's sad. That's exactly what college does. It makes you feel like you're worth nothing. You are one little fish in a big pond and, if you're lucky, you'll get a job after college. Now why am I leaving college with a $15,000 debt if I'm not going to find a job? I might as well go home and work.

While she was not suicidal, Tiana always felt stress around trying to find a social/academic balance in her life. In fact, she missed many of our interview appointments and was constantly rescheduling for which she apologized: "...but you see how I run around everywhere." She indicated that low self-esteem was probably behind much of her behavior and that she sabotaged herself.

Finances came to the fore as one of the major stressors for some of the Searchers, unlike the Pleasers. Tiana had to rely on her friends to provide such things as copying: "Like I don't have money to make copies. My teachers just don't seem to understand that there are people with no flex accounts." Yasmin had a problem with credit card debt because she had to take an advance on her credit card to help out her married sister back home who had young children. She complained that her family assumed that because she had a job, she had money to loan. Martine struggled with financial aid to clear up problems with missing paperwork, but ended up having to work to make ends meet.

Several Searchers complained that their parents, because they were immigrants, pressured them for academic success. They were working to appease them: "I do get stressed from the work but I know what I have to do because if not, I feel like I'm disappointing myself and my friends and my family, especially." Others, like Laila, wistfully wished to return to the security of home:

> At some point, I just wish that I could go home and lie on my bed, not a dorm bed. Watch my TV at home. I have a TV here, but it's not the same. Sometimes I get really homesick and I can't keep my feeling to myself....I'll just tell him [her HEOP counselor] how my classes are going and if I'm discouraged at this point and if I'm thinking of dropping out or something. Like last week, I was so discouraged. "I'm taking the next bus home." [Laughs.]...I agree that the work loads are supposed to be challenging, so that you'll be able to meet the needs of the working career and such. I agree that it's challenging, but I sometime question how far I can meet those challenges.

Ironically, the lack of time was identified as contributing to stress as frequently as the unfamiliar abundance of time: "I have too much down time. That's the problem with college. Things are so spread out. Time is given to you and you do whatever you want with that time."

The Skeptics seemed the least surprised by the stress of the college environment and resigned themselves to working hard. In fact, Sybill indicated that she was too busy to be stressed; she didn't have time to think about it. Teresa recalled that when she was heavily involved with athletics in high school, she also felt this way: "Life was so much more simpler. I didn't have all the extra time to have all these strange complexes. I didn't really worry about half the stuff I worry about now." Of the Skeptics, she sounded the most affected by stress. She had trouble with her throat and her doctor diagnosed it as anxiety and stress related. In trying to identify why she felt so much stress, Teresa stated:

> The stress that I can see is that sometimes I feel that it's not fair because other kids can like do average in classes without worrying about losing aid, but I have to keep a "B" average in order to stay in school because even though HEOP is only paying like $700 of my tuition, that's $700 that I don't have to pay. So, I'm like, okay, I'm running around here losing my mind cause I'm getting "C's" on my tests and other kids are like completely failing and they're having a ball. I know it's not the right thing to be jealous of, but it is kind of stressful when you have to constantly not worry, but I have to work twice as hard as everybody else cause I have to maintain a certain grade average.

Of course, other students had to maintain passing grade levels or face probation or suspension from their programs or loss of financial aid, but Teresa perceived more stress on HEOP students because their participation in HEOP could be terminated if they did not maintain their grades.

Coping Strategies

The students employed a variety of strategies in order to cope with stress. Some preferred solitude, a function of individualism. Among the Pleasers, Paolo indicated that he ran whenever he really felt bad. In addition, he was the only one of the Pleasers who indicated that he drank, and he admitted that he did this rarely and only when he was really down. Veronika indicated that when she was stressed she would study (!) and listen to music. Her single room allowed her the solitude to work through her anxieties. Others relied on the bonding functions for relief and release, which meant talking and sharing experiences with friends from common backgrounds.

Most of the Searchers indicated that they didn't have too much time to relieve stress, which was part of the stress. However, the solitary pursuit of art was helpful to two of the young women. Martine found little time for things other than work, but described herself as "...a big music person." When she felt stressed, she wouldn't discuss it with friends; she coped by herself: "If I can't cope with it, I have a book and I'll just write it down. I'll write, 'I am so pissed!', the date and time." Jason found some of his stress alleviated by his bonding friendships with other male Asian students. He spent most of his evenings with them in the library, a comfortable routine.

Because few of the Skeptics spoke about stress, few methods for coping were shared. While Nicole, who was eager to graduate because she felt "frustrated" by being on campus, indicated that hanging out and talking with friends made her feel better, Teresa spent time with the more solitary outlets of music and writing, and couldn't talk with her family about what she was feeling. A number of the HEOP students felt that their families were unable to comprehend the type and depth of stress they felt in this academic environment. Stacey felt that "tuning out" was a popular response: " A lot of people just decide, like OK, listen, I'm stressed. I'm not doing anything. I'm going to sit here and just chill."

The HEOP students constructed lifestyles within the confines of their new environment that would allow them to cope as effectively as possible with the tremendous pressures of being a student in this rarified space. Some, as individuals, naturally chose coping strategies that allowed them to recharge their batteries alone in quiet reflection, while others found strength and comfort in bonding with friends who were experiencing similar stresses.

TAKING A STAND: FLASH POINT OF ACTION

Even though academics and emergent student relationships consumed most of the students' early months on campus, they were not apathetic and oblivious to the political world around them, contrary to the picture of apathetic students that is often painted by the popular media. The rising awareness of the complexity of the social and political mores and attitudes that impacted the daily lives of these students indicated an increasingly active engagement with the larger issues of life beyond academics, issues that may have not been consciously noticed up to this point. Several of them pointedly critiqued the American Dream, even though most of them believed that if one worked hard enough, one could achieve success, however the person defined it. There was an awareness of the benefits attributed to affirmative action and a felt need to counter the stigmatization that arose from the perception that the HEOP students were only admitted *because* of affirmative action. They found themselves frequently "fronting," assuming an academic or social identity that proved to others their right to be at Ivy University. They also experienced a fatigue of representation, always expected to speak for and behave in ways that represented their respective minority group(s).

Throughout all of this, how did students locate agency, the ability to act within a system that often demanded one oppose it in order to maintain one's identity? Lawrence Grossberg (1993) calls agency the urge to create "...maps of identification and belonging" (p.96) on the part of modern individuals whose identities are composed of: "...the subject as a unified source of knowledge and experience; the agent as a position of activity; and the self as the bearer of a social identity" (p. 95). Grossberg indicates that these maps are "...mattering maps, which define where and how one can and does invest, and where and how one is empowered, made into an agent" (p. 101). What he refers to are maps of power, how power is allocated within a space, and how individuals become agents for shifting the allocation of power.

A serendipitous event occurred during the second semester of my research that served as a "**flash point**" of agency for the HEOP students. Opening the local newspaper one morning, I was treated to a photograph from the previous day that featured one of the HEOP students from my study participating in a sit-in at the Ivy University administration building. This event captured a sense of Philip Altbach's (1993) observations of the contemporary college culture, but provided fresh hope where he saw little:

> [T]here is a kind of struggle going on for the soul of the university in the United States. Although there is no flash point of political crisis, as was the case in the 1960s, the American university is profoundly divided. Undergraduate students are bifurcated into increasingly separate ethnic and racial enclaves. A not insignificant proportion of white students resent perceived "special opportunities" for underrepresented minority students and fear undue competition from high-achieving Asian-American students. With many students working while studying and most more concerned with private concerns than with community issues, there is no center to campus life (p. 219).

This sit-in attracted students from all racial and ethnic groups represented on campus. As Altbach states, there may be no discernible "center" to contemporary campus life, but this incident proved that there are still issues around which the majority of students can unite.

While I was conducting the interviews on campus fall semester, there were rumblings of discontent with how the administration was (mis)handling issues of deep concern to the members of the "minority" community. As spring semester commenced, the student body president wrote an editorial for the student paper that blasted the leadership of the university for "increasingly put[ting] students' concerns about diversity at the bottom of their institutional agendas." She listed several examples of the administration's lack of concern about diversity and how damaging this was to the quality of educational discourse on the campus. The president of Ivy University fired back a response in the next issue of the student paper and indicated that all of her concerns were being addressed, although he admitted that they had not moved with enough speed on some concerns. He closed by emphasizing the priority of diversity initiatives to him personally and the campus as a whole. Within two weeks, the minority student board (composed of students from Black and Latino/a groups on campus) had distributed hundreds of flyers around campus pointing to the longstanding racism of the institution. They claimed to have taken this action because they were frustrated by the lack of movement and communication over the last year and a half when they'd been trying to get the administration to address issues. An article in the student newspaper at this time contained responses from university officials to five of the stated concerns on the flyer. When responding to the issue of the small number of minority freshmen, the director of admissions stated that, "We're doing as much, or a little more, than in the past....I think it's just a perception problem." Other concerns were the lack of African Studies, a discrepancy in the security charges levied on minority and "majority" social events, a lack of institute programming that recognized significant cultural events for Blacks and Latinos/as, the paucity of minority administrators, and the inadequate allocation of resources for the HEOP, including their physical space in the basement. While the flyer incident provoked considerable backlash due to its inflammatory nature, an editorial in the student paper claimed that this was the most political activity the campus had witnessed in years. It also claimed that a perpetual lack of communication between the leadership of the university and the students had created much of the problem.

The sit-in occurred several days after this last round of public airing of the university's dirty linen. It now became visible to not just the campus community, but to the larger community in which Ivy University resides. The 200 plus students who participated in the four hour sit-in presented the president with a list of demands which were negotiated in private, but on the spot, and produced an agreement that the institute would address all of the students' concerns in a timely fashion (usually within the year) that would include students on many of the decision making committees and groups. Members of the administration and the student news reporters complimented the students for their "peaceful" demonstration. This evoked howls of outrage from the HEOP students at a focus group a month later:

> *Sybill:* Yeh, that really offended me. People were like, "I just can't believe you were so peaceful." What did they think we were going to do, like break out the windows?

> *Nicole:* I mean like, when we first came in there, were you like, when we first came in, did you hear everyone like locking their doors? Like closing their doors, locking their purses up, you know? It was just like...

> *Stacey:* I know. We attend the same school. I mean, I sit in classes with some of these people. You don't have to act like that.

The president of the student body, who chose not to attend the sit-in because she had "personal misgivings" about demonstrations of this kind, regretted that decision. In a follow-up article for the student paper, she stated, " A lot can be learned from the students who were at the sit-in—lessons of determination, courage and conviction. They sure taught me."

Months before this event, several of the HEOP instructors and counselors had shared ideas about the growing political awareness of the students. An instructor observed that:

> [A] lot of them were so afraid of this, so afraid of their own power, for whatever reason. Maybe they had been discouraged at high school. They didn't want to step outside of those boundaries for fear they would be punished.

And a HEOP counselor expressed her delight when students finally begin to assume some political savvy:

> [O]ne of the things that makes you extremely proud is when a student sits here and says, "You know, I just figured it out. Politics isn't just about voting and it's not just about setting policies and stuff like that. But, politics is about everyday life," he says, "where you work at, where you go to school at, how it's run." He says, "Everything has politics involved in it in some shape or form or another." I was like, "Wow, that's phenomenal!" It's basically how the power structure works and power doesn't necessarily mean all the people with the money.

This sit-in, the flash point that united students and brought them to new levels of political consciousness and agency, was almost as meaningful for the HEOP personnel as the students. They were proud of the students' mobilization and that the students coordinated the event without their help and involvement, which could have placed the office in an awkward position between the administration and the students.

The organizers of the sit-in wrote a letter to the editor of the student paper that week that revealed the depth of their awareness of the oppression within the institution:

> Subtle institutionalized racism is a real facet of American society. It manifests itself in the way we feel when our needs are ignored—it is when we face barriers in this institution that cause us to struggle, it is the lack of role models, the lack of this institution's support, the lack of fulfilled promises which causes us to feel this way.

Although the students were members of the academic community, they felt consigned to the margins and, as a result, ironically forced into the eye of the storm. These students were able to create a "mattering map" that united them as agents under one banner for a moral cause. One of the students in a sit-in photo carried a banner that read: "Don't verbalize, strategize!" They were using their collective identity to "battle for resources made scarce by elite control" (Zinn, 1980, p. 574), developing yet another strategy of resistance that could ultimately assist in the achievement of their goals. Stuart Hall (1998) recognizes this process:

> I speak of the process of identification, of feeling yourself through the contingent, antagonistic, and conflicting sentiments of which human beings are made up. Identification means that you are called in a certain way, interpolated in a certain way: "you, this time, in this space, for this purpose, by this barricade with these folks." That's what is at stake in political struggle... (p. 290).

It was remarkable that these students, some Black, some Latino/a, some White, and a few Asian (although noticeably smaller in number), from different historical, geographical, and experiential locations, were able to come together for this brief time to unite in this political move. "Education has always been considered...an extension of a political project" (Torres, 1996, p. 315). This was truly a flash point on this campus.

Chandra Mohanty (1989) acknowledges the challenge that "marginal people" experience within higher education when attempting to carve out spaces for *education*, not just schooling (Shujaa, 1994), within the academy. She would see the students' demands for more diversity within the student and faculty bodies, and more courses that reflect their histories and interests, as part of the emancipatory work that needs to be done on campuses. The results of this labor could be that: "...new analytic spaces [are] opened up in the academy, spaces that make possible thinking of knowledge as praxis, of knowledge as embodying the very seeds of transformation and change" (p. 185). Like other researchers (Apple, 1979, 1995; Bourdieu & Passeron, 1977; Freire, 1973; Giroux, 1983; Grossberg, 1993; Hall, 1998; Morrow & Torres, 1998; Torres, 1996, among others), Mohanty sees education as a political struggle where power is a fundamental source of friction as groups of people vie for recognition within the limited resources of curriculum and pedagogical space. I was heartened to see that the students did not back away from this challenge and responsibility and, for at least that day, were able to engage in a praxis of collective opposition.

Most of the HEOP freshmen participated in this political act, but, as noted above, there were few Asian students involved. The Asian student organizations were not a part of the minority student board who organized the sit-in. They also were not considered underrepresented as a collective group because they were attending Ivy University in a higher percentage than is present in the larger society. It is conceivable that they were perceived to be a threat to the organizing groups because of their numbers and their stereotyped "model minority" status, along the lines that Altbach (1993) observed.

HEOP: A SUPPORTIVE SAFETY NET

Without HEOP, I question whether these freshmen students would have rallied together to support the sit-in. The summer program began the students' relationship with HEOP, and the fall semester continued through the creation of some sort of supportive community feeling for most of the HEOP students. They have shared how many of them nurtured their friendships and the bonds that were created with fellow HEOP students. These bonds were critical to their ability to mobilize politically. There was unity in their shared membership in HEOP.

Amid the decisions and daily conflicts that faced the HEOP students, the HEOP program positioned itself as a central resource for accessible student support and guidance. The HEOP staff provided ongoing advising for each student, and workshops on various aspects of college were held periodically throughout the semester. All HEOP students were invited to attend these sessions, and they drew primarily first year students, but always some upper level students as well. In addition, there were newsletters several times a semester and a web site that kept the students informed of what was happening within the HEOP office.

In one way or another, each HEOP student utilized the resources of the program. Beyond the financial assistance with tuition, room and board, and books for first year students, the counseling and workshops were of primary interest. The Pleasers seemed to make the most consistent use of this resource. Mai indicated that, "I have my own counselor, so I can go here every time I feel stressful." She also found the workshops about financial aid and final exams helpful. Luc appreciated the assistance with course selection that was extended, especially with the difficulty she was having integrating with her department. She felt lucky that there was a casual, open-door policy that made it non-threatening for students to use services. Most of the Pleasers took advantage of the range of free services that were offered, from counseling, to tutoring and study groups. Many would drop in at the office at least once a week, and Tran commented that, "...we get first priority, all kinds of stuff to help us." He met with his HEOP advisor once or twice a week to discuss problems with courses and some personal issues. Several of the students made strong connections with an advisor because of their similar ethnic origins, and they were upset when she left the university. The difficulty of finding appropriate role models on campus increased the sense of loss when one of them left.

The Searchers echoed many of the Pleasers' comments, but seemed somewhat more guarded in reaching out for the support and assistance that was extended to them. While many of the Pleasers were frustrated that HEOP was viewed by many other students as an affirmative action program for less able students, they were less inclined to let this bother them than the Searchers. It was more difficult for the Searchers to separate themselves from the perceived stigma around the program. Most of them pointedly discussed their embarrassment about the tuition support and the stereotype that they were less qualified to be on this campus. Alicia had quickly separated herself from HEOP, the program (other than the financial assistance) and students, and admitted that this made her transition to college by herself difficult. Laila best expressed the discomfort that many of the Searchers revealed by describing HEOP this way: "So, you're given a stereotype that being a HEOP student, that's the only way you were able to come to this school, that you would never have the credentials to come to this school otherwise—automatically if you're a minority, like being African-American in the HEOP program." Despite this perception, most of the Searchers saw their HEOP counselors on a consistent schedule and attended some of the workshops and other activities. They valued the personalized support that they received. Jason became proud of his ability to receive all of this support and financial aid that allowed him to escape his past and take advantage of all that Ivy University could offer. Martine avoided mentioning that she was part of HEOP to other students, but was bothered that she was always trying to justify her presence on this campus and in this program: "I know I'm working hard, and it's not even about the grades. It's more about the financial aid. That's why I feel I'm in HEOP." The Searchers struggled to find a comfortable space for themselves within the contexts of HEOP and Ivy University.

The Skeptics forged tight bonds with their HEOP peers and counselors, and expressed not just an awareness of the stereotyping of HEOP participants, but an anger toward the injustice of these misperceptions. Damon advised me to not get him started on the cons of HEOP, but launched into a heated explanation of the stigmatization of HEOP:

> I have big problems with HEOP. It's a good program, don't get me wrong. But, there's EOP for the state schools and HEOP for the regular [private] schools....You have to have a academic disadvantage to get in EOP in the state schools. HEOP is not really that way, and you also have to have a financial need. So, therefore, the HEOP people think that because you don't have millions of dollars you don't have the mental capacity to be on the same level of other students. That is the biggest bunch of "B.S." I've ever heard in my life....And there's also the perception that every HEOP student is African-American, which is totally untrue. There's just not enough African-Americans in NY State. There's more Caucasians than African-Americans in NY State. So, I mean it's been associated with a program for poor, ignorant African-American and Hispanic. That's what it's been labeled as and it's not

that, and it's not supposed to be that, but state schools confirm that. I'm really upset with that.

In this excerpt, Damon refers to HEOP allowing some private schools to have higher academic admission standards for their HEOP students than state schools. Among the private schools, HEOP does attract a more diverse population than EOP at state schools, but it would be untrue to say that EOP was strictly African-American and Hispanic. The mission of HEOP is to provide educational opportunity for students from economically and educationally disadvantaged backgrounds, but the guidelines for recruiting these students become a little murky when different institutions have different standards to which they are held. In addition to Damon's ire, Teresa has already expressed her irritation and high levels of stress over being held to higher academic standards than many of the non-HEOP students once she was admitted to Ivy University. However, she felt pride in her ability to hold her own with other students, despite her minimal high school preparation.

Regardless of the stereotypes and stigma surrounding HEOP participation, the Skeptics did not let this prevent them from making appropriate use of the resources. Stacey indicated that HEOP was value-neutral: "I don't mind. I don't like the label that other people give it. Like it's nothing to be ashamed of. There's no real good or bad thing about it." She found it easy to connect with the counselors and didn't hesitate to talk with them about problems. Teresa and Nicole doubted whether anyone else at the university would provide the kind of support they'd received from the HEOP staff. Sybill recognized that students had to take the initiative in seeking out the support, but talked about the strong academic and personal support that she'd received. In looking back on his four years in the program, James was most grateful for the tutoring that HEOP provided. He found it comical that other Ivy students complained to him that they hadn't received this level of support: "I'm like, what are you complaining about? You're saying your father pulls in a half a million dollars a year, and you're upset that the university isn't giving you as much financial aid? Come on!" Vanessa explained that because she had to fight to get into HEOP, she was motivated to work hard, to do her best, and to achieve strong grades.

In conjunction with HEOP, the learning support department that had been centrally involved in the summer program offered an in-depth study skills course that began mid-semester and ran for seven weeks. Students voluntarily signed up and received one credit for attending the class twice a week. The advertised intent of the course was to develop personalized strategies for any type of academic work. Very few of the HEOP students had registered for the fall session. Only Ileana and Tiana indicated at the second interview that they were enrolled in this course. Ileana's expressed goal was to learn to manage her time. Tiana indicated that it wasn't helping yet and that she found it "tedious." Stacey and Teresa were interested in the course but had missed the fall session because they were confused about when it was offered. And Clarissa realized in hindsight that this might have been a helpful option. She revealed that her courses were not going as well as she had expected and speculated about the reasons for this: "I've been thinking about this all week.... It's partly, I guess I'm not studying enough, but even when I do study enough, I don't see the grades coming up. Unless it's that I'm not studying the proper way or something." Of interest to me was the lack of involvement by the HEOP students in this well-publicized course. A possible explanation is that the students viewed this as a remedial course that would further stigmatize them as academically deficient. However, most of them felt that they were working hard, but doing well grade-wise in this first semester. At mid-semester, most of them did not perceive a need for this course. The fact that over half of the HEOP students were on the dean's list at the end of the first semester was testament to the effectiveness of their efforts, buoyed by the support and encouragement they received from the HEOP staff. The open-door, casual, and confidential support of this office was comfortably accessible and the students relied on it to be their constant in a sea of rolling inconsistencies. With the number of adjustments to college life that demanded immediate assessment and action from these students, their levels of confusion and perplexity were often quite high. HEOP was the port in the raging storm that extended a hand to intervene and assist them with academic or personal dilemmas. Ironically, it was a source of increased stigmatization for the HEOP students, but it was also a source of collective identity that enabled them to become agents for success.

CONCLUSION

In trying to live up to the expectations of parents, professors, and one's self-image, these students all experienced high levels of stress. This was one of the shared experiences of all the HEOP students. Even though they realized that college would be an intellectual challenge, many of them were surprised by the amount of stress that they were experiencing. In order to prove themselves, most of these students responded by trying harder, studying longer and trying to work more strategically. This, in turn, often increased the level of stress. Developing coping mechanisms became another task in learning how to be a college student. The significant outcome was that they all developed successful coping strategies, and they never threw up their hands and quit. Pride and perseverance could have been group mottoes.

The well-orchestrated sit-in at the administration building that attracted the participation of most of the HEOP students spoke volumes about this group of individuals. It was a risky, political act, but the sheer mass of students who participated made it less intimidating. However, the fledgling political mobilization was not entirely successful. Their network of support was missing a significant group, the Asian students. Whether their lack of inclusion was one sided, or reciprocal, is difficult to determine. But, it points out the difficulty of rallying all subordinated groups to any single cause when resources are perceived to be competed for because they are limited (McCarthy, 1988). Nonetheless, the resulting orderly and calm demonstration earned the president's signature on the students' list of five demands, all related to improving minority visibility on campus. The HEOP students perceived that the administration's resolution of these demands could have a dramatic effect on the quality of their educational experience, improving the academic and social environment. Perhaps they had begun to realize what bell hooks (2000) so eloquently expressed about her experience at Stanford:

> Slowly, I began to understand fully that there was no place in academe for folks from working-class backgrounds who did not wish to leave the past behind. That was the price of the ticket. Poor students would be welcome at the best institutions of higher learning only if they were willing to surrender memory, to forget the past and claim the assimilated present as the only worthwhile and meaningful reality (p. B16).

The HEOP students were not willing to "surrender memory" or assimilate elite standards that would require them to compromise their identities. This demonstration was a stand, a significant learning experience, a flash point that united most of the diverse student body in a political act of resistance to oppression and marginalization within the academic setting.

The extent of identity work in which these students engaged on a daily basis, the negotiations that were required each and every day which tapped the functions of bonding, buffering, code switching, and bridging, made a "home" base a necessity, not a luxury, if one were to maintain aspects of one's individuality and to survive the critical first months of college. Most of them found this in HEOP. They recognized the irony of their situation, that the very program that provided them a safe haven and compassionate understanding on this campus was also one of the major sources of stigmatizing stereotypes. However, some of their best role models and empathetic mentors came from the HEOP personnel who were among the few employees on campus who truly understood aspects of these students' experiences. Most of the students responded positively to this support and used it as a springboard for success. They were active agents, working strategically with the available resources, especially HEOP, to achieve their goals at this institution and to prove what they already suspected to be true, that they were, in fact, "good enough."

CHAPTER 8

Conclusion

By identity, I mean an evolving nexus where all the forces that constitute my life converge in the mystery of self: my genetic makeup, the nature of the man and woman who gave me life, the culture in which I was raised, people who have sustained me and people who have done me harm, the good and ill I have done to others and to myself, the experience of love and suffering—and much, much more. In the midst of that complex field, identity is a moving intersection of the inner and outer forces that make me who I am, converging in the irreducible mystery of being human.

–Parker Palmer, The Courage to Teach (1998)

Within the structured confines of an elite university, students from socioeconomic and educationally disadvantaged backgrounds construct their identities amidst mixed cultural messages that invite them to participate in this academic experience, yet pressure them to surrender their former identities in order to survive in this rarified atmosphere. In adjusting to this environment, the students experience culture shocks that force them to question who they are and how much they are willing to compromise in order to achieve their academic and career goals. This book has explored the struggles, challenges, responses, successes, and failures of a group of 23 students from the Higher Education Opportunity Program (HEOP), a compensatory program co-sponsored by New York State and by Ivy University, the private university these students attended. Their narrations of their initiations into this college experience provide insight into the remarkable character and tenacity of these young adults living on the margins of campus culture as they devise strategies and coping mechanisms that enable them to retain their core identities and to become resilient learners. The HEOP students have earned their places at the table of this elite university.

The conclusions I derived from the time I spent observing and interviewing these students are a result of their dialogues viewed through my interpretive lens that has been shaped by years of experience within the higher educational system and by my exposure to the plentiful research and theorizing that has bloomed in the many areas of critical, cultural sociology and education. Two pivotal themes emerged from a synthesis of all of the narrations and observations. First, and most central, is that these students' identities are far more complex and resilient than what is conveyed through research, media, and assumptions held within educational communities. These entities do not know these students well and do not expend much effort to get to know them better. While there is a wealth of work that explores aspects of various groups of students, this work is often limited to the deficit model that explores why students don't succeed within our societal systems rather than examining the students who are succeeding and the conditions necessary to ensure their success.

In chapter 1, the term "disadvantaged" was given an historical context of referring to students who were deficient in background and/or ability. Throughout this text, I have applied a different context for this term. I define this group to be disadvantaged by institutionalized systems within society that have devalued their cultural capital (Bourdieu, 1977) and worldviews. Rather than a deficit model that blames the victims, my perspective finds that these students have been marginalized by oppressive power systems (Ivy University in this case) that function to preserve the dominant ideologies and status quo. In doing so, the identities of these students are rarely noticed or taken into consideration when designing educational programs that include them. This group is often ascribed monolithic characteristics that mask and collapse vibrant cultural identities. Only a highly visible student disturbance evoked the appropriate level of institutional response to the needs of these students. This flash point held the potential to shift the power dynamics, even if only so slightly.

The second theme is that in order to maintain these complex identities and to achieve their educational goals, these students construct systems of *strategic instrumentalism* that resist and oppose the institutionalized academic and social orders that frequently stigmatize and oppress them. These systems are in fact strategic when the students are then able to function successfully within these contexts. However, the trial and error process subjects the students to inevitable non-strategic behaviors that can derail their efforts along the way. Higher education can help with the success and retention of marginalized students if we understand how to assist, not block, their efforts and how to teach students to become more strategically effective.

Implications of this research for educators, institutions of higher education, and educational policy makers are many and will be pointed out in the next section. Toward the end of the chapter, the limitations of this study and further questions will be highlighted. These HEOP students teach us valuable lessons about social justice and equitable access to opportunity for all members of our society and they need to be better understood.

SIGNIFICANT FINDINGS AND LESSONS LEARNED

Resilient Identities

I began this book by identifying the students who participated in my research as resilient (Ward, 1999, 2000) learners who actively engage in the construction of their identities from the margins of an oppressive elite university. I defined identity construction as "an individual and collective pursuit that coalesces around an orchestration of contextual elements that are experienced through the family, society, and within one's geographical, historical, and situational location" (p.3). In the introductory quotation for this chapter, Parker Palmer attributes more humanistic aspects, especially the concept of "mystery," into the complexity of identity. In this research, I learned that these students are truly a mystery, sometimes to themselves, and usually to those around them on this elite campus. Taking apart pieces of this mystery as they were revealed and coming to better understand the significance of these pieces in the educational setting, was important work and the heart of this project.

Complex Identities within Three Distinct Groups

The tremendous diversity of the HEOP population, especially in terms of ethnic affiliations and countries of origin, is virtually unexplored and unrecorded, yet it is significant to the educational outcomes for these students. In chapter 2, the family histories of these students revealed three differently situated groups, based on their immigration status. Their experiences, even within these three groups, were not uniform. However, there were some striking differences between these groups and how their families operated within their locations in economic and educational systems of this country, which was explored in chapter 3.

The first group of nine students, the "Pleasers," were all first generation immigrants who were born in countries other than the United States. Three of them claimed Black racial/ethnic identities, two were Latino/a, and four were Asian (three of whom were refugees from Vietnam). The Pleasers often found school in the United States less challenging than their "home" schools and were able to navigate the educational systems fairly successfully on their own. Concurrently, teachers generally found these new immigrants easier and more enjoyable to work with (Suarez-Orozco, 1991). Their parents inherently believed in the "American Dream," that the road to success (i.e. status mobility) was a public throughway open to all, but that education was the magic ticket that would take their children farther and faster. These families held a positive dual frame of reference (Ogbu, 1991), the perspective of having lived somewhere else and, by comparison, perceiving that the United States held more opportunity. The major educational stumbling block could be attributed to subtle discrimination in how schools accommodated the different language needs of these students (Suarez-Orozco, 1991) resulting in inappropriate placement either in classes designed to teach non-English speakers or in holding students back because they were perceived to lack the necessary skills/ability to be placed in age appropriate classes. The parents were genuinely interested in the education their children received, but they often lacked the time or skills to intervene.

The seven "Searchers," the second group, were second generation immigrants whose parents had been born outside of the United States, but immigrated before the students were born. These students had always been citizens of the U.S. and their racial/ethnic identities were more difficult to express. Five were of Latino/a descent, one was Black, and one was a mix of Asian and White parentage. Although this group also held a positive dual frame of reference (Ogbu, 1991), their families had experienced the leveled aspirations of having lived in the United States for a generation and they were not as optimistic as the Pleasers. They were the most complicated group in terms of experiences and behaviors, a point that has not escaped a number of researchers, most notably Alejandro Portes (1995) and Ruben Rumbaut (1996). Both of them have described the "segmented assimilation" patterns of the second generation immigrants, how these immigrant groups choose different ways to assimilate (or not) into the mainstream culture. Their work demonstrates that assimilation is not a given for immigrants, but upward or downward status mobility hangs on these choices. The Searchers verified this dilemma and, to counter the negative effects of assimilating into the "wrong elements" of the culture, their parents practiced "selective acculturation" (Portes & Rumbaut, 1996) by limiting their children's exposure to what they perceived as the negative environmental factors of their urban neighborhoods and schools. Their dream was to escape the fate of becoming permanent members of the "underclass" by selectively taking advantage of the opportunities provided in this society and by avoiding the pitfalls. Schooling was not free from problems, but this group of parents had a better vantage point from which to navigate the system and assist their children, and their children escaped most of the transitional problems that the Pleasers experienced.

Both of the Pleasers and the Searchers were *voluntary* immigrants (Ogbu, 1991), arriving in the United States through choice and expecting to find a better life here than in their countries of origin. On this, they differed distinctly from the third group, the "Skeptics." These seven students were from families who had been historically disenfranchised within this society for generations, all of them claiming African American identities—John Ogbu's *involuntary* immigrants. These families had *negative* dual frames of reference (Ogbu), having experienced generations of leveled aspirations in this society and understanding that this was not a temporary situation that would be removed solely by achieving educational credentials. Some Skeptics spoke of how their educational achievements were viewed negatively by their peers and that they had to counteract this pressure to not succeed in school, much like Signithia Fordham (1997) and John Ogbu (1988, 1991) have reported. The Skeptics positioned themselves, as best they could in urban schools with limited resources, to be on the top academic tracks, despite a number of teachers who tried to limit their options from early on.

Family dynamics were determined by the effects of immigration, cultural beliefs and values, and the composition of the family. It was significant that eight of the nine Pleasers had two parent families, while this was true for only four of the Searchers, and one of the Skeptics. In addition, three students were raised by their grandmothers in the absence of their parents. A number of the Pleasers had lived apart from their parents who came ahead to seek employment in the United States. Despite the tremendous variation of educational achievement among the parents of all of these students, most of them were in the volatile service economy, which meant that they were vulnerable to unemployment or lack of benefits and disability pay when health problems arose. If they had educational credentials, they were devalued in the United States and these families worked hard to just survive. There was little time for the "luxuries" of traditions, celebrations, and family bonding experiences. A loss of adolescence was evident for many of these students who had little opportunity for the carefree youth that is often associated with the growing up years. Instead, they were occupied with rigorous school work, academic activities associated with school, care of younger children in their families, household responsibilities, and paid employment.

Some parents were unable to participate in their child's schooling due to language or cultural barriers, or because they were absent from their children's lives. In these situations, the students did the best they could in the schools that were available to them, given their addresses in less than desirable neighborhoods in the urban centers. Even though the

Searchers and Skeptics were not immediately viewed as favorably by the schools as the Pleasers, all of the HEOP students indicated that they found someone in their educational experience who saw their potential and nurtured their learning. Many of them were propelled into advanced classes and activities that enhanced their college preparation. As these students explained to me, they came to college ready to work hard because they had always worked hard, in one way or another. This study demonstrates that, contrary to perceptions that fuel academic discussions about students entering college lacking skills and polish and unwilling/unable to work hard (the deficit model), it is truly the educational and societal systems that are deficient in providing the appropriate resources for properly preparing and nurturing students. Students from backgrounds of family deprivation and challenge, who cling to dreams of making it, however that is conceived within their minds, can succeed when provided the opportunities and support they need.

Unexplored Identities

Just as research has spent little time exploring the identities of diverse students, these students have had little opportunity for self-exploration. When I posed specific questions about identity, they were met by lengthy silences—not the type of silence indicating that there would be no forthcoming answer, but silence that allowed time to ponder and construct a response to a question never thought about at a conscious level. It seemed hard for students to look underneath their outer identities or to express the more individual aspects of identity, away from the collective descriptions of their families and earlier lives. The Asian students particularly avoided speaking too intimately about themselves. Cultural humility and shyness may be a part of this but, for most students, identity seems relatively unexplored at a conscious level. Their responses evidenced rather convoluted, circular thought around identity. When asked to locate themselves racially or ethnically, the students had limited one word responses, or confused and uncomfortable replies. However, when asked questions about their cultures, the responses were rich, meaningful, lengthy, and informative. These responses told so much more about the person than their confined racial/ethnic responses of "Black," "Asian" or "Hispanic." Some of them did not use racial and/or ethnic descriptors for their friends. Their cultural and socioeconomic locations seemed as important as race/ethnicity when choosing friends. Race truly is a social construct, and one that is not uniformly agreed upon within a society. Despite their difficulty in describing aspects of their identities, many of the students enjoyed the opportunity to discuss these complexities and would benefit from and make a tremendous contribution to courses about cultural/social issues. They are often undervalued resources on campuses with unrecognized and/or unmet needs. The students sacrifice a tremendous amount financially and personally to attend institutions like Ivy University. What does or can an institution do to meet the students half-way? Providing them space and opportunity for self exploration and development seems a worthy task for higher education.

Actively Producing Identity

The college years are a fertile time for the production of identity. These students were constructing and redefining their identities daily, shaped by their interactions with family, friends, academicians, their gender, race, and class positions, and the larger systems of politics, economics and culture that positioned them. Students continuously changed identities, defining themselves by what they perceived they were and what they perceived they were not. They looked around and critiqued others to add refinement to who they were becoming. While some of the self identity formation was subconscious, the students showed a growing consciousness of how others positioned them and imposed upon them aspects of identity. As Stuart Hall (1991) noted: "Identity is a structured representation which only achieves its positive through the narrow eye of the negative. It has to go through the eye of the needle of the other before it can construct itself" (p. 21).

By going through the "eye of the needle of the other," these students often felt stigmatizing responses from others. Higher education tends to try to smooth over differences by forcing some types of conforming behaviors. When these students did not fit the "mold," they had to deal with the reality of life in an elite institution. In order to remain and survive at this university with identities of their choosing, they needed to find *space*, both for the construction and the expression of their identities. HEOP provided some space for establishing safe relationships and for exploring the challenges they faced. The students often banded together for support and learned how to shift identities depending on the context (Fernandez-Kelly & Schauffler, 1996). In many respects, they were forming the hybridized identities that Antonia Darder (1998) attributed to subordinate cultural groups who were responding to cultural oppression and domination in the United States:

> This is to say that their histories of forced interaction with the dominant culture have required consistent forms of adaptional behaviors which have, in many instances, eroded, restructured, and reconstructed the language system, cultural beliefs, and social traditions of these groups (p. 130).

Even though the students could not avoid being changed in their interactions with the dominant forces within the university, they actively resisted being oppressed "victims" in this interchange and chose to adapt, but not "sell out."

Resisting Assimilation

Families of the HEOP students took "segmented" approaches to assimilation (Portes & Rumbaut, 1996) into the dominant US culture, and experienced minimal levels of success in becoming upwardly mobile. Observing this, these students were not interested in becoming "American" as defined by the dominant, Anglo-European majority. They were learning and actively engaged in constructing identities that were authentic to their backgrounds, experiences, and desires. Students with this level of independence, who don't seek to be at the competitive center, but who can sometimes exist comfortably and confidently at the margins, finding strength within their purpose and with those who choose to reside at the fringe with them, are sometimes perceived as a threat to members of the dominant group who are confused by this resistance to "belonging," being part of the in crowd. Even though the dominant group holds most of the power and does little to include these margin residents, as chapters 4, 5, and 6 illustrated for the HEOP students, they are still at a loss to understand why these students may choose to be self-segregating or uninvolved in many campus activities. bell hooks (2000) described her experience with White dorm mates in college, which captures this confusion:

> Nothing they did to win me over worked. It came as a great surprise. They had always believed black girls wanted to be white girls, wanted to possess their world. My stony gaze, silence, and absolute refusal to cross the threshold of their world was total mystery; it was for them a violation they needed to avenge (p. B15).

There is a tendency, especially for Whites in this society, to be offended when others do not seek to be exactly like them. Feelings of offense or rejection interfere with healthy communication and often lead to actions that create even more problems for resistant, subordinate groups. Elite status groups set the standards for what the academic world views as cultural capital (McDonough, 1998), and bucking this establishment takes courage.

Institutions can assist students in meeting these challenges by attempting to provide an environment that does not push conformity and assimilation. All students would benefit from space to develop strong identities through a range of opportunities for intellectual, physical, and emotional growth. Flexible workshops and extracurriculars that convene when students want and need them, springing up around timely issues and developmental stages, are all too rare. Courses need to find ways to teach students about the development of identity, cultural competency, and mutual respect. These efforts could have a bridging effect between groups of students, and even faculty. We all need to continually grow and learn how to communicate with each other.

Strategic Instrumentalism

Concurrent with the first theme of the active, ongoing construction of their identities, the second theme emerged as the HEOP students created a repertoire of strategies to deal with the cultural discontinuities they experienced both in their academic and social environments, as identified in Chapters 4 through 7. They and their families had little experience with negotiating political systems like higher education. They lacked previous experiences with and awareness of this level of bureaucracy, elitism, relationships, and politics. And they were quickly learning that it was all political! HEOP students engaged in "class jumping," going from the unemployed or poor working class to preparing for professional careers, like doctors or lawyers.

The HEOP students gathered their strength from whatever resources were available to them to engage in their struggle to survive in the foreign college culture at Ivy University. The prefreshman summer program that was mandated by HEOP was an opportunity to begin this work of marshaling resources through the bonds they created and the acquisition of skills to help them master the academic code. Programs such as these are not without their detractors (Gose, 1998) who view them as counterproductive to the goals of higher education.

Central to their defense was the application of William Cross and Linda Strauss's (1998) five identity functions that served to provide strategies for dealing with the stigma that these students encountered in their daily lives at college, described in Chapter 4. These five functions—buffering, bonding, bridging, code-switching, and individualism—describe the stigma reducing behaviors in which the students engaged. While this model was developed to explain the behaviors of African American students, it translates appropriately to all of the HEOP students because they all face stigmatizing situations on a regular basis, be it from their racial/ethnic, gender, or socio-economic locations. Examples of each of these functions are evident in Chapters 4 through 7. This model and Beverly Tatum's (1997) discussions of minority student development substantiate the need for the self-segregating behaviors that are apparent within college populations. They also explain the break-down in communication and the confusion that is created when students respond to what they perceive as environmental threats to their identities.

Beyond the management of stigma, the students acquired strategies that enabled them to maintain their identities, resist assimilation into the dominant culture on campus, and still achieve the academic and career goals that they had set. This *strategic instrumentalism* employed aspects of resistance and opposition, but if the students were truly strategic in the use of these techniques, they enhanced their ability to succeed. Daniel Solorzano and Octavio Villalpando (1998) identify what they call "critical resistant navigational skills" that have the flavor of strategic instrumentalism, without describing specific skills in which students engage. Chapters 4 through 7 highlighted the trial-and-error creation of specific coping techniques which resulted in each student developing a "bag of tricks" that shared some common elements with most successful students, but took on an individual cast dictated by the peculiar needs of each student. Some acquired these strategies more quickly and effectively than others, but there were also ample illustrations of the students experimenting with non-strategic ploys, both academically and socially.

Institutional Response: Helping Students Succeed

To most of the HEOP students, Ivy University seemed cold. HEOP was one of the few institutional structures that seemed responsive to them. The students compensated by using the resources that were available to them to become as successful as possible in this environment. However, it was clear that this was an elite environment that did little more than admit these students into a competitive space where they could either sink or swim. The institutional reform plan that had recently been initiated to bring Ivy University more into line with Ivy League schools had made admissions more selective and the intake of students smaller. A repercussion of this policy was that the campus became more homogeneously White and upper-middle class as fewer minorities qualified under the raised expectations. Hence, the few who were admitted became more visible and had fewer peers of similar backgrounds with which to associate. There was a compression and displacement of cultural identity on campus as people were collapsed under rubrics of Black or Latino/a. Elitism forced more conformity into narrow spaces with not much room for expression and voice. This plan seemed like an attempt to (mis)manage race (Mohanty, 1989) rather than address what it means to be a White elite establishment. The largest group of minorities was Asian, which provided little comfort for the few Asian students in HEOP who struggled with cultural differences that were unacknowledged on campus. The loss of a number of graduate students as the graduate program was reduced impacted on the valuable mentoring factor and role model influence that older students could provide.

The campus itself seemed divided as to whether this change was positive or negative. People seemed to either love the plan because they perceived that the students were now more serious and teachable, or hated the plan because the campus had become more elite and lost some of the energy generated by diverse participants. The most acerbic comments came from instructors who were graduate students themselves and who were quite critical of the Ivy League "wannabe" culture that provided a rigorous education but not much opportunity for critical thought and ethical reflection.

The students raised pedagogical questions about the nature of courses at Ivy University that did not allow much exploration or creation of knowledge. They found the introductory courses very structured large lectures for the most part. Lecture courses overwhelmed and bored many of the students. In these courses, they felt distanced from the professors and they were more likely to deal with teaching assistants than professors who they found inaccessible and inflexible. The HEOP students appreciated discussion courses which were harder to find. The students reported that different learning styles and needs were rarely considered in their classes, except the smaller social science, composition, or humanities sections where they were noticed and given room to develop a voice.

What becomes clear as these students narrate their experiences is that there is a capital mismatch (Bourdieu, 1977) between the HEOP students and this elite university. By virtue of qualifying for HEOP, they lack true economic capital and may be short on educational capital due to the limitations of urban schools, so the material and symbolic resources that are currency in this system are not readily available to them. Their major strength is that they arrive with ample cultural capital, but they soon discover that their cultural capital is not highly valued within this social economy despite some rhetoric to the contrary. So, the HEOP students need to rapidly acquire political and social capital in order to be true members of this community, and they are given few assists in this undertaking. In fact, institutional barriers are constantly erected that prevent them from amassing the valued capital. This sets up the "culture war" that Laura Rendon (1998) articulates. The "universal" standards set up by the dominant White majority are based on a model of meritocracy rather than a model of social justice, which advocates the sharing of "wealth" (at Ivy University that might translate as educational, political, and social capital) rather than competing for limited resources. In the social justice model, difference is an asset, not a deficit. The HEOP office became one of the HEOP students' few allies in building valued capital, and most of the students recognized this.

Breaking Points

The efforts that are expended by this group of students in becoming strategic members of this elite community come with an emotional cost. The "imposter syndrome" was raised as an issue for those students who were attempting to fit in by changing their identities, sometimes temporarily by code-switching or fronting, but sometimes by trying to become someone they were not. They felt like they were imposters who were out of their element and who were terrified of being unmasked. Many of the HEOP students did not identify with this syndrome and worked hard not to front and force a fit that was not meant to be. These students were remarkable in their high self esteem, respect for themselves and others, and measure of independence

However, all of the students felt stressed. Some were most stressed over identity issues and the pressures of being in an elite environment, so foreign from what they had always known. Many, but especially the Pleasers, felt pressured to succeed by their parents, although the families had little conception of what life at Ivy University was like for them. Immigrant parents, even for the second generation Searchers, saw education as the key to a brighter future for the student and the family (Ogbu, 1991). The Skeptics, with their leveled expectations, were not as optimistic about the brightness of the future, but understood that there would be better, although not equal, opportunities with the credentials from Ivy. Another major stressor was the financial aid that was contingent on maintaining high grades. And, if that was not pressure enough, the red tape of financial aid put many students over the top in stress levels. Individual coping strategies varied from solitary pursuits to social bonding, but all of these students accepted that they would just have to work hard, and harder than many of the students at Ivy University, to achieve their educational goals.

In their second semester, and having just enough time to get a sense of the pressures of this environment and some of the wind knocked out of them, most of the students participated in a sit-in at the administration building, requesting the president's attention to their demands for more minority recognition on campus. This was a flash point of political engineering that was one of the most strategic maneuvers in which they could have engaged. Not only did it capture the attention of the campus, but it advertised to the community surrounding the university that there were issues that had gone too long unattended and for which the administrators would now be held accountable. Student groups exercised united agency behind the banner of "Don't just verbalize, strategize!" and pushed their agenda that demanded more sharing of power on the campus. These students refused to be victims and unleashed a storm of political unrest that would have lasting effects on their college experience by forcing an institutional response. This was strategic instrumentalism at its finest. However, situations need not escalate to this point in order to be addressed. Building a caring community of learners, where each individual is respected and listened to, and student needs, not just financial status and reputation, are a factor in the construction of policy and procedure, are all steps that can alleviate the need for demonstrations to defuse pent up hurts and hostilities.

IMPLICATIONS

This study speaks to the dire need for educational institutions, even those (perhaps especially those) that consider themselves "elite," to assume their central responsibility for building communities of learning that include all of their members. Students who are marginally admitted, like those in HEOP, quickly become shunted to the outskirts amidst bureaucratic structures and stifled curricula. The institution admits the students, but then is unresponsive to who they are and what needs they may have. Little changes as policies, courses, and traditions seem to go on as usual, with surprised and confused raising of administrative eyebrows when questions surface about altering the status quo. There seems to be little concern about understanding the students who are populating their campus. Or, perhaps they understand too well and are electing the meritocratic gatekeeping function of higher education. As Michael Reichert (2000) learned when an elite boys' school decided to admit "less privileged boys": "...the school had invited these boys into their community but had not otherwise opened itself up to them. The deck, in the eyes of the recruits, remained stacked in favor of the traditionally privileged identities. Apart from their physical inclusion, the school expected little else to change in its curriculum and practice" (p. 7). These words could be describing Ivy University.

Institutions must be responsive to change. Populations and demographics change and mandate corresponding revision of policies and curriculum. The HEOP students voiced numerous ways that curriculum and personnel could enhance their educational experiences instead of creating roadblocks and pedagogical nightmares. Their ideas should be solicited and valued in academic discussions about visions for the university. They, like all students, should become players in the decision-making roundtables. Educational institutions cannot afford to become concerned only when negative publicity threatens exposure of hegemonic practices. And just inviting the same few "minority" students to these discussions over and over, defeats the purpose of hearing diverse perspectives and creates the fatigue of group representation of which these students complain. As this study has shown, there is tremendous diversity within each of the racial/ethnic clusters of students. The institution needs to become acquainted with these differences that can only enhance the educational experience if they are recognized. Statistics and surveys tell only part of the story. Student voices need to be heard. Students, like most people, love to talk about themselves, but are infrequently asked about things that are meaningful to them. Too many beautiful songs go unsung in these hallowed spaces.

Institutional "fit" is the responsibility of the entire institution and all of the individuals who work and live there, not just the students. The HEOP summer program was an excellent beginning for creating the institutional and individual bonds that enhance the academic and social fit. But the ball is then dropped by the university and thrown into the lap of the HEOP staff to keep up in the air. The likelihood of "fit" and integration into the academic environment would increase dramatically with the addition of some type of freshman and transfer student seminar course that would continue through at least the first full semester of classes. In addition, required courses throughout the college years that deal with communication skills and that explore cultural and social issues would assist all of the students in making transitions to the global culture of which we are all a part. Many students come to college from sheltered, homogeneously populated high schools. Even the HEOP students found relating to the student body, including other HEOP students, challenging. Few students (and faculty and staff) innately understand how to bridge over differences and open meaningful conversations with people from diverse backgrounds. These are skills that can be taught and can be learned and need to become valued components of the curriculum.

Compensatory programs like HEOP have a place in higher education and play a vital role in providing some measure of democratic access, equitable opportunity and education for students who are as deserving of opportunity as those from affluent families. What these 23 students have shown is that they are a hard-working, deserving group of students who have high goals and aspirations that they will achieve as long as barriers are not rebuilt around them as quickly as they find strategies to break through them. These are resilient students who have earned a place on this campus. They have cultural and intellectual assets that the university should treasure and go out of its way to retain. Their performance refutes the argument that "disadvantaged" students, like those who qualify for HEOP, are better served at community colleges. Some may be, but these students are seriously engaged in a quest for knowledge. They have professional aspirations; they've worked hard to get to this university; and, they succeed in overwhelming numbers.

Aside from the access that HEOP provides these students, it is there as a safety net and as a supportive resource. Although the students are stigmatized by student and faculty misperceptions that this is an affirmative action or academic welfare program, they rely on the HEOP staff to provide what the rest of the institution cannot or will not provide—care, compassion, honest concern, a safe space. There is controversy over the divisiveness of programs that cater only to certain racial or ethnic populations, but there is ample justification for the bonding function that they serve. A critical political mass and space is created that serves to form a collective identity for these students, building the energy and resiliency to overcome an oppressive environment. The type of support and political space that is engendered by this program is so valuable that it could be useful for all students admitted to the university. Having a precollege experience to orient oneself to the campus, its resources, and to other students, followed up by strong advising and support systems, would help any student feel more a part of an academic community. These should not be stigmatizing experiences, like HEOP students are sometimes made to feel. Institutions want and need to retain their students, and would prefer to have alumni who are loyal to the values and goals of the university. Caring for the student body is sound educational policy, all the way around.

A final institutional implication is a warning raised by Chandra Mohanty (1989) and echoed in the voices of these students, that diversity is not something to be managed. Educators and policy makers cannot afford to view diversity as a problem that must be reduced, or behaviors that must be made standardized and predictable. In other words, institutions cannot "domesticate race and difference" (p. 200). One of the lessons of the sit-in was that students who view themselves as "different" from the dominant groups on campus, who reside at the fringe of membership, will resist attempts to mold, control, and shape them to the university's conception of what an elite student should be. They demand a voice in this community and, as long as they remain mysteries to the people who work there, they will be viewed as unpredictable and uncontrollable "problems". They see through the university's attempts to add on lip-service "solutions" to their requests for more representation in the student body, the faculty, and the curriculum. One-day workshops or speakers do not significantly alter the soul of the university. Admitting minuscule numbers of students from underrepresented groups and hiring a few new faces from different places smacks loudly of tokenism. These students want sincere and genuine efforts to respect, value, understand, and include those things *they* hold dear in the daily workings of this place where they reside. When the main character in the movie *School Ties* was told by a superior that he must violate a Jewish holy day in order to win a school football game that was "tradition," he replied: "Your tradition or mine, sir?" That is the crux of the matter. Whose traditions are valued and honored on an elite campus?

LIMITATIONS, FIRE ALARMS, AND BURNING QUESTIONS

In the tradition of most ethnographic research, this study faced a number of limitations related to the resources of time, energy, and finance. These students had a tremendous amount to say, which resulted in an overwhelming quantity of fascinating data. As a "lone ranger" researcher, I had to make a number of expedient choices in order to rein in this project, especially because I lacked the time and funding to consider every nuance and ramification of every piece of data. I have listened and observed carefully, and I have obsessed over accurately and fairly representing what the participants revealed. However, given this type of research, I am certain that I have overlooked or underanalyzed some things that others would find significant.

Beyond the implications listed above, I find that a number of questions are raised by this research, but certainly not answered. Further studies may address these issues, but honest *work* on the part of all stakeholders in higher education may be of greater value. Speaking truth to what it means to be a student at an elite university dominated by Anglo-European traditions and values is needed. However, hearing and acting upon that truth is praxis that is too frequently absent on college campuses.

One question that was generated by the students concerns the current intense focus on math and science programs in high school. Does this distort and limit students' vision, or does this focus provide more opportunity? A number of students felt this focus detracted from learning to communicate, especially in the written format which was criticized by faculty and staff as well as the students. The social implications of steering students into math, science, and technology fields are that there will be fewer minorities in the "pipelines" to do the vital work of humanitarian and social service sectors, including teaching, because they will be off to higher paying jobs that offer faster returns and greater status. There is no end in sight for our need for more diverse representation on campuses and in schools, both in the student body and the faculty. Where will teachers from diverse backgrounds come from? Why would campuses be more attractive venues for employment than businesses and corporations? We need to carefully examine this situation and its long term repercussions.

Another question that begs more study is, where are the males from underrepresented groups? The HEOP population had dramatically fewer males than females, and the trend around the country is that these males are not in college in great numbers. We must ask if it is because of their leveled career aspirations (Fine & Weis, 1998), if it is because such high numbers of them reside in the prison system, or is it because they are rarely offered access to higher education? In this study, many of the fathers were unwilling or unable to support and/or connect with their children. What are the implications for the future when fathers are alienated from their children and from educational opportunities? The struggles the males in this study voiced may be too much for other males to endure. What are the cultural issues that make elite campuses inaccessible for minority males? How can campuses better accommodate them?

Further, we need to explore who will be the leaders and decision makers in our country. While they are as qualified as anyone for programs such as HEOP, more of the recent voluntary immigrants are taking part in HEOP which closes out opportunities for those who have been traditionally disenfranchised in our country, the involuntary immigrants (Ogbu, 1991). HEOP's stated purpose is not to provide educational opportunities for a specific racial/ethnic group, but it was born from the Civil Rights era when social justice demanded that those who had been left out for so long be given the chance to participate. At that time, the intended recipients were Black. Today, HEOP ironically perpetuates the historically disenfranchised "underclass" that it was designed to eliminate, even though the immigrants filling the limited admissions slots are justly qualified and deserve the opportunity as well. This sets up a competition between groups for limited resources where the stakes are high. The chance for professional careers that will provide upward status mobility for the students and their families, as well as place them in decision making positions in this country, is much stronger for those who graduate from Ivy University than those graduating from schools with fewer resources. So, another irony is that the HEOP students, who are often stigmatized and forced to the margins within universities, have the potential through their education and career achievements to significantly impact power relations in this country. But, will the historically disenfranchised be increasingly shut out of these opportunities?

As the societal winds blow to the conservative right, there is justified fear that programs like HEOP may have to, once again, battle for survival. If this type of support and access to higher education is reduced or disappears all together, there will be a significant loss of bright, energetic, and vibrantly diverse voices to participate in the leadership of this country. Can the United States afford this loss? Will the citizenry, including the students, be able to mobilize for more equitable access and for social justice? Compensatory programs provide the means for social justice through democratic access, and they need serious support.

Beyond the questions that have been raised, there are many directions to which this study points for further exploration. Comparing these three groups of students to a group of White students on campus who do not receive need-based financial aid, would add a counterpoint perspective to the lived experiences of students on an elite campus. Similarly, comparing this group of HEOP students to a group of EOP students at a public university, would provide greater insight into how elite, private institutions structure their environments differently from public institutions, and the effect this has on student agency. Also worthy of exploration is a longitudinal study that would follow this group of students through graduation, into the careers or graduate schools that follow, and further down the road as they establish more mature adult lives.

Students in programs like HEOP have much to tell us about how people develop both resilient spirits that refuse to be oppressed by societal structures and the tenacity to muster strength from their marginal spaces. Their stories inform institutional practices that can lead to enhanced retention and diversification of student bodies. Research that focuses its attention on these students is a matter of social justice, as Maxine Greene (2000) so eloquently defines it:

> Thinking about our thinking, imagining things for ourselves, seeking a community of concern in a public space: These may be the phases of our striving for social justice, our striving for collectivity, our striving for what is always in the making—what we call democracy. These may be our ways of reaching toward each other in safe and unsafe spaces, seeking equity, seeking decency, seeking for a common world (p. 303).

The students seek this kind of world, and researchers and educators can choose to assist them in this arduous work of creating a society in which all members are valued, not marginalized, for their unique contributions.

Bibliography

AAUW [American Association of University Women]. (1992). *How schools short-change girls*. NY: Marlowe & Co.

Acosta-Belen, E. & C. E. Santiago. (1998). Merging borders: The remapping of America. In A. Darder & R. D. Torres (Eds.), *The Latino studies reader: Culture, economy, and society* (pp. 29–42). Malden, MA: Blackwell.

Akoto, A. (1994). Notes on an Afrikan-centered pedagogy. In M. J. Shujaa (Ed.), *Too much schooling, too little education* (pp. 319–340). Trenton, NJ: Africa World Press.

Alford, S. M. (1995). An exploratory study of peer relationships among students in the SEEK compensatory educational programs at two four-year urban commuter colleges. (Doctoral dissertation, Columbia University, 1995). *Dissertation Abstracts International, 56*, 4342.

Allsup, C. (1995). Postmodernism, the "politically correct," and liberatory pedagogy. In C. E. Sleeter & P. L. McLaren (Eds.), *Multicultural education, critical pedagogy, and the politics of difference* (pp. 269–290). Albany: SUNY Press.

Altbach, P. G. (1993). Students: Interests, culture, and activism. In A. Levine (Ed.), *Higher learning in America: 1980–2000* (pp. 203–221). Baltimore: Johns Hopkins University Press.

Althusser, A. (1971). Ideology and ideological state apparatuses. In L. Althusser (Ed.), *Lenin and philosophy and other essays* (pp. 121–173). NY: Monthly Review.

Altman, A. H. (1973). A preliminary study of the relationship between the characteristics of Higher Education Opportunity Program students and three selected private higher educational institutions. (Doctoral dissertation, State University of New York at Buffalo, 1973). *Dissertation Abstracts International, 34*, 6401.

American Federation for Suicide Prevention. *About suicide.* (1/13/01). <http://208.205.107.31/about/epidemio.htm>

Apple, M. W. (1979). *Ideology and curriculum.* London: Routledge & Kegan Paul.

Apple, M. W. (1982). *Education and power.* London: Routledge & Kegan Paul.

Apple, M. W. (1993). Constructing the "Other": Rightist reconstruction of common sense. In C. McCarthy & W. Crichlaw (Eds.), *Race, identity and reproduction in education* (pp. 24–39). NY: Routledge.

Apple, M. W. (1995). Book review: *Education policy: A critical and poststructural approach. Education Policy, 9* (4), 426–428.

Apple, M. W. & Beyer, L. E. (1988). Values and politics in the curriculum. In L. E. Beyer & M. W. Apple (Eds.), *The curriculum: Problems, politics, and possibilities* (pp. 3–13). Albany, NY: SUNY Press.

Apple, M. W. & Weis, L. (Eds.). (1983). *Ideology and practice in schooling.* Philadelphia: Temple University Press.

Aronowitz, S. & Giroux, H. A. (1991). *Postmodern education: Politics, culture, and social criticism.* Minneapolis: University of Minnesota Press.

Asante, M. K. (1990). *Kemet, Afrocentricity and knowledge.* Trenton, NJ: Africa World Press.

Bankston, C. L. (1997). Education and ethnicity in an urban Vietnamese village. In M. Seller & L. Weis (Eds.), *Beyond Black and White: New faces and voices in U.S. schools.* 207–230.

Bean, J.P. (1980). Dropouts and turnover: The synthesis and test of a causal model of student attrition. *Research in Higher Education, 12* (2), 155–187.

Birnbaum, R. (1991). Value of different kinds of colleges. In J. L. Bess (Ed.), *Foundations of American higher education* (pp. 111–129). Needham Heights, MA: Simon & Schuster.

Bourdieu, P. (1977). Cultural reproduction and social reproduction. In J. Karabel and A. H. Halsey (Eds.), *Power and ideology in education* (pp. 487–511). NY: Oxford University Press. (Original work published 1973)

Bourdieu, P. & Passeron, J. C. (1977). *Reproduction in education, society and culture.* Beverly Hills: Sage.

Bowen, W. G. & D. Bok. (1998). *The shape of the river: Long-term consequences of considering race in college and university admissions.* Princeton: Princeton University Press.

Bowles, S. & Gintis, H. (1976). *Schooling in capitalist America: Educational reform and the contradictions of economic life.* NY: Basic Books.

Boyer, E. (1993). Campus climate in the 1980s and 1990s: Decades of apathy and renewal. In A. Levine (Ed.), *Higher learning in America: 1980–2000* (pp. 322–332). Baltimore: Johns Hopkins University Press.

Bureau of Higher Education Opportunity Program. (1998–1999). *HEOP works: Annual report.* Albany, NY: University of the State of New York, State Education Department.

Cabrera, A., Castaneda, M. B., Nora, A., & Hengstler, D. (1992). The convergence between two theories of college persistence. *Journal of Higher Education, 63* (2), 143–164.

Carrington, B. (1982). Sport as a side-track: An analysis of West Indian involvement in extra-curricular sport. In L. Barton & S. Walker (Eds.), *Race, class and education* (pp. 40–65). Croom Helm.

Centrie, C. (2000). Free spaces unbound: Families, community, and Vietnamese high school students' identities. In L. Weis & M. Fine (Eds.), *Construction sites: Excavating race, class, and gender among urban youth* (pp. 65–83). NY: Teachers College Press.

Chan, S. & Wang, L. (1991). Racism and the model minority: Asian-Americans in higher education. In P. Altbach & K. Lomotey (Eds.), *Racial crisis in American higher education* (pp. 42–66). Albany: SUNY Press.

Collins, P. H. (1990). *Black feminist thought: Knowledge, consciousness, and the politics of empowerment.* NY: Routledge.

Connell, R. W., Dowsett, G. W., Kessler, S., & Ashenden, D. J. (1982). *Making the difference: Schools, families and social division.* Sydney: George Allen & Unwin.

Cross, W. E. (1991). *Shades of Black: Diversity in African-American identity.* Philadelphia: Temple University Press.

Cross, W. E. (1995). The psychology of Nigrescence: Revisiting the Cross model. In J. G. Ponterotto, J. M. Casas, L. A. Suzuki, & C.M. Alexander (Eds.), *Handbook of multicultural counseling* (pp. 93–122). Thousand Oaks, CA: Sage.

Cross, W. E. & Strauss, L.. (1998). The everyday functions of African American identity. In J. K. Swim & C. Stangor (Eds.), *Prejudice: The target's perspective* (pp. 267–279). San Diego: Academic Press.

Cross, W. E. & Strauss, L. (1999). African American identity development across the life span: Educational implications. In R. Hernandez-Sheets & E. Hollins (Eds.), *Racial and ethnic identity in school practices: Aspects of human development* (pp. 29–47). Mahwah, NJ: Lawrence Erlbaum.

Darder, A. (1998). The politics of biculturalism: Culture and difference in the formation of *Warriors from Gringostroika* and *The New Mestizas.* In A. Darder & R. D. Torres (Eds.), *The Latino studies reader: Culture, economy, and society* (pp. 129–142). Malden, MA: Blackwell.

Darder, A. & Torres, R. D. (1998). Latinos and society: Culture, politics, and class. In A. Darder & R. D. Torres (Eds.), *The Latino studies reader: Culture, economy, and society* (pp. 3–26). Malden, MA: Blackwell.

Davidson, A. L. (1997). Marbella Sanchez: On marginalization and silencing. In M. Seller & L. Weis (Eds.), *Beyond Black and White: New faces and voices in U.S. schools* (pp. 15–43). Albany: SUNY Press.

Delpit, L. D. (1988). The silenced dialogue: Power and pedagogy in educating other people's children. *Harvard Educational Review, 58* (3), 280–298.

Evans, S. M. & Boyte, H. C. (1986). *Free spaces.* NY: Harper & Row.

Feinberg, W. & Soltis, J. F. (1992). *School and society.* NY: Teachers College Press.

Felder, R.M., Felder, G.N., Mauney, M., Hamrin, C.E., & Dietz, E.J. (1994). *Gender differences in student performance and attitudes. A longitudinal study of engineering student performance and retention.* (Report No. NCSU–94A) Raleigh, NC: North Carolina State University. (ERIC Documentation Reproduction Service No. ED368 553)

Fernandez Kelly, M. P. & Schauffler, R. (1996). Divided fates: Immigrant children and the new assimilation. In A. Portes (Ed.), *The new second generation* (pp. 30–53). NY: Russell Sage.

Fine, M. (1991). *Framing dropouts: Notes on the politics of an urban public high school.* Albany: SUNY Press.

Fine, M. & Weis, L. (1998). *The unknown city: Lives of poor and working-class young adults.* Boston: Beacon Press.

Fine, M., Weis, L., Weseen, S., & Wong, L. (2000). For whom? Qualitative research, representations, and social responsibilities. In N. K. Denzin & Y. S. Lincoln (Eds.), *Handbook of qualitative research* (pp. 107–131). Thousand Oaks, CA: Sage.

Fordham, S. (1997). "Those Loud Black Girls": (Black) women, silence, and gender "passing" in the academy. In M. Seller & L. Weis (Eds.), *Beyond black and white: New faces and voices in U.S. schools* (pp. 81–111). Albany, NY: SUNY Press.

Foucault, M. (1995). *Discipline and punish: The birth of the prison.* (A. Sheridan, Trans.). NY: Vintage Books. (Original work published 1975)

Frankenberg, R. (1993). *White women, race matters: The social construction of whiteness.* Minneapolis: University of Minnesota Press.

Freire, P. (1973). *Education for critical consciousness.* NY: Seabury.

Freire, P. (1995). *Pedagogy of the oppressed.* NY: Continuum. (Original work published 1970)

Gardner, J. N. (1992). *Your college experience: Strategies for success.* Belmont, CA: Wadsworth.

Gee, J. P. (1999. April). *Learning language as a matter of learning social languages within discourses.* Paper presented at the meeting of the Conference on College Composition and Communication, Atlanta, GA.

Gibson, M. A. (1991). Minorities and schooling: Some implications. In M. A. Gibson & J. U. Ogbu (Eds.), *Minority status and schooling: A* comparative study of immigrant and involuntary minorities (pp. 357–381). NY: Garland.

Giroux, H. A. (1981). *Ideology, culture, and the process of schooling.* Philadelphia: Temple University Press.

Giroux, H. A. (1983). *Theory and resistance in education: A pedagogy for the opposition.* S. Hadley, MA: Bergin & Garvey.

Giroux, H. A., Lankshear, C., McLaren, P., & Peters, M. (1996). *Counternarratives: Cultural studies and critical pedagogies in postmodern spaces.* NY: Routledge.

Goodwin, L. L. (2001) Resilient spirits: Identity construction among socioeconomically and educationally disadvantaged freshmen at an elite university. (Doctoral dissertation, State University of New York at Buffalo, 2001). UMI Number:3010827.

Gordon, B. M. (1994). African-American cultural knowledge and liberatory education. In M. J. Shujaa (Ed.), *Too much schooling, too little education* (pp. 57–78). Trenton, NJ: Africa World Press.

Gose, B. (1998, Sept. 4). Do minority orientations encourage segregation? *Chronicle of Higher Education,* A67–68.

Greene, H. R. (1998). *The select: Realities of life and learning in America's elite colleges.* NY: Cliff Street Books.

Greene, M. (2000). Lived spaces, shared spaces, public spaces. In L. Weis & M. Fine (Eds.), *Construction sites: Excavating race, class, and gender among urban youth* (pp. 293–303). NY: Teachers College Press.

Gross, E. J. (1990). *Opportunity program administrators: An analysis of higher education in New York State.* Bristol, IN: Wyndham Hall Press.

Grossberg, L. (1993). Cultural studies and/in new worlds. In C. McCarthy & W. Crichlow (Eds.). *Race, identity, and representation in education* (pp. 89–105). London: Routledge.

Gutek, G. L. (1997). *Philosophical and ideological perspectives on education.* Boston: Allyn & Bacon.

Hall, R.M., & Sandler, B.R. (1982). *The classroom climate: A chilly one for women?* (Project on the Status and Education of WOMEN). Washington, D.C.: Association of American Colleges. (ERIC Documentation Reproduction Service No. ED215 628)

Hall, S. (1991). Ethnicity: Identity and difference. *Radical America, 23:* (4), 9–21.

Hall, S. (1998). Subjects in history: Making diasporic identities. In W. Lubiano (Ed.), *The house that race built* (pp. 289–299). NY: Vintage Books.

Haraway, D. J. (1991). *Simians, cyborgs, and women: The reinvention of nature.* NY: Routledge.

Hegel, G. W. F. Translated by Leo Rauch (1988). *Introduction to the philosophy of history.* Indianapolis: Hackett Publishing.

Helms, J. E. (Ed) (1990). *Black and White racial identity: Theory, research and practice.* Westport, CT: Greenwood.

Hirschman, C. (1996). Studying immigrant adaptation from the 1990 population census: From generational comparisons to the process of "Becoming American." In A. Portes (Ed.), *The new second generation* (pp. 54–81). NY: Russell Sage.

Hochschild, J. L. (1995). *Facing up to the American dream: Race, class and the soul of the nation.* Princeton: Princeton University Press.

Holland, D. C. & Eisenhart, M. A. (1990). *Educated in romance: Women, achievement and college culture.* Chicago: University of Chicago Press.

hooks, b. (2000, November 17). Learning in the shadow of race and class. *Chronicle of Higher Education,* B14–16.

Horowitz, H. L. (1987). *Campus life: Undergraduate cultures from the end of the eighteenth century to the present.* Chicago: University of Chicago Press.

Hurtado, S. & Inkelas. K. (1998). New dilemmas of access and implications for national data use. In U.S. Department of Education, National Center for Education Statistics. *Reconceptualizing access in postsecondary education: Report of the Policy Panel on Access, NCES 98–283,* for the Council of the National Postsecondary Education Cooperative, Subcommittee on the Policy Panel on Access, Washington, DC.

Jaschik, S. & Lederman, D. (1996, March 29). Appeals court bars racial preference. *Chronicle of Higher Education,* A26–27.

Jones, D. J. & Watson, B. C. (1990). *High-risk students and higher education.* Washington, D.C.: George Washington University.

Jones, S. (1995). Voices of identity and difference: A qualitative exploration of the multiple dimensions of identity development in women college students. (Doctoral dissertation, University of Maryland, 1995). *Dissertation Abstracts International, 57,* 1045.

Josselson, R. (1987). *Finding herself: Pathways to identity development in women.* San Francisco: Jossey-Bass.

Karabel, J. & Halsey, A. H. (1977). *Power and ideology in education.* NY: Oxford University Press.

Kozol, J. (1995). *Amazing grace.* NY: Harper Perennial.

Lara, J. (1992). Reflections: Bridging cultures. *New Directions for Community Colleges, 80,* 65–70. San Francisco: Jossey-Bass.

Lather, P. (1991). *Getting smart: Feminist research and pedagogy with/in the postmodern.* NY: Routledge.

Lee, Y. (1991). Koreans in Japan and the United States. In M. Gibson & J. Ogbu (Eds.), *Minority status and schooling: A comparative study of immigrant and involuntary minorities* (pp. 131–167). NY: Garland.

Levine, A. (1993). Diversity on campus. In A. Levine (Ed.), *Higher learning in America: 1980–2000* (pp. 333–343). Baltimore: Johns Hopkins University Press.

Levinson, B. A., & Holland, D. (1996). The cultural production of the educated person: An introduction. In B. Levinson, D. Foley, & D. Holland (Eds.), *The cultural production of the educated person* (pp. 1–54). Albany: SUNY Press.

London, H. B. (1989). Breaking away: A study of first-generation college students and their families. *American Journal of Education, (97) 2*, 144–170.

London, H. B. (1992). Transformations: Cultural challenges faced by first-generation students. *New Directions for Community Colleges, 80*, 5–11. San Francisco: Jossey-Bass.

Lorde, A. (1984). *Sister outsider.* New York: Crossing Press.

Luttrell, W. (1996). Becoming somebody in and against school: Toward a psychocultural theory of gender and self-making. In B. Levinson, D. Foley & D. Holland (Eds.), *The cultural production of the educated person* (pp. 93–117). Albany: SUNY Press.

MacLeod, J. (1995). *Ain't no makin' it: Aspirations and attainment in a low-income neighborhood.* Boulder, CO: Westview.

Mangione, T. L. (1998). An ethnography of working class female students at a private, comprehensive college. (Doctoral dissertation, State University of New York at Buffalo, 1998). *Dissertation Abstracts International, 59*, 0129.

Marcia, J. (1966). Development and validation of ego identity status. *Journal of Personality and Social Psychology,3*, 551–58.

Matute-Bianchi, M. E. (1991). Situational ethnicity and patterns of school performance among immigrant and nonimmigrant Mexican-descent students. In M. A. Gibson & J. U. Ogbu (Eds.), *Minority status and schooling: A comparative study of immigrant and involuntary minorities* (pp. 205–247). NY: Garland.

McCarthy, C. (1988). Rethinking liberal and radical perspectives on racial inequality in schooling: Making the case for nonsynchrony. *Harvard Educational Review, 58* (3), 265–279.

McClelland, P. (1996). Economic developments. In U. Bronfenbrenner, P. McClelland, E. Wethington, P. Moen, & S. Ceci (Eds.), *The state of Americans: This generation and the next* (pp. 51–89). NY: Free Press.

McDonough, P. M. (1998). Structuring college opportunities: A cross-case analysis of organizational cultures, climates, and habiti. In C. A. Torres & T. R. Mitchell (Eds.), *Sociology of education: Emerging perspectives* (pp. 181–210). Albany: SUNY Press.

McRobbie, A. (1978). Working class girls and the culture of femininity. In University of Birmingham: Center for Contemporary Cultural Studies,

Women take issue: Aspects of women's subordination (pp. 96–108). London: Hutchinson.

Meyers, L. (1996). Rethinking romance: cultural construction of female gender identity at a prestigious, private university. (Doctoral dissertation, State University of New York at Buffalo, 1996). *Dissertation Abstracts International, 57,* 2691.

Moffatt, M. (1989). *Coming of age in New Jersey: College and American culture.* New Brunswick, NJ: Rutgers University Press.

Mohanty, C. (1989–90, Winter). On race and voice: Challenges for liberal education in the 1990s. *Cultural Critique,* 179–208.

Morrow, R. A. & Torres, C. A. (1998). Education and the reproduction of class, gender, and race: Responding to the postmodern challenge. In C. A. Torres & T. R. Mitchell (Eds.), *Sociology of education: Emerging perspectives* (pp. 19–45). Albany: SUNY Press.

Mow, S. L. & Nettles, M. T. (1990). Minority student access to, and persistence and performance in, college: A review of the trends and research literature. *The handbook of higher education* (pp. 35–105). NY: Agatha Press.

National Mental Health Association. (1997). *Suicide: Teen Suicide.* (1/13/01). <http://www.nmha.org/infoctr/factsheets/82.cfm>

Nora, A. & Rendon, L. (1988). Hispanic student retention in community colleges: Reconciling access with outcomes. In L. Weis (Ed.), *Class, race and gender in American education* (pp. 126–143). Albany: SUNY Press.

Ogbu, J. U. (1988). Class stratification, racial stratification, and schooling. In L. Weis (Ed.), *Class, race and gender in American education* (pp. 163–182). Albany: SUNY Press.

Ogbu, J. U. (1991). Immigrant and involuntary minorities in comparative perspective. In M. Gibson & J. Ogbu (Eds.), *Minority status and schooling* (pp. 3–33). NY: Garland.

Okun, B. F., Fried, J., & Okun, M. L. (1999). *Understanding diversity.* Pacific Grove, CA: Brooks/Cole Publishing.

Omi, M. & Winant, H. (1994). *Racial formation in the United States.* NY: Routledge.

Ottinger, C. (1991). College going, persistence, and completion patterns in higher education: What do we know? *Research briefs, 2* (3), 1–11.

Padilla, F. M. (1997). *The struggle of Latino/a university students: In search of liberating education.* NY: Routledge.

Palmer, P. J. (1998). *The courage to teach.* San Francisco: Jossey-Bass.

Pascarella, E. T., Terenzini, P. T., & Wolfle, L. M. (1986). Orientation to college and freshman year persistence/withdrawal decisions. *Journal of Higher Education, 57* (2), 155–175.

Pessar, P. (1997). Dominicans: Forging an ethnic community in New York. In M. Seller & L. Weis (Eds.), *Beyond Black and White: New faces and voices in U.S. schools* (pp. 131–149). Albany: SUNY Press.

Phinney, J. (1993). A three-stage model of ethnic identity development in adolescence. In M. E. Bernal & G. P. Knight (Eds.), *Ethnic identity: Formation and transmission among Hispanics and other minorities* (pp. 61-79). Albany: SUNY Press.

Population Estimates Program. (2000). *Resident population estimates of the United States by sex, race, and Hispanic origin: April 1, 1990 to July 1, 1999.* Washington, DC: U. S. Census Bureau, Population Division. <http://www.census.gov/population/estimates/nation>

Portes, A. (1995). Children of immigrants: Segmented assimilation and its determinants. In A. Portes (Ed.), *Economic sociology of immigration* (pp. 248–280). NY: Russell Sage.

Portes, A. & Rumbaut, R. G. (1996). *Immigrant America: A portrait.* Berkeley, CA: University of California Press.

Raissiguier, C. (1994) *Becoming women, becoming workers: Identity formation in a French vocational school.* Albany: SUNY Press.

Reichert, M. C. (2000). Disturbances of difference: Lessons from a boys' school. In L. Weis & M. Fine (Eds.), *Construction sites* (pp. 259–273). NY: Teacher's College Press.

Rendon, L. I. (1992). From the barrio to the academy: Revelations of a Mexican American "scholarship girl." *New Directions for Community Colleges, 80,* 55–64. San Francisco: Jossey-Bass.

Rendon, L. I. (1998). Access in a democracy: Narrowing the opportunity gap. In U.S. Department of Education, National Center for Education Statistics. *Reconceptualizing access in postsecondary education: Report of the Policy Panel on Access, NCES 98–283,* for the Council of the National Postsecondary Education Cooperative, Subcommittee on the Policy Panel on Access, Washington, DC.

Richardson, R. C. & Skinner, E. F. (1992). Helping first-generation minority students achieve degrees. *New Directions for Community Colleges (80),* 29–43. San Francisco: Jossey-Bass.

Root, M. P. (1997). Multiracial Asians: Models of ethnic identity. *Amerasian Journal (23)* 1, 29–41.

Rumbaut, R. G. (1996). The crucible within: Ethnic identity, self-esteem, and segmented assimilation among children of immigrants. In A. Portes (Ed.), *The new second generation* (pp. 119–170). NY: Russell Sage.

Ruppert, S. S. (1998). Reconceptualizing access: A review of the findings from the NPEC/ACE policy panel on access and its data systems ramifications. In U.S. Department of Education, National Center for Education Statistics. *Reconceptualizing access in postsecondary education: Report of the Policy Panel on Access, NCES 98–283,* for the Council of the National Postsecondary Education Cooperative, Subcommittee on the Policy Panel on Access, Washington, DC.

Sadker, M. & Sadker, D. (1994). *Failing at fairness: How America's schools cheat girls.* NY: Charles Scribner's Sons.

Seller, M. S. (1988). *To seek America: A history of ethnic life in the United States.* Englewood, NJ: Ozer.

Shor, I. (2000). Illegal literacy. *Journal of Basic Writing, 19* (1), 100–112.

Shor, I., & Pari, C. (Eds.). (1999). *Critical literacy in action.* Portsmouth, NH: Boynton/Cook.

Shujaa, M. J. (1994). Education and schooling: You can have one without the other. In M. J. Shujaa (Ed.), *Too much schooling, too little education: A paradox of Black life in White societies* (pp. 13–36). Trenton, NJ: Africa World Press.

Sleeter, C. E. (1993). Power and privilege in white middle-class feminist discussions of gender and education. In S. Biklen & D. Pollard (Eds.), *Gender and education* (pp. 221–239). Chicago: University of Chicago Press.

Sleeter, C. E. & McLaren, P. L. (Eds.). (1995). *Multicultural education, critical pedagogy, and the politics of difference.* Albany: SUNY Press.

Smith, H. H. (1991). The impact of supportive services on performance of disadvantaged students attending a predominantly white university. (Doctoral dissertation, Cornell University, Ithaca, 1991). *Dissertation Abstracts International, 52,* 2102.

Smithson, I. (1990). Introduction: Investigating gender, power, and pedagogy. In I. Smithson (Ed.), *Gender in the classroom: Power and pedagogy* (pp. 1–27) Urbana, IL: University of IL Press.

Solomon, R. P. (1988). Black cultural forms in schools: A cross national comparison. In L. Weis (Ed.), *Class, race and gender in American education* (pp. 249–265). Albany: SUNY Press.

Solorzano, D. G., & Villalpando, O. (1998). Critical race theory, marginality, and the experience of students of color in higher education. In C. A. Torres & T. R. Mitchell (Eds.), *Sociology of education: Emerging perspectives* (pp. 211–224). Albany: SUNY Press.

Stavans, I. (1995). *The Hispanic condition: Reflections on culture and identity in America.* NY: Harper.

Suarez-Orozco, M.M. (1991). Immigrant adaptation to schooling: A Hispanic case. In M. Gibson & J. Ogbu (Eds.), *Minority status and schooling* (pp. 37–61). NY: Garland.

Suarez-Orozco, M. M. (1997). "Becoming Somebody": Central American immigrants in U.S. inner-city schools. In M. Seller & L. Weis (Eds.), *Beyond Black and White: New faces and voices in U.S. schools* (pp. 115–129). Albany: SUNY Press.

Suzuki, B. H. (1994). Higher education issues in the Asian American community. In Justiz, R. Wilson, Bjork (Eds.) *Minorities in higher education* (pp. 258–285). Phoenix: Oryx Press.

Tatum, B. (1997). *Why are all the Black kids sitting together in the cafeteria?* NY: Basic Books.

Tierney, W. G. (1993). The college experience of Native Americans: A critical analysis. In L. Weis & M. Fine (Eds.), *Beyond Silenced Voices* (pp. 309–323). Albany: SUNY Press.

Tinto, V. (1987). *Leaving college: Rethinking the causes and cures of student attrition.* Chicago: The University of Chicago Press.

Torres, C. A. (1996). State and education revisited: Why educational researchers should think politically about education. In M. Apple (Ed.), *Review of research in education, 21* (pp. 255–331). Washington DC: American Educational Research Association.

Trotman, R. E. (1998). Success of academic intervention on female single-parent Educational Opportunity Program and non-Educational Opportunity Program students. (Doctoral dissertation, Walden University, New Jersey, 1998). *Dissertation Abstracts International, 59,* 2304.

U. S. Census Bureau. (2001). *Census 2000 Brief: Overview of race and Hispanic origin.* (4/15/01). <http://www.census.gov/prod/2001pubs/c2kbro1-lpdf>

Valdes, G. (1998). The world outside and inside schools: Language and immigrant children. *Educational Researcher, 27* (6), 4–18.

Walleri, R. D. (1988, May). *Case studies of non-traditional high-risk students: Does social and academic integration apply?* Paper presented at the Twenty-Eighth Annual Forum of the Association for Institutional Research, Phoenix, AS. [ERIC Documentation Reproduction Service No. ED 298 861]

Walsh, J. (1993, Fall Special Edition). The perils of success: Asians have become exemplary immigrants, but at a price. *Newsweek, 142, 55–56.*

Ward, J. V. (1999). Resilience and resistance. In A. Garrod, J. V. Ward, T. L. Robinson, R. Kilkenny (Eds.), *Souls looking back* (pp. 173–185). NY: Routledge.

Ward, J. V. (2000). *The skin we're in.* NY: Free Press.

Waters, M. C. (1996). Ethnic and racial identities of second-generation Black immigrants in New York City. In A. Portes (Ed.), *The new second generation* (pp. 171–196). NY: Russell Sage.

Webster, C. (1997). It's not enough to be smart: Distinctions among female high school peer groups as they narrate their gender identity construction in the context of extracurricular activities (Doctoral dissertation, SUNY Buffalo, 1997). *Dissertation Abstracts International, 58,* 2881.

Weis, L. (1990). *Working class without work: High school students in a de-industrializing economy.* NY: Routledge.

Weis, L. (1992). Discordant voices in the urban community college. *New Directions for Community Colleges, 80,* 13–27. San Francisco: Jossey-Bass.

Wexler, P. (1988). Symbolic economy of identity and denial of labor: Studies in high school number 1. In L. Weis (Ed.), *Class, race and gender in American education.* Albany: SUNY Press.

Wexler, P. (1992). *Becoming somebody: Toward a social psychology of school.* London: Falmer.

Willis, P. (1977). *Learning to labour.* London: Saxon House.

Youssef, N. H. (1992). *The demographics of immigration: A socio-demographic profile of the foreign-born population in New York State.* NY: Center for Migration Studies.

Zhou, M. (1997). Social capital in Chinatown: The role of community-based organizations and families In the adaptation of the younger generation. In M. Seller & L. Weis (Eds.), *Beyond Black and White: New faces and voices in U.S. schools* (pp. 181–205). Albany: SUNY Press.

Zinn, H. (1980). *A people's history of the United States.* NY: Harper & Row.

Index

* Student research participants